ACT AND IDEA
IN THE NAZI GENOCIDE

ACT AND IDEA
IN THE NAZI GENOCIDE

BEREL LANG

THE UNIVERSITY OF CHICAGO PRESS
CHICAGO AND LONDON

Berel Lang is professor of philosophy and humanistic studies and chair
of the Department of Philosophy at the State University of New York
at Albany.

The University of Chicago Press, Chicago 60637
The University of Chicago Press, Ltd., London
© 1990 by The University of Chicago
All rights reserved. Published 1990
Printed in the United States of America
99 98 97 96 95 94 93 92 91 90   5 4 3 2 1

Library of Congress Cataloging-in-Publication Data
Lang, Berel.
   Act and idea in the Nazi genocide / Berel Lang.
      p.   cm.
   ISBN 0-226-46868-2   ISBN 0-226-46869-0 (pbk)
   1. Holocaust, Jewish (1939–1945)—Moral and ethical aspects.
2. Genocide—Moral and ethical aspects.   I. Title.
D810.J4L267 1990
940.53′18—dc20   89-37320
                                                            CIP

♾ The paper used in this publication meets
the minimum requirements of the American National
Standard for Information Sciences—Permanence of
Paper for Printed Library Materials, ANSI Z39.48-1984.

For my mother, Sarah Stamm Lang,
   for whom memory inscribes the present

Contents

Acknowledgments

I wish to express my appreciation to a number of friends and colleagues who from their readings in the manuscript of this book or through conversations or correspondence have generously contributed to it. Beyond their learning, and even when they found themselves in disagreement, they provided a sense of community which for the harsh issues addressed here was itself reassuring. They are not responsible, of course, for what I have made of their suggestions—although I should insist, on the other side of this disclaimer, that without their help the book's failings would be larger still. My thanks, then, to: Aharon Appelfeld, Emil Fackenheim, Saul Friedländer, Victor Gourevitch, Philip Hallie, Joel Kraemer, Ulrich Maché, Nathan Rotenstreich, Tuvya Shlonsky, Gary Stahl, Kenneth Seeskin, Roger Smith, Richard Stamelman, Marx Wartofsky, Hayden White, and Leni Yachil. Albert Hofstadter and Terrence Des Pres can no longer be thanked; the loss of their counsel extends far beyond these pages. My wife, Helen S. Lang, was here as always both a generous and an acute reader; her efforts to imagine the book as it might be are often reflected in what it is. My daughters, Ariella and Jessica, who became aware of the events that are the book's subject during the years in which it was written, were for me a constant incentive. I am grateful also to the Center for the Humanities at Wesleyan University, the Lucius N. Littauer Foundation, and the State University of New York at Albany for support which they have provided.

Introduction:
Writing between Past and Present

It seems obvious to me that anything written now about the Nazi genocide against the Jews that is not primarily documentary, that does not
uncover new information about the history of that singular event, requires special justification. Other writing about the same subject, as it is
meant to convey the common or a personal sense of horror, serves too
often as a rhetorical incentive for memory, assuming a role of surrogate
in which voice substitutes for conscience so that the need to feel displaces reflection, or substitutes even for feeling itself. Even for writers
conscious of this danger, moreover, there remains the divided challenge
of justice and sentiment; they can hardly balance their own imagined
lives against the histories of those who spoke—or for that matter, who
were silent—within the events of the genocide.

It may seem that writing in general, not only writing about moral
enormity on the scale of the Nazi war against the Jews, faces this same
challenge. Wherever it appears, literary representation imposes artifice,
a figurative mediation of language, and the contrivance of a persona—
that is, a mask—on the part of the writer. To this extent, *all* writing requires justification; it is at the very least an obtrusion on its subject. But
if these conditions hold in general, they are especially compelling when
the occasion for writing makes its own mark, when the facts "speak for
themselves." In such circumstances—and if they ever occur, the Nazi
genocide against the Jews is an instance—artifice tends to become con-

ceit, and the writer's intervention, whatever else it does, draws attention
away from the subject itself. Even for discourse that proposes to *think*
rather than to feel or imagine this event, to measure it against the abstraction of theory or explanation, a related objection holds. For
abstraction is also contrivance, and the attempt at objectivity or disinterest by an author itself becomes part of the view of his subject. Just so,
Kierkegaard described an audience who, when a clown ran out on stage
and shouted at them that the hall they were sitting in was on fire,
laughed; he repeated his warning, and they laughed harder. But the hall
was on fire, and the clown wanted only to warn them of this.

I refer to these constraints on writing about the subject of this book
with an awareness that they have not always been observed here, although also with the suggestion that even the violations which occur
reflect a different conception of writing from the one which would usually account for them. In this more common view, a premise of the
written word is its intention to be read *through;* it is designed to enable
readers to see what they would otherwise see differently or perhaps not
at all. The motif of the studies that follow here, in contrast, is "intransitive" (in Barthes's term), where an author does not write to provide
access to something independent of both author and reader, but "writes-
himself." This conception of writing denies the distances among the
writer, text, what is written about, and, finally, the reader; they all converge on a single point. In the traditional account, the writer is conceived
as first looking at an object with eyes already expectant, patterned, and
then, having seen, as representing it in his writing. For the writer who
writes-himself, writing becomes itself the means of vision or comprehension, not a mirror of something independent, but an act and
commitment—a doing or making rather than a reflection or description.

This conception, it should be noticed, has its own precedents. One
early example appears in the Passover Haggadah and the requirement
which accompanies it of the recitation, on each anniversary of Passover,
of the history of the Exodus from Egypt—the ritual of storytelling for-
malized in the Seder. Why, we might ask, this unusual manner of recital
in which there are only speakers and no audience, where no one listens,
where each person is responsible for recounting the story? Not mainly, it
seems, as a means of collective learning or exchange, but to enable each
reciter, everyone present, to see himself, to *tell* himself. It is one thing to
hear or to read an account related by someone else; the act is quite different for the person who recites the story, who speaks and hears the events
in his own voice. Even then, of course, the narrator does not create the
event; but his voice, the at once literal and metaphorical voice that
sounds the words, takes on the shape of its subject, much as a hand does

with its grasp. The voice here becomes the expression of its subject, not its source or cause.

It is unlikely that the assertions of act and idea which constituted the Nazi genocide will ever be accommodated within a single account of that event. It seems to me, however, that this fact should also be taken as an incentive for retelling the event rather than for attaching a sense of failure (at least of *that* failure) to its limited versions. We cannot predict the forms of these versions—but there is no uncertainty about the outcome if those recitals should cease, if the historical event should slip from consciousness by only as much as would be entailed by the decision to listen to others speak of it rather than to address it ourselves. The irony intrinsic to the concept of memory insists on the present as a means to the past; without that basis, if memory did not originate in the active voice of the present—"I [*now*] remember"—it would not be memory that was disclosed, but an imaginary or hypothetical set of events, the beginning of fiction. The act of memory, moreover, cannot be carried on vicariously; each self must remember for itself, and thus the retelling is always, for each person, begun anew.

These constraints on writing about the Nazi genocide against the Jews reflect a sense of moral obligation: both that the writing should be done and that its form must itself expect to stand judgment. These "oughts" also extend to the historical subject itself. As the Haggadah places every Jew at Sinai, instructed to recount the events of the Exodus as though they had been part of his own life, the presence of all Jews is also fixed within the events of the genocide—those born after it as well as those who died in it or who lived despite it. The consequences of historical events extend both backward and forward, and in retelling the Nazi genocide, the narrator tells himself not only as a speaker in the present but also as a character of the narrative, living in the text recited. Writers do not usually think of their readers as themselves writers. For me in this writing, however, the greater failing would be to have readers who did not do this, who might think to avoid retelling what was written because they were reading. Even if what emerges in such revisions moves away from or against what is said in these pages, this would be more consistent with the ideal of moral discourse—discourse not about moral issues, but *as* moral—than would writing which requires that writer and reader distance themselves from their subjects, as aesthetic expression (poetry, fiction) distances itself from the immediacy of will and emotion, or as the generalizations of scientific or philosophical theory distance themselves from their specific objects.

The proposal that each Jew should tell the story of the genocide as though he or she had passed through it is based on more than an interpretive legend. For many Jews, the import is literal: it was no more than chance, the impulse of an ancestor who had seen or visualized a map, that they, too, were not among the actual victims, murdered or, less directly, unborn because of the murder of their "parents." As for the traveler who is accidentally detained and then misses a plane which crashes, the arbitrariness of such survival marks all later history as contingent and improbable. But more than this: as the Nazis willed the expulsion of the Jews not only from one country or another, not only from certain occupations or social roles, but from existence itself, it is quite specifically the life of each Jew who lives now and after this that was willed to extinction. Had the Nazis succeeded in their design, the Jews would not *be*.

This is not an easy possibility to imagine, let alone to live. The difficulty here reflects not mainly the growing distance in time from the occurrence of the genocide, but the nature of the intention itself. Those Jews who faced the threat directly, even when it was about to destroy them, often seemed to have no more definite a conception than is now possible of its reality—and there is obviously much more at issue here than the allegedly passive response of the Jews confronted with that threat. *Should* a human imagination be able to conceive of the possibility that it is being willed out of existence, not for something it has done or been, but only because of its existence? An imagination which fully anticipated this possibility would, it seems, be that of the agent, not of the victim; the effort required to imagine this, moreover, seems hardly slighter now, long after the possibility became actual, than it was before. That the Jew who lives today knows the reality of genocide in a way that Jews of earlier ages did not nonetheless leaves the matter of moral knowledge, of deciding how now to act on that possibility, still to be given a content. The reckoning must be done by each person anew, from the beginning; moral character, as it makes decisions in the present, also takes responsibility for rehearsing a particular past.

I do not feel able to argue with the same conviction for a gesture of identification by those who look back now on the Nazi genocide and who are not Jews. The sense of individual agency or identity that is a condition of moral consciousness cannot be imposed from the outside; still more pertinently, no one acts or speaks in moral terms as a universal consciousness. If the history of ethics has any single lesson to teach, it is that the status of moral agents is determined by their own places in space and time: they act always, if not only, as individuals and always and only in a context. To propose as an ideal that they should escape this particularity is to propose also that they should be quite different beings. In the Nazi genocide against the Jews, the lines are drawn around a *genos* as a group, and as a particular group at that; whatever the direction in which reflection on the Nazi genocide moves, it cannot ignore this first one of its features.

The rejection of the ideal of universalization as a basis for moral judgment does not preclude a moral role to the imagined self, to imagining oneself in the guise of another. The prospect here is of a joining. It is no small thing to propose to view the Nazi genocide against the Jews as a human rather than a Jewish cataclysm, as arguing that the acts of the Nazis condemn all mankind to a future of concern, since as human, any other person might have been present at the site and in the time of that event. It seems clear enough that in one sense everyone alive now shares this aftermath; the reality of genocide is in effect a new premise of experience, since brief as its history has been, it is difficult to conceive the present or future without it. When Cain killed Abel, murder became a new element of consciousness, a then constant expectation which put its mark on individual experience and social institutions alike. Analogously, the prospect of genocide is now also inevitable and common: there is no way of avoiding it, and the variations of its past history include everyone, all of humanity, in its future.

Even granting the breadth of this consequence, however, it should not be mistaken for the whole—since its individual parts remain which cannot be touched by the general view. It was not as "human beings" but as Jews that the victims of the Nazis were murdered, and it was not as human beings in general but by an avowal of their own supposed particularity and destiny that the Nazis acted. We have here to take history at its word—and that word is not mankind or human nature.

This does not mean that there can be no such larger community. In the face of the Nazi genocide, people to whom Jewish identity was hardly less alien than to the agents of the genocide yet pronounced that identity for themselves, as part of their own. But even acts such as these involve a joining that affirms underlying differences and that is effective, morally and practically, just because of this. It is not, in any event, an affirmation of the idea of a "person-in-general." There are times when joining in the identity of another is the only way that people, individually or collectively, can preserve their own; but even this reflects rather than displaces the differences among them.

I was not myself immediately caught by the Nazi genocide. I was born in the United States near the end of 1933, and during the next twelve years which saw the rise and then the defeat of Hitler's Germany, the Jewish community in the small Connecticut town in which I lived did not know, or in any event did not pay much attention to, what was happening during that time to the Jews of Europe. Large numbers of the Nazis' victims came from the same cities and towns in Lithuania and Poland from which members of the community, one or two generations before, had set out for America. But a certain forgetfulness of the past was evidently part of what seems also to have been a forgetfulness of the present; the distance between Norwich and the villages of Eastern Europe was as large in consciousness as it was in space.

It may be that I missed or that I have forgotten expressions of concern or outrage. Perhaps there were such moments, private or collective, that escaped a young boy, even a watchful one, living in a household which sooner or later heard versions of almost everything that was said elsewhere in the town. But none of my memories of the time recalls protests or discussions of what was happening to the Jewish communities in Europe, nor does that silence seem to have been disingenuous—the result of a decision at once to know something and not to know it. The circumstances were, I believe, even harsher than this: little was said because little was known or thought, and still less imagined.

Other memories of the war from those years are still strong, in reference both to the Jewish community and to the community outside it; these add to my sense that if there had been an attentiveness to what was happening to the Jews of Europe, it would be part of those memories. A number of Jewish men from the town served in the American armed forces; several were killed in action. I remember in particular the day when the news came that the plane in which one of them flew as a bombardier had been shot down. He was the son of the owners of the bakery which stood across the street from where we lived. When I was sent into the bakery the next morning, the pain of the workers and the customers in the shop was evident, unrestrained and sharp. But not there or in our own house or in the talk around the town, then or in the period afterward, was there a sense that the flier had been killed in a war which affected the Jews in a special way. It was the American war against the Germans and the Japanese that the young man had fought in; together with the sorrow at his death, there was a certain pride in the loss— mingled, it seems to me, with a certain resentment that a Jew had died in an American war. This last feeling reflected the sense that the largely immigrant community did not yet count itself fully at home; but if that was understandable, it is more difficult to grasp now that the Jews of the town did not recognize how much more was at stake for them in the war against the Nazis than for others in the town or beyond it.

I do not have an explanation for this blank space in local history, apart from the evident one that the strategy of "quiet diplomacy" adopted by the national Jewish organizations would foster the appearance of normalcy to anyone who was not in on the secret—this, together with the

difficulty that continues to this day but was much greater then, in imagining the events themselves even once they were known. At any rate, the
effect of this blank space on me four decades later was of a reproach, for
what should have filled it but did not. I *ought* to have been present, it
seemed to me, at least by being conscious. Here was an event which basically affected my own past and present, but which had scarcely been
acknowledged in them. If I did not have consciousness to reach back to
by way of memory, I would, by writing, be present *now*. In this way, the
past might be entered even when it was otherwise, unalterably, over.

Such autobiographical comments obtrude on a subject that requires no
introduction and to which personal history is largely irrelevant. But
there is, it seems to me, the contrary view to this that is still more troub-
ling and that prevails in much recent philosophical writing, about this or
other subjects. On this conception, philosophy may be written and read
quite apart from reference to the writer or the process by which he comes
to his subject. The assumption here is that philosophy would say the
same things it does even if history—recent or past, personal or general—
were quite different from what it was. This assumption often passes un-
said and unnoted; the allure of an escape from history helps to conceal it.
But it is dangerous in practical terms and a source of obscurity in thinking. The alternative to it does not imply that philosophy has to take
account of *all* historical events—or of those it does answer to, equally.
But it does imply that one test of philosophy will be found in its acknowledgment of its own historical ground, even or perhaps especially
of the most extreme events to be found there, since these are a test of
whatever is concluded also about lesser, more restrained ones.
    It is not, then, a general justification that is most pertinent for assess-
ing the work of philosophy, but one directed to its individual appearances. This is all the more evident when the conception of philosophy
applied denies that there are any distinctively "philosophical" questions
or methods. The history of philosophy itself, it seems to me, discloses
philosophy only as talking further and less restrictively than other forms
of discourse about questions in and of the world of common experience.
It is true that philosophy in the last century has become profes-
sionalized, a "discipline" no more resistant to the lure of science than
other areas of thought. I have assumed here, however, that there are
other and more telling directions in which philosophy may turn. In any
event, except for certain parts of chapters 6 and 7, no special philosophical "knowledge" is presupposed here; nor, on the other side, is
familiarity assumed with the extensive scholarship that has the Nazi
genocide against the Jews as its subject. Much can be learned from these

sources that bears on the latter subject, and some of this will be introduced; but my main purpose has been to construct a framework within which the evidence of the Nazi genocide can be imagined and thought, and which would thus provide in the present a means of approach to the combination of conceptual assertion and historical experience constituting that moral enormity. That the Nazi genocide was more than an idea or set of ideas is obvious; no less obviously, it was also more than a thoughtless or accidental series of historical events. The convergence in it of act and idea seems undeniable, and it is the relation between those two as they met in the phenomenon of genocide that is the focus of the discussion here.

This does not mean that the questions raised by philosophy can avoid abstraction. But the aspects of the conceptual structure outlined in the present volume, although they themselves move in various directions, return constantly to a single focus at their center—the Nazi genocide, which was, it is now generally recognized, a fundamental and not an incidental part of the Nazis' overall design. The focus here, then, is on the phenomenon of genocide as it represents, literally and emblematically, the intentions of the Nazis during the years of the Third Reich. The point from which the discussion sets out is not the issue of uniqueness in relation to that phenomenon, but the more basic question of what it is that identifies, historically and morally, the phenomenon of genocide. The studies in part 1, "The Presence of Genocide," address this general question by following a sequence of subordinate questions that converge on it: What is the relation between genocide and the other forms of killing to which it is compared, and indeed between the act of genocide and wrongdoing more generally? To what extent does genocide presuppose a motivating intention? Can wrongdoing *as such* be intentional—and how does the specific character of genocide bear on this question? These questions, impelled by the evidence of the Nazi genocide, are addressed in chapter 1, "Intending Genocide," and chapter 2, "The Knowledge of Evil and Good." Chapter 3, "The Decision Not to Decide," turns the phenomenon of genocide to a different perspective, viewing it through the decisions and responses it forces on its victims.

It may be objected, even from this brief summary, that what is proposed does not focus on the particular historical occurrence at all, that also here the Nazi genocide serves as an occasion for raising other, quite general philosophical questions. In such terms, the historical event would almost certainly become distanced or naturalized, its distinctiveness obscured. I am aware of points in these studies to which this objection applies, but my intention to move in the opposite direction should nonetheless be evident. The focus on the Nazi genocide is

not as one among a group of examples which together yield philosophical generalizations—but for the particularity of that event, its own
historical and moral place. Moral or practical discourse differs in just
these features from theoretical discourse: the one begins and concludes
with particulars; the other begins with particulars and concludes with
generalization. The goal of the one is practice or doing, the goal of the
other, theory or knowing; evaluation in the one is by criteria concerned
with goals set for human conduct—in the other by external (and impersonal) standards of theory. The two forms of discourse cannot avoid
meeting at certain junctures, but it is clearly the second that has domi-
nated recent philosophical and ethical discourse—and it is the first that
I attempt to bring to bear here.

One aspect of this last issue—the relation between a subject of discourse and the forms of its representation—is itself the focus of part 2,
"Representations of Genocide." For as the events that constituted the
Nazi genocide pose distinctive issues for ethical understanding, so also
the representation of those events (in their "imaginative" reconstruc-
tions as well as in their historical retelling) will reflect those issues,
including the "boundary question" of whether the events of the genocide can or should be represented at all. Insofar as the attempt at
representation is made, the question of how the moral status of its subject affects representation becomes a central concern—in relation, for
example, to the standard requirements of scholarly disinterest or of aesthetic distance in fictional representation. The latter topic comes into
view from more than one direction. For although such representations
have usually been articulated from the perspective of the victims of the
genocide, they also disclose the perspective from which the perpetrators looked out at those events. Thus, chapter 4, "Language and
Genocide," considers the role of the language of the Nazis as implicated
and expressive in the genocide. Chapters 5 ("Jabès and the Measure of
History") and 6 ("The Representation of Evil") address the issue of
the representation of evil in imaginative and historical writing about
the genocide. The privileging of historical discourse becomes part of
the overall thesis here.

The last part of the book, "Histories and Genocide," examines a
number of institutional questions—some bearing on the history of
ideas, some on more immediately social and religious issues—that intersect with the occurrence and then with the aftermath of the Nazi
genocide. Memory, whether personal or collective, religious or scholarly, is itself a form of institutionalization; in one sense, the most basic of
all institutions. Anyone who has attempted to trace *the* history of the
genocide, furthermore, will recognize that many lines or histor*ies*

constitute the whole, and that these reflect a process of social definition that precedes the event itself and continues to have consequences in its aftermath. Institutionalization originates with or even before the event—and chapter 7, "Genocide and Kant's Enlightenment," thus considers the development of certain Enlightenment ideas or motifs as nonetheless "affiliated" with the much later and in other ways remote Nazi genocide. The aftermath of the genocide is constituted for the present (that is, now) by the embodiments of history and memory in social institutions: in formal memorials, but also in social ideals and policies, in education and scholarship, in artistic and religious themes. The two concluding chapters of the book—"Zionism in the Aftermath" and "Speaking, Writing, Teaching"—consider a number of instances of these "external" representations in the nearly half century since the Nazi genocide occurred.

Are these distinctively *philosophical* issues? And quite aside from that, is there any way of settling them or, before that, even of gaining agreement on their formulation? It would be significant, it seems to me, if the moral issues themselves could be made sufficiently explicit to constitute a framework of reference for addressing the prior facts and evidence of the Nazi genocide—in contrast to the more usual form of theoretical analysis which imposes an explanatory structure on a complex (and otherwise independent) assembly of evidence. This contrast once again reflects the difference between moral and theoretical judgment; it also reflects the attempt made here to render the events of the Nazi genocide and the issues related to them imaginable: not *easier* to imagine, but as disclosing what the work of the imagination must have been in order that those events should have unfolded as they did. Together with the historical improbabilities that were features of the Nazi genocide and notwithstanding the impersonal factors that contributed to it, it is also evident that what took place was and had to be imagined—and then thought and willed. This is no less the case if the acts and ideas constituting the genocide stood at the very boundary between what was and what was not imaginable, between what could or could not be thought and willed— and even if, as also seems true, the phenomenon of genocide was itself intended to test the limits by which these had previously been confined. To understand this process is obviously a task of great difficulty, unlikely to be realized in any one account. But it is unavoidably the standard by which writing about the Nazi genocide must expect to be judged.

The reader of this Introduction will have noticed the absence of the term "Holocaust" where it would usually be expected to appear. Admittedly, the original meaning and connotations of that term have to an extent been superseded by its recent usage; few contemporary readers would fail to recognize its main current application to the Nazi attempt to exterminate the Jewish people. But its historical connotations persist even in this recent usage (quite recent, it is important to note; the earliest published references in the United States date from the late 1960s; the first appearance of "Holocaust" in the *New York Times Index* is in 1970). The main connotations of the term derive from the use in the Septuagint of *holokaustoma* ("totally consumed by fire")—the Greek translation of the Hebrew *olah,* which designates the type of ritual sacrifice that was to be completely burned (as in *Leviticus* 1:3 ff.). The English usage of "holocaust" in the sixteenth and seventeenth centuries elaborated this literal sense of a religious burnt offering; secondarily, the term began to appear as a metaphor for sacrifice more generally. In the seventeenth and eighteenth centuries, the term characteristically appears in reference to the complete destruction of an object or place or group, most often by fire, but also by other (mainly natural) causes. The latter usage predominated until the events of "the Holocaust" itself. But—as against the usage— the Nazi genocide against the Jews had none of the properties of a sacrifice except for its design of willful destruction: no intentionality on the part of those "sacrificed," no sense of loss or of giving by those "offering" the sacrifice, no evocation of a good to be redeemed by the act itself. Nor did it have anything in common with the character of natural catastrophe except, again, for a large and gratuitous loss of life. Even the latter feature, moreover, does not reflect the specific bearing on the "Holocaust" of the role of genocide. Both the Hebrew designation *shoah* ("wasteland" or "destruction," as in *Isaiah* 10:3 and *Proverbs* 3:25) and the Yiddish variation of the Hebrew *churban* ("destruction")—the latter traditionally applied to the destruction of the Temples and then reapplied metonymically to other destructions—are more accurately descriptive than "Holocaust," because they imply a breach or turning point in history (*and* because they reject the connotations of "sacrifice"). But these references, too, have theological or at least mediating overtones, they are confined to the viewpoint of the victims, and they fail to suggest the specific role of genocide as it figured in the deeds of the Third Reich. I refer in the studies that follow, then, to the Nazi genocide against the Jews; the few appearances of other terms (including "Holocaust") are accounted for in context.

It may be well in this connection also to refer briefly to the writing in this volume—specifically to certain variations in form among the parts and chapters. These do not reflect differences in their own histories; with one exception, the book was written with the whole in mind. Such variations have to do rather with differences in the topics addressed and in the purposes of the individual chapters or parts. As the discussion in part 2 proposes that the subject of writing is intrinsically related to its form, no special justification should be required for the evidence of that relation as it appears in the writing here.

The idea of an author "writing himself" mentioned above may seem to suggest that only the present is at stake in writing, that the past has no hold on it. I hope it will become clear that the studies here come from the opposite direction, supposing and asserting that the past, even if it is not (or ever will be) "settled," weighs continuously on the present, whether as writing or as being written about. This is an added reason for rejecting the view that the reader or writer about moral issues ought to assume the role of an ideal or "universal" moral consciousness. For moral discourse, even the most abstract topic loses by being viewed only abstractly; in any event, this perspective could only distort what is to be seen and known now of the Nazi genocide, with its origins and ideas rooted in specific historical intentions and circumstance. The suggestion will be elaborated here, in fact, that one element in the background of the genocide itself was the pressure exerted by the ideal of ethical objectification and universalization—what a recent writer has named "The View from Nowhere." Against this, it can be shown, again and again, that the most pressing concerns of ethics originate and conclude in the particularity of historical events and in the particularity of the agents involved in them. The writing of ethics ought, it seems, to take seriously this condition of its own possibility.

Albany / W. Hartford and Jerusalem
March, 1989

I

THE PRESENCE OF GENOCIDE

1

Intending Genocide

The hard decision had to be made that this people should be caused to disappear from the earth. . . . Perhaps, at a much later time, we can consider whether we should say something more about this to the German people. I myself believe that it is better for us—us together—to have borne this for our people, that we have taken the responsibility for it on ourselves (the responsibility for an act, not just for an idea), and that we should now take this secret with us into the grave.

HEINRICH HIMMLER, Secret Address to SS Officers, at Poznan, 10 June 1943

The term "genocide" has come to be used when all other words of moral or political opprobrium fail, when the speaker or writer wishes to indict a set of actions as extraordinary for their malevolence and heinousness. The pathology of everyday political life has left no shortage of candidates for this designation or of accusers, with good reason or not, who have been ready to confer it. So we find the term assigned to the policies in Nicaragua first of the Somoza government and then of the Sandinistas—no less categorically than to the actions of the Turks against the Armenians in 1915–17; to the role of the United States in Vietnam and to policies toward ethnic minorities within the USSR; to the political structure imposed by the Afrikaners on nonwhite South Africans, or again to the social definition in the United States of blacks living there; to the intentions of Israelis with respect to Palestinian Arabs and of the Palestinians with respect to Israelis; to policies and decisions in Canada,

Tibet, Chile, Australia, Paraguay, Bangladesh[1]—and, of course, to the lasting exemplar of the war of the Nazis against the Jews during the rule of the Third Reich.

It is noteworthy that quite different, often conflicting designations have been given for each one of the situations mentioned; the difficulty of finding anything common among these uses, except for their referral to violence and mass death, makes it clear that the term "genocide" has become largely emotive in meaning. This conclusion is itself not without significance: curses, too, disclose principles and commitments. But this diffuseness also suggests the need to provide an analysis of genocide itself, if only in order to determine what in that phenomenon supports the connotations of extraordinary wrongdoing which the term unmistakably carries with it. For genocide *is* distinctive, not, as has often been claimed, in the "uniqueness" of its occurrence—since we know that there may have been, and even more surely can be, more than one of these—but as an idea and act of wrongdoing, and thus too for its place in the history of ethics.

The academic tone of this thesis may seem to clash with the moral enormity of its subject. But when ethical issues are confronted in their historical settings rather than as hypothetical, the distance between act and description, between idea and exemplification, becomes a feature of the discourse itself. Undoubtedly, writing is also a form of action, at times perhaps of moral action; but where moral experience is the subject, and more certainly where the moral facts are so compelling as to speak for themselves, talking or writing about those facts must always seem to open itself to invidious comparison.

1. The Idea as History

The history of the concept of genocide provides a number of important clues for the analysis of genocide, and two principal sources are relevant to that history: the first, the writings of Raphael Lemkin; the second, the legislation of the United Nations Convention on Genocide. The word "genocide" itself first appears in print in 1944 in Lemkin's book

1. See, e.g., Robert Davis and Mark Zannis, *The Genocide Machine in Canada* (Montreal: Black Rose Books, 1973); Rodney Y. Gilbert, *Genocide in Tibet* (New York: American-Asian Education Exchange, 1959); Carlos Cerda, *Génocide au Chili* (Paris: Maspero, 1974); Tony Berta, "Relations of Genocide: Land and Lives in the Colonization of Australia," in Isidor Wallimann and Michael N. Dobkowski (eds.), *Genocide and the Modern Age* (Westport: Greenwood, 1987), 237–52; Kalyan Chandhuri, *Genocide in Bangladesh* (Bombay: Orient Longmans, 1972); Richard Arens (ed.), *Genocide in Paraguay* (Philadelphia: Temple University Press, 1976).

Axis Rule in Occupied Europe.[2] In that work, which he began to write in 1940, Lemkin, a Polish Jew whose family would perish almost in its entirety in the few years after that, reviews what was then known of the actions by the Nazis against noncombatants in countries they had conquered or occupied. Still earlier, in 1933, with grim prescience, Lemkin, at the Fifth International Conference for the Unification of Penal Law in Madrid, had introduced resolutions proposing definitions for two new international crimes: "barbarity"—"oppressive and destructive actions directed against individuals as members of a national, religious, or racial group"; and "vandalism"—"the destruction of works of art and culture." Those resolutions were not adopted by the Madrid Conference; when in his 1944 formulation Lemkin joins under the single, broader heading of "genocide" the two crimes to which he had previously attempted to call attention, he notes that the earlier proposals would have provided legal instruments for judging the actions of the Nazis in the years since.

By 1944, in any event, the need and applicability of such legislation were only too evident. Provision had long been made for judging military actions against civilians as individuals, Lemkin points out, as in the Hague Conventions of 1899 and 1907. But the actions of the Nazis were marked by a pattern of violence different from anything anticipated in those Conventions. For the Nazis were not only persecuting noncombatants; they were persecuting at least some of them solely on the basis of their membership in certain cultural and religious groups, with the intention of destroying those groups as groups. The purpose of these quasi-military operations differed from those in which individual "enemy" civilians were harmed, even willfully, by an occupying force. The concept of genocide—the killing of a race, the members of a common "descent," more broadly, of a "kind"—was intended to represent this difference. The rights of individual noncombatants and of defeated soldiers, Lemkin asserts, had been clearly defined and to some extent protected, but the "fate of nations in prison . . . has apparently not

2. Raphael Lemkin, *Axis Rule in Occupied Europe* (Washington, D.C.: Carnegie Endowment for International Peace, 1944). Lemkin also served as a consultant in the drafting of the UN Convention (see Raphael Lemkin, "My Battle with Half the World," *Chicago Jewish Forum,* Winter 1952). On the historical and conceptual background of genocide, see also Uriel Tal, "On the Study of the Holocaust and Genocide," *Yad Vashem Studies* 13 (Jerusalem, 1979), 7–52; Irving L. Horowitz, "Many Genocides, One Holocaust?" *Modern Judaism* 1 (1979), 74–89; Leo Kuper, *Genocide: Its Political Use in the Twentieth Century* (New Haven: Yale University Press, 1981); Yehuda Bauer, "The Place of the Holocaust in Contemporary History," in J. Crankel (ed.), *Studies in Contemporary Jewry.*(Bloomington, Ind.: Indiana University Press, 1984); Wallimann and Dobkowski, *Genocide.*

seemed to be so important as to call for supervision of the occupational authorities" (84).

In formulating the concept of genocide, Lemkin cites mainly the "national" but also the "ethnic" and the "religious" group as examples of the *genos* against which the act of genocide might be directed. He does not indicate in these comments, however, exactly how these "kinds" are themselves to be defined: what features distinguish them among the considerably larger variety of groups which appear within most social structures. A second and related issue, also mentioned and left unresolved by Lemkin, concerns the nature of the destruction—more literally, the "killing"—indicated in the term "genocide." He addresses the latter issue by citing eight aspects of group existence that are liable to destruction: the "political," "social," "cultural," "economic," "biological," "physical," "religious," and "moral" structures of a group. Early in his book, Lemkin suggests that genocide is effected by a "synchronized attack" (xi) on *all* these aspects. Subsequently, he proposes that only some of them must be attacked in order for the charge of genocide to be warranted, but he does not even then distinguish among the aspects or compare them in their bearing on the charge of genocide.

The two questions thus raised—what groups can be the victims of genocide, and what aspects of such groups are the objects of the act of genocide—are central to any consideration of the phenomenon of genocide. They pose theoretical difficulties, on the one hand, for defining the concept (could, for example, the limited *genos* of the family be the "occasion" of genocide?); they give rise, on the other hand, to practical difficulties for legislation or judicial proceedings that address its historical occurrence. The United Nations Convention on the Prevention and Punishment of the Crime of Genocide, initiated by a resolution passed in the General Assembly in 1948,[3] constitutes the principal legal state-

3. The text of the United Nations Convention on the Prevention and Punishment of the Crime of Genocide, together with a history of its formulation and a commentary, appears in Nehemiah Robinson, *The Genocide Convention* (New York: Institute of Jewish Affairs, 1960). The United States, an original signatory and advocate for the resolution in the General Assembly in 1948, did not ratify the Convention until February 1985; proposals for Senate ratification either died or were defeated on four separate occasions previously (1970, 1973, 1973, and 1976). Even in voting to ratify in 1985, the Senate attached "reservations" that effectively block international jurisdiction over charges that might be brought against the United States by another country or a group outside the United States. The legislation for implementing the qualified United States ratification, required before the resolution could be transmitted to the United Nations, was not enacted until October 1988. A contrast bears mentioning: in 1973, the Senate and the House of Representatives passed the Endangered Species Act on its first presentation, without dissent in the Senate and with four dissenting votes in the House of Representatives.

ment that has been formulated about genocide; it is important, although also problematic, for the responses it proposes to these two questions.

After a dramatic opening which asserts that "genocide, whether committed in time of peace or in time of war, is a crime under international law," the UN Convention defines the potential victim of genocide as a "national, ethnical, racial, or religious group"; genocide, then, is "committed with intent to destroy, in whole or in part" any such group. As versions of destruction, the Convention cites, in addition to the outright killing of members of the group, four other sufficient conditions: "causing serious bodily or mental harm to members of the group"; "deliberately inflicting on the group conditions of life calculated to bring about its physical destruction in whole or in part"; "imposing measures intended to prevent births within the group"; and "forcibly transferring children of the group to another group." Even the last of these conditions—and more obviously, the other four—underscores the basic emphasis of the Convention on the *physical* destruction of a group as characteristic of genocide. (The motion initiating the UN Convention was passed in the General Assembly over objections to its failure to include political genocide, a category that had been included in an earlier draft of the resolution.)

This emphasis of the UN Convention makes explicit what will also be elaborated here as the distinguishing features of genocide; these are themselves linked, however, to a number of historical issues. One of the latter concerns is the historical occurrence of genocide. For even if the term or, more generally, the concept of genocide does not appear prior to the events of World War II, the phenomenon itself obviously could have—and has been alleged to have—occurred before then. One precedent in particular has been widely referred to, namely, the attempted destruction by the Turkish government in 1915–17 of the Armenian population in Turkey. Lemkin himself cites this, as well as a number of much earlier examples, among them the Roman destruction of Carthage in 146 B.C., the conquest of Jerusalem by Titus in A.D. 72, and a conglomerate of the brutalities of Genghis Khan. These, together with the other references mentioned in the opening paragraph of this chapter, are no doubt all arguable as instances of genocide, although it is also clear that the evident differences among them suggest the need for gradations within the concept itself. In the attack of the Turks on the Armenians, for example, the Turks sometimes (although in no systematic way) allowed the Armenians the alternative of conversion to Islam as a means of saving themselves—in effect substituting the intention of religious or cultural genocide (ethnocide) for physical genocide. Moreover, the attacks of the Turks on the Armenian populace were confined to the boundaries of Turkey—thus imposing a geographical constraint on the intentions of genocide.[4] In a more extreme form of genocide, national or geographical boundaries might be a constraint in fact but not in principle; the option of emigration or of finding refuge elsewhere would be denied even as a possibility.

It is important that typologies should be elaborated of the historical and possible instances of genocide which would take account of these differences. Such typologies would be required for assessing responsibility in specific instances of genocide; no less importantly, their analysis of the variable features in genocide is a necessary step in constructing social or political models designed to anticipate or prevent the occurrence of genocide, and a number of attempts have been made along these lines recently.[5] But the emphasis in the present discussion is not on distinguishing among different forms of genocide, but in characterizing what will be claimed here to be as yet its most explicit and fully determined occurrence, namely, the Nazi genocide against the Jews. For it is in this exemplification that the distinctive conceptual and moral features of the phenomenon of genocide most fully appear; if one can speak of a "paradigm" of moral enormity, it is here that the paradigm of genocide is found.

This claim, it should be noticed, is not a claim even for historical, let alone for metaphysical, uniqueness. In any other than the trivial sense in which every event is unique, historical descriptions would be more precise in restricting their reference to events as "unprecedented"—since the past notwithstanding, there always remains the future possibility of identical or closely comparable events. Even if it should be concluded that the Nazi war against the Jews represents one and so far the only actual instance of genocide—or, more restrainedly, that it is if not the only, the most explicitly intended and documented instance of genocide—one historical judgment concerning the status of genocide would still take precedence over any metaphysical one: the obvious but urgent inference that if genocide happened once, it can happen twice,

4. See Yehuda Bauer, *The Holocaust in Historical Perspective* (Seattle: University of Washington Press, 1978), 36; Helen Fein, *Accounting for Genocide* (New York: Free Press, 1979), 10–18; David M. Lang, *The Armenians* (London: George Allen and Unwin, 1981).

5. See, e.g., Vahakn N. Dadrian, "A Typology of Genocide," *International Review of Sociology* (1975); Helen Fein, "Scenarios of Genocide: Models of Genocide and Critical Responses," in Israel W. Charney (ed.), *Toward the Understanding and Prevention of Genocide* (Boulder, Colo.: Westview Press, 1984), 3–31; Leo Kuper, *International Action against Genocide* (London: Minority Rights Group, 1982), and *The Prevention of Genocide* (New Haven: Yale University Press, 1986); Roger W. Smith, "Human Destructiveness and Politics: The Twentieth Century as an Age of Genocide," in Wallimann and Dobkowski, *Genocide,* 21–39. See also the typological distinction between "genocide" and "Holocaust" in Bauer, *Holocaust,* chap. 2—and the denial (and also, it seems to me, refutation) of that distinction in Alan Rosenberg, "Was the Holocaust Unique: A Peculiar Question?" in Wallimann and Dobkowski, *Genocide,* 153–56.

that genocide is possible because it has been actual. Any claim for historical distinctiveness made in reference to a particular act of genocide has
also to take into account this sobering feature of history itself.[6]

A second point of reflection on genocide as an historical phenomenon
contributes to a thesis concerning the history of ethical concepts more
generally; namely, that ethical judgment has a history of development
that differs markedly from the progressive view often given of it. Genocide may not be entirely an "invention" of twentieth century; but it was
even for the Nazis sufficiently alien (and even for them, one infers, sufficiently terrible) that they did not set out with the goal of genocide clearly
fixed before them. They came to it, at the levels both of idea and of practice, by a succession of steps, each opening onto further historical
possibilities and only later, by this cumulative progression, affirming the
intention for genocide. The establishment of concentration camps within Germany in the first year of the Nazi regime (1933); the implementation of the Nuremberg Laws in 1935 by which the Jews of Germany were denied certain features of civil protection; the invasion
of Poland in 1939 and the concurrent establishment there of Jewish
ghettos; the invasion of Russia in June 1941 and the accompanying
("Commissar") order to violate the conventions of war in the treatment
of prisoners; the starting up of the death camps at the end of 1941 and
the explicit formulation of the plan for the Final Solution at the Wannsee
Conference in January 1942: the sequence here is cumulative and (it shall
be argued) intentional—but it also represents a series of individual steps
each of which causally influences the one following it. The explicit "deduction" of the goal and practice of genocide appears only rather late in
this progression and in any event years after the Nazi accession to power.

Admittedly, an alternative description to this one has argued that the
future genocide against the Jews was explicitly indicated early on—in
statements by Hitler himself, for example, in *Mein Kampf* (1924–26) or
even before that, in the late nineteenth-century sources of anti-Semitism
that would then influence Hitler.[7] (The term "anti-Semitism" itself first

6. On the issue of the uniqueness of the Nazi genocide, see, e.g., Nathan Rotenstreich,
"The Holocaust as a Unique Historical event," *Patterns of Prejudice* 22 (1988), 14–20; Ste-
ven T. Katz, "The 'Unique' Intentionality of the Holocaust," in Katz, *Post–Holocaust
Dialogues* (New York: New York University Press, 1983), 287–317; Kenneth Seeskin,
"What Philosophy Can and Cannot Say about Evil," in Alan Rosenberg and Gerald E.
Myers (eds.), *Echoes from the Holocaust* (Philadelphia: Temple University Press, 1988), 91–
93.

7. See in support of this claim George L. Mosse, *The Crisis of German Ideology* (New
York: Grosset and Dunlap, 1964), 138–45, and *Toward the Final Solution* (New York:
Howard Fertig, 1978), chaps. 12 and 13; Lucy Dawidowitz, *The War against the Jews,
1933–1945* (New York: Bantam, 1976), 156–58; and Joachim Fest, *Hitler*, trans. Richard
and Clara Winston (New York: Harcourt Brace Jovanovich, 1974), 679. Among the other

appears in the latter period, impelled by the "League of Anti-Semites" formed by Wilhelm Marr.) There are, furthermore, conceptual and practical difficulties in fixing the historical point at which an intention becomes an intention—even for a single person, let alone where group or corporate intentions are in question. (This issue is especially pertinent to the claim advanced recently by a number of historians that the genocide against the Jews was in its origins never specifically intended by the Nazis, that it occurred almost spontaneously, as the outcome of a series of unrelated, and so undirected, decisions.)[8]

Notwithstanding these counterclaims and issues, however, the weight of evidence argues that the design for the extermination of the Jews of Europe emerged as an explicit intention only gradually, becoming fully formed and definite in the period between 1939 and 1941; *and* that as this design unfolded, it disclosed certain features of genocide that had not previously appeared in any historical formulation of political purpose, either in the classical or in the modern worlds. Contrary to such casual assertions as Sartre's, that "the fact of genocide is as old as humanity,"[9] genocide thus conceived had arguably never before been intended; the idea and the act which are joined in the Nazi effort to annihilate the Jews—to annihilate them not only in one or several lands but wherever they might be—represented an innovation in the concept of genocide which in effect brought that concept to completion. With the definition that the Nazis gave to the concept of genocide, there was nothing more that *could* be added to it.

It is usually acknowledged that certain ethical ideals (for example, the concept of "natural rights") evolved over a period of time, influenced by a variety of cultural and intellectual sources. But evil or the "ideals" of wrongdoing have been accorded no parallel history—apparently on the grounds that evil, unlike good, is all one, or, alternatively, that the

---

evidence against this thesis, one passage in particular in *Mein Kampf* is worth noting. Hitler, who makes constant use of hyperbole in excoriating the historical role of the Jews, writes of the difference it would have made to the course of World War I and its aftermath if "twelve or fifteen thousand Hebrew corrupters of the people had been poisoned by gas before or during the war." At the time, those evidently seemed to him very large numbers.

8. See, e.g., Martin Broszat, "Hitler and the Genesis of the Final Solution," *Yad Vashem Studies* 13 (1979), 61–98; and Hans Mommsen, "Die Realisierung des Utopischen: Die 'Endlösung des Judenfrage' im 'Dritten Reich,'" *Geschichte and Gesellschaft* 9 (1983), 381–420. For concise statements of the disagreement between the "Intentionalist" and the "Functionalist" accounts of the Nazi genocide, see Eberhard Jäckel, *Hitler in History* (Hanover, N.H.: University Press of New England, 1984), esp. 29–46; and Saul Friedländer, Introduction to Gerald Fleming, *Hitler and the Final Solution* (Berkeley: University of California Press, 1982).

9. Jean-Paul Sartre, *On Genocide* (Boston: Beacon Press, 1968), 57.

mechanisms of evildoing leave no room for innovation. But the recent history of the phenomenon of genocide argues against this assumption; it moves in the opposite direction, in fact, by demonstrating that evil, too, is open to historical revision and conceptual "advance." The imagination, we thus learn, has no native ties to moral conscience—and references to the progress of moral concepts (as for example, in Whitehead's description of the evolving opposition in Western societies to slavery)[10] must also leave room for a progression of quite a different kind. Genocide is portentous not only for its occurrence *in* history but for the shape it gives *to* history.

A number of quasi-legal conditions concerning the definition of genocide warrant mention before its more basic structure is analyzed. The term "genocide" itself, it will be recognized, differs from its etymological analogues (as in "homicide" or "fratricide") in that the action of killing—denoted by the suffix "cide"—need not be fully realized for the term to apply. Legal and moral judgment; characteristically distinguish between homicide and attempted homicide, implying that the latter, because of its difference in consequence, ought also to be judged differently. Genocide would obviously be charged to actions that destroy a group in its entirety, but neither Lemkin's formulation nor the UN Convention cites this as a necessary condition; on those accounts, the term applies if the intended killing of a "kind" is no more than partly realized, or indeed if only the intention itself is demonstrated.[11] (The UN Convention complicates—and to an extent, confuses—this issue by stipulating that the charge of genocide would be warranted even if the intention to commit genocide were directed not at a group as a whole but only at part of a group.) This ascription of culpability to intentions even when they are not realized undoubtedly adds to the requirements for proof in certain possible instances of genocide; but the charge of genocide is no different in this respect from other charges in which an agent's intentions are a significant consideration.

As has already been mentioned, neither Lemkin's analysis nor the more narrowly focused UN Convention on Genocide provides specific criteria for identifying the "national, racial, or religious" groups that may be the objects of genocide. (As noted, the General Assembly vote on the UN Convention in 1948 deliberately excluded the category of "political genocide"; but this exclusion—itself based on political considerations—narrows only slightly the definition of the groups to which

10. Alfred North Whitehead, *Adventure of Ideas* (New York: Macmillan, 1933), 13–31.
11. It is difficult to imagine but not logically impossible that such an intention could be made explicit without the killing of *any* member of the group.

the Convention applies.) It seems likely in fact that necessary and sufficient conditions may not be ascertainable for the phenomenon of
genocide, mainly because of the difficulty already mentioned in identifying such conditions for the concept of a *genos*. The possibility of a
definition is further hindered by the fact that the type of "destruction"
will also vary in relation to the group specified: a group that defined itself
in terms of a common linguistic tradition, for example, would become a
victim of genocide if a ban were effectively imposed on the use of the
language. Yet notwithstanding the vagueness of certain distinctions
used to refer to the phenomenon of genocide, there is nothing intrinsically problematic about the concept or, much more obviously, its
appearances. Some exemplifications of genocide have been only too
clear, and the emphasis in the UN Convention on Genocide on the
physical destruction of a group defined by (allegedly) biological traits—
the definition represented in the Nazi genocide against the Jews—suggests a basis for their definition.

Before considering further the two primary factors in the concept of
genocide (the specification of the group and the intention related to its
destruction), it is important to recognize the implied relation between
these factors, on the hand, and the likely agents of genocide, on the
other. That genocide entails the destruction of a group does not imply
that the act of genocide itself must be the act of a group; but the practical
implementation of a design for genocide would almost necessarily be so
complex as to assure this. Admittedly, the same technological advances
that make genocide increasingly possible as a collective action also have
increased the possibility that an individual acting alone could initiate the
process. (When the push of a single button can produce cataclysmic effects, we discover an order of destruction—"omnicide"—even larger
than genocide.)[12] But the opprobrium attached to the term "genocide"
seems also to have the connotation of a corporate action—as if this act or
sequence of acts would be a lesser fault, easier to understand if not to
excuse if one person rather than a group were responsible for it. A group
(we suppose) would be bound by a public moral code; decisions made
would have been reached collectively, and the culpability of individual
intentions would be multiplied proportionately. Admittedly, corporate
responsibility is sometimes invoked in order to diminish (or at least to
obscure) individual responsibility; so, for example, the "quagmire" effect that was appealed to retrospectively by defenders of the United

12. Larger in one sense, but conceptually and morally dependent on it. See Berel Lang,
"Genocide and Omnicide: Technology at the Limits," in Avner Cohen and Steven Lee
(eds.), *Nuclear Weapons and the Future of Humanity* (Totowa, N.J.: Rowman and Allanheld,
1986), 115–30.

States' role in Vietnam. But for genocide, the likelihood of its corporate origins seems to *accentuate* its moral enormity: a large number of individual, intentional acts would have to be committed and the connections among them also affirmed in order to produce the extensive act. Unlike other corporate acts that might be not only decided on but carried out by a single person or small group of persons, genocide in its scope seems necessarily to require collaboration by a relatively large number of agents acting both collectively and individually.

The pressure to ascribe individual responsibility for genocide is a reflection of this pattern in the act of genocide, and the UN Convention anticipates the latter point when, in article IV, it claims the liability to punishment for anyone who commits genocide, "whether they are constitutionally responsible rulers, public officials or private individuals." Admittedly, this stipulation only defers the issue of accountability as between the corporate and the individual agent: does responsibility extend to everyone serving in an army which in only some of its units is carrying out the orders that specifically involve genocide? to the citizens who pay taxes to a government which through its armies or other agencies effects the policy of genocide? to the nation as a whole? But these are standard and difficult examples for assessing responsibility in *every* instance of corporate action. They are distinctive in respect to genocide only as the enormity of an act may affect the degree of culpability (the more serious the crime, the greater the blame), and thus also as it heightens the importance of assessing responsibility. In any event, it needs to be said once again that the fact that it may be impossible to demonstrate agency or responsibility for some instances of genocide does not mean that for other instances or agents such judgments may not be certain—as certain, in any event, as moral judgments ever can be.

2. Genocide as Principle

The reason for emphasizing the feature of physical destruction in the structure of genocide is evident. Where life itself remains, as in cultural genocide or ethnocide, the possibility also remains of group revival; but this is not the case where genocide involves physical annihilation. A conceptual relation has already been asserted, furthermore, between the *genos* subjected to genocide and the type of destruction involved in that act. Here again, physical destruction would also result in cultural genocide, but the converse does not hold: for a group which is defined genetically, physical destruction is the one form that genocide can take. Thus genocide in which both the *genos* and the means of destruction are defined in biological terms represents genocide in its most extreme and unequivocal form; it is, in effect, the "paradigm" of genocide. This is, we recognize, the form that the Nazi genocide against the Jews took, as that also remains, for other reasons, the most explicitly articulated and fully documented instance of the idea and act of genocide. Any general claims about genocide as a phenomenon, including the contention which follows here of the moral distinctiveness of genocide, can thus be measured against the structure—in intention and act—of the Nazi genocide.

In itself, the claim for the distinctiveness of the Nazi genocide in these terms still faces many of the standard questions relevant to other and less extreme instances of morally culpable decisions. Here, too, the question recurs of how an agent's intentions can be determined and of how important a role intentions have in the ascription of responsibility; here, too, the question is unavoidable of how culpability is to be measured in relation to the consequences of an act. Insofar as these considerations bear on ethically relevant decisions in general, the distinctiveness of the Nazi genocide must lie elsewhere. It seems clear, moreover, that such distinctiveness is not to be based only on the number of victims involved, although the reference in "genocide" to a group or kind suggests that that number is likely to be large. The total number of noncombatant victims of the Nazis in World War II, for example—killed in concentration and death camps, by forced labor, massacres, bombings—has been estimated to be on the order of twenty million. (The figure itself guarantees that it is at most an approximation; but this is not the immediate issue.) The size of that figure and the enormity of the acts which produced it can be acknowledged, however, without maintaining that all the people included in it were victims of genocide. Obviously, the term used to designate an act of killing makes little difference to the victim. But there remains a significant distinction, conceptually and morally, between mass murder and genocide—a distinction that does not depend on numbers at all. (This does not mean that the question of numbers will not have psychological or even moral force. In 1949, for example, the American Bar Association—which remained until 1973 a consistent and influential opponent to American ratification of the UN Convention on Genocide—recommended to the United States Senate a reservation to be appended in the event that the Senate did vote to ratify the convention, to the effect that a minimum number of people [in the "thousands"] should be fixed for defining the groups covered by the Convention.)

What distinguishes the concept of genocide in its extreme form, then, is its requirement of the physical destruction of a group of people as a consequence of their membership in an allegedly "natural" (biologically defined) group. There are two implications which follow from the convergence of these identifying features. The first implication is that the persons against whom the genocide is directed retain, neither as individuals nor as a group, any agency in the rationale or justification for that process. No personal deed or possession of the victims is at issue; the persons who constitute the group can do nothing, short of revising their biological history, to alter the terms of genocidal intention. They cannot affect that intention by renouncing a cultural or religious identity, or by proposing ransom or compensation; they cannot ask or be offered the options of exile or conversion or assimilation as "assurances" against the future. Genocide singles them out by their identification with a group quite apart from any choices they have made of identity or character and indeed aside from all individual characteristics other than the biological feature(s) which (allegedly) mark them as group members. Apparent individual divergences from the stereotype of the group can only be interpreted as superficial and accidental: the verdict against such "exceptions," like the broader one against "ordinary" members of the group, follows from the claim of a *generic* essence that is irrefutable at the level of individuals.

This status of the victim of genocide is linked to the second implication: that the agent of genocide requires nothing from his victims except their destruction and that in setting this condition he acts on a principle that is categorical and nonutilitarian. He is not motivated here by the hope of gain, like a robber who might be satisfied to acquire the money for which he commits robbery by other means; he differs also from a murderer who anticipates a reward for his act or who has a personal score to settle or even one who acts on sadistic impulse. Evidently, these or similar motives may influence individual agents of genocide, but by themselves they could not account for the distinguishing features of that act.

It may be objected that the decision to destroy a group and its members can be, and at times has been, based on categorical premises which are nonetheless utilitarian. This argument has been made, in fact, in respect to the Nazi genocide—on the basis of the claims by the Nazis that the existence of the Jews was a threat to the well-being of other groups in the society or of the society as a whole. Defended on these grounds, the extermination of the Jews would then be warranted or even obligatory, for instrumental or possibly "moral" reasons.

It is important to note against this line of reasoning, however, that the utilitarian justification for the policy of genocide, so far as it was a factor at all, was inconsistently applied by the Nazis both in practice and in principle. This inconsistency, moreover, was not an accidental lapse but was symptomatic of a rejection of the utilitarian rationale within the

Nazi ideology itself. There is a variety of evidence for this contention, but it appears most clearly in respect to the medical or biological metaphors that Nazi ideologists frequently employed in their public attacks on the Jews.[13] In these metaphors, the Jews were compared to various types of bacilli or disease: cancers, plague, tuberculosis. On the basis of these analogies, the extirpation of the Jews would then represent a cure; genocide would in effect be a requirement of public health.

The inconsistency that appears in connection with this justification is not in the use of these analogies or metaphors, however, but in the context of justification of which they are part. Had the Nazis held consistently to the values implied by the metaphors of disease, the value of self-preservation—the ostensive reason for attacking agents of disease—would have been a dominant motive for them, and the genocide against the Jews would then follow justifiably from that premise. But on a number of occasions when the policy of genocide conflicted with the requirements of self-preservation that became progressively more urgent in the general war the Nazis were fighting, it was the former, not the latter, that won out. It can be stated as a general conclusion, in fact, that the Nazis were willing to increase the risk that they would lose the wider war—with whatever consequences this would have for their survival individually or as a nation—in order to wage their war against the Jews. That this order of priorities was a matter of policy and not simply a result of circumstance is clear from a number of statements and decisions. So, for example, the Minister for Occupied Eastern Territories who had ordered the extermination in those territories of Jews who might have been used for forced labor to support the war effort con-

13. The use of the disease metaphor recurs in Nazi ideology. So, for example, in *The Jew in German History,* a German army indoctrination booklet from 1939 (cited in Dawidowitz, *War Against the Jews*), the Jews are a "plague," "poisonous parasites." Hitler in a letter of 16 September 1919 writes that the "effect of Jewry will be racial tuberculosis of nations"; and in *Mein Kampf,* he speaks of them as "germ carriers," as an "abscess." A remarkable extension of the metaphor appears in a speech by Hitler in February 1942 (cited by Fest, *Hitler,* 212): "The discovery of the Jewish virus is one of the greatest revolutions which has been undertaken in the world. The struggle we are waging is of the same kind as in the past century, that of Pasteur and Koch. How many diseases can be traced back to the Jewish virus? We shall regain our health only when we exterminate the Jews." Alex Bein points out that the disease metaphor was used to reinforce the distinction between the Jews and "inferior races" who nonetheless remained human ("The Jewish Parasite: Notes on the Semantics of the Jewish Problem with Special Reference to Nazi Germany," *Yearbook of the Leo Baeck Institute* 9 (1964), 3–40. See also the discussion of the disease metaphor by Saul Friedländer, "On the Possibility of the Holocaust," in Yehuda Bauer and Nathan Rotenstreich (eds.), *The Holocaust as Historical Experience* (New York: Holmes and Meier, 1981), 7–8.

firmed that order with the assertion that "as a matter of principle no consideration should be given to economic interests in the solution of this problem" (Nuremberg Document PS-3666). A similar statement would be made by Himmler himself in 1944, when the course of the war was still more obviously going against the Nazis.[14] It was in that year also that the evidence most frequently cited for the claim that the Nazis were willing to sacrifice their own interests appears; this is the use by the Nazis, even on the brink of defeat, of badly needed railroad transport to convey Jews (mainly during this period, the Jews of Hungary) to the death camps. At his trial in Jerusalem, Eichmann was to appeal to this fact as evidence of the disinterested and self-sacrificing "principles" that had motivated him.

Additional reasons for rejecting Nazi references to the Jews as pestilence or disease as a consistent rationale of their acts are suggested by the history of the metaphors themselves. The most immediate implication of the nineteenth-century discovery of the "germ theory of disease" was that the way to fight disease would be to attack the organisms which caused it or their carriers. The medical campaigns based on these premises spoke of immunizing or curing the individuals affected by disease, or at most of "sanitizing" certain geographical ares—but virtually never of eradicating the source of the disease.[15] (These more modest goals undoubtedly reflected what were seen as the realistic possibilities of medical science at the time.) It was only late in the nineteenth century

14. See Yitzhak Arad, *Belzec, Sobibor, Treblinka* (Bloomington, Ind.: Indiana University Press, 1987), 133. *This* emphasis is in flagrant contrast to one of the main reasons given by the Allied governments for their negative responses, while the Nazi genocide was being committed, to proposals for the rescue of the Jews. So, for example, in a memo from the British Foreign Office (15 December 1943): "The Foreign Office are concerned with the difficulties of disposing of any considerable number of Jews should they be rescued from enemy or occupied territory . . . [including the] difficulties of transportation, particularly shipping . . ." (cited in David Wyman, *The Abandonment of the Jews* (New York: Pantheon, 1984), 182.

15. Medical histories have not focused on this issue, but see, e.g., Robert P. Hudson, *Disease and Its Control* (Westport, Conn.: Greenwood Press, 1980), chaps. 8 and 9; and Arturo Castiglioni, *A History of Medicine* (New York: Knopf, 1985), 692–93. Bein points out ("Jewish Parasite") that biological metaphors (e.g., "parasite") go back at least to the eighteenth century. But parasites do not themselves *cause* disease: the step toward that identification comes after the development of the germ theory of disease in the nineteenth century. Thus the medical prescription for eradicating the source of disease and the impulse for genocide have a proximate historical—and more than metaphorical—relation. Consider in respect to this background, for example, the statement by Paul Legarde (1887): "One does not negotiate with trichinae and bacilli; trichinae and bacilli are not chosen to be educated, they are exterminated quickly and as thoroughly as possible." (cited in Bein, "Jewish Parasite," 32).

and in the early twentieth century that the possibility was envisioned that a disease-related organism might be exterminated *as a kind*.

The difference between preventing or curing a disease, on the one hand, and eliminating its cause, on the other hand, approximates the relation in political terms between common warfare and genocide. The historical development of these two forms of "defense" was so closely linked chronologically, moreover, that the developing idea of political genocide might have contributed to the goal of medical prevention as well as the more obvious other way around. It could be argued, still more extremely, that use of the concept of disease as a political metaphor is itself a foreshadowing of the phenomenon of genocide. For the latent content of that metaphor seems almost calculated to provoke the genocidal reaction: that the members of a particular group pose a mortal danger because of their inherent characteristics; that those characteristics cannot be controlled by the people who "have" them or anyone else—and thus that attempts either to change or to quarantine the group would necessarily fail; that there are no compensating features among the group; and that extermination is the obligatory response to the danger they pose. The group and its members are in effect irremediable.

Viewed in these terms, the disease metaphor employed by the Nazis is symptomatic of the structure of genocidal intention most basically in denying any semblance of humanity or personhood to members of the group singled out. It is not necessary to settle the disputed question of what those features of humanity or personhood are to recognize that they will in some form involve an individual power of agency and self-determination, a sense of continuing identity or character, and a capacity of intersubjective rationality or power of discourse. Where the individual person is considered only as the member of a group—and the group itself defined by characteristics over which the individual has no control—nothing remains to any of these aspects of the person qua person. Not self-determination or individual identity or the capacity for shared discourse is admitted for members of the group, and this reiterative denial of the self makes the disease metaphor appropriate symptomatically to the act of genocide in which the *genos* is to be destroyed, with the individuals within the *genos* entirely incidental. (The Nazi order of 17 August 1938 that German Jews whose first names were not already on an approved list should "legally" take common names— "Israel" for the men, "Sara" for the women—was itself a step in this direction.)

What emerges from analysis of the utilitarian justifications proposed by the Nazis for their genocide against the Jews is a basis *in principle* which contradicts those supposedly prudential arguments. A bitter

irony appears here in the form of an inverted conception of moral agency: the agent of genocide does not treat his victims as a means; he attacks
them as ends in themselves and on grounds of principle rather than of
inclination. There is no use that the agent wishes to make of his victim,
nothing he requires or wants of the latter except to deprive him of all
claims of selfhood. In the act of physical destruction on the basis of
group identity, all claims of the individual are denied: the agent is here
entitled, even obligated, to act toward his victims in a way that demonstrates that they have no claims as persons. To act otherwise—to take
account of the individual as a person or even to allow this as possible—
would in these terms be a fault, a moral parody in the sense that anthropomorphism always is. The principle applied here asserts that
certain persons may—more strongly, *ought*—to be treated not as ends in
themselves, but as the negation of ends in themselves. The individual is
attacked not for anything he himself is or does, but for his relation to a
group, a relation over which he has no control; the reason for the attack
is not personal interest, gain, or inclination, but the principle that membership in the group itself suffices to exclude him from the domain of
humanity. This principle may not itself *require* the physical destruction
of the group—but annihilation is the one way of affirming the principle
that leaves no doubt either about the principle or about its applicability
to the group.[16]

   This aspect of genocide suggests the surprising conclusion that there
may be differences among wrongdoers in respect to the measure of humanity they acknowledge in the persons of their victims. To be sure, a
robber violates the person of his victim, treating the victim as a means.
But insofar as the robber wants what his victim *has,* he is not attacking or
denying everything that the victim *is;* this condition holds also for the
thief who steals simply for the pleasure of the act: here, too, there could
be surrogates or substitutes. Even a murderer may be responding (however disproportionately) to something his victim possesses or has done
as an individual. It is only where a person is defined in every essential
characteristic by an abstraction of group membership beyond the person's own choosing, and where the attack on the group is itself raised to
the level of principle, that all sense of individual agency in the victim—
choice, deliberation, the potentiality for change—is denied. It is only

16. Such a principle is presupposed in statements such as that by Hitler, in his political
Last Will and Testament (29 April 1945), written hours before his death and with the
thousand-year Reich in ruins around him: he could still urge (one wonders whom) that
"above all I charge the leaders of the nation and those under them to scrupulous observance of the laws of race and to merciless opposition to the universal poisoner of all
peoples, international Jewry."

here, in genocide, that the victim is no longer, except in an accidental physical sense, a person at all.

No other morally relevant action can be consistently described in these terms, and it is in this that the distinctiveness of genocide consists. Most wrongdoing is directed against individuals as individuals and against groups only insofar as those groups reflect the deliberate histories or traits of their members. Even where group identification beyond the control of individual members affects the choice of the victim (for example, in sexual attacks), the act will usually be emotionally expressive—for example, the means of revenge—not a matter of principle. Anger or hatred often lead to actions which conflict with the practical interests of the agent, but then, too, the agent chooses among interests; he does not forego them in the name of principle. It is extraordinary, moreover, that actions directed against classes or groups of people should call for their complete destruction, wherever they might go or be; here, too, the sense of individual agency is denied. So long as *some* alternative is proposed (e.g., ransom, religious or cultural conversion), or where the "punishment" itself follows an alleged injury, the sense remains that compensation is being exacted for something the members of the group are held responsible for. When, however, identification in the group is entirely out of the hands of its members, when the act of destruction is directed against individuals entirely as members of the group, willing the extinction of both as a matter of principle and oblivious to even self-interested consequences, there we have a distinctive act, one in which physical destruction or murder has become an end in itself.

It might be objected that to identify the act of genocide with a process of *de*humanization, even for the Nazi genocide but more obviously as a general rule, begs the question. What is at issue in the ideological structure of genocide as represented in Nazi policy, for example, might be judged a consequence of bad science, not of moral criminality—since if the Nazis genuinely believed that the Jews *were* a disease, there would be no force to the charge of dehumanization: the Jews would not have been human to begin with. Nor would there be any basis for the more general claim that genocide was for the Nazis nonutilitarian and a matter solely of principle. Since (in this view) the Jews posed a grave threat, their destruction, like any other act of self-defense, could be justified on prudential or even moral grounds.

But this interpretation faces an objection identical to the one cited before against the view of Nazi genocide as based on more general utilitarian considerations. The contention that the Jews were not human was not consistently maintained by the Nazis, and the inconsistencies are so flagrant that they undermine any force that the contention would otherwise have. The conclusion is difficult to avoid, in fact, that it was a deliberate and systematic feature of Nazi policy to dehumanize the victims of the genocide they were implementing—and this feature of their policy itself suggests a quite different starting point than the premise that the Jews were not human.

There is undoubtedly some basis for attributing this belief to the Nazis; the Jews, in contrast to the Slavic peoples, who according to the Nazi typology were *inferior* human beings, were formally classified as *sub*-human, i.e., not human at all. But there is substantial evidence beyond that already cited that the Nazis themselves did not either consistently credit this claim or, more to the point, act on it. I refer here not only to the many expressions of awareness on the part of the Nazi leadership, in quite conventional terms, that their policies were open both to serious moral and to scientific question, but more importantly, to the *practice* of dehumanizing their victims that was so constant a part of the Nazi design. For a period of more than eight years from the time that they came to power, Nazi policy did not initiate the systematic extermination of the Jews. It was, in fact, only in October 1941 that the emigration of German Jews from Germany was formally prohibited; before that, forced emigration had been the principal feature of the "Solution" proposed by the Nazis to the "Jewish Question." (In the period between 1933 and 1938, about a third of the German Jewish community did in fact leave Germany, something that would have been impossible if the policy of extermination had even been anticipated.) But neither during that time nor subsequently was there any doubt about the systematic brutality and degradation which figured in Nazi policy and which itself, by a cruel inversion, testifies more strongly even than extermination itself to the essentially human status accorded the Jews to begin with. In the face of alleged danger, a justification for violence based on the right of self-defense can plausibly be invoked. But a systematic pattern of torture and degradation is only intelligible on the premise that the victims are not essentially dissimilar from the perpetrators and that something much more morally complex than self-defense is at issue. When Franz Stangl, the commandant of Treblinka, was asked, after his capture, why, if it was clear that the Jews were to be killed anyway, such extremes of cruelty and humiliation were made part of that process, he responded that this was done in order "to condition those who actually had to carry out the policies."[17] Even if one accepts this response as cred-

17. In an interview with Gitta Sereny, recorded in Gitta Sereny, *Into That Darkness* (New York: Random House, 1983), 101.

ible, it acknowledges that those "who actually had to carry out the policies" saw (and recognized that they saw) in their victims a shared humanity, not nonhumans threatening them with mortal danger.

3. The Form of Intention

The process of systematic dehumanization requires a conscious affirmation of the wrong involved in it—that is, that someone who is human should be made to seem, to become, and in any event to be treated as less than that. And this step is not, it seems, only a feature of the Nazi attacks on the Jews, for in its more general form, it marks the distinctiveness of genocide as well: that here the agent of the act is voluntarily choosing to do wrong as a matter of principle—what is wrong even by *his* lights. This is a large claim to make, and the evidence for it will be considered more fully in chapter 2. But in the immediate context of what has been said about the occurrence of genocide, the basis for the claim can be seen in the stages of deliberation which the act of genocide presupposes and without which neither the idea nor the act embodying the idea is possible. One stage of deliberation is required in order to identify apparent individuals in terms of a generic and collective essence—that is, to "see" individuals not as individuals but as exclusively defined by their membership in a group. A second stage is presupposed in the claim that this generic essence represents an imminent danger, and that it has this character not as it happens, but necessarily: a judgment is made that the essence is intrinsically a menace. A third stage of deliberation is required for the decision that only extermination of the danger, now fixed intrinsically in the *genos,* can be an adequate response to it.

Each of these stages entails a process of reflection which, as the stages succeed each other, concludes with the intention of genocide. Each of the steps requires the agent's denial of a burden of evidence, a denial in which conceptual analysis and evaluation merge: the denial, first, of an individual nature and the capacity for individual agency in human beings; the denial, secondly, of qualities in the group or its members that would allow an alternative response (deportation, imprisonment) to "problems" associated with the group; thirdly, the rejection of claims of self-interest or even self-preservation in the face of what is then asserted as the "principled" demand for genocide. (The last of these denials may seem to be a distinctive feature not of genocide as such but of the Nazi genocide in particular. But where a human *genos* becomes the object of annihilation, the feature appears as a general one; the principle is required as part of the justification.) Hannah Arendt, responding to criticism of her conception of the "banality of evil" in the actions of Eichmann, expanded on that reference by describing Eichmann as "thoughtless," as not having understood and thus of not having willed or chosen the consequences of the acts that made him so central a figure in the Nazi genocide. The difference between the "banality" of evil in an Iago and the profundity of evil in a Satan is for Arendt the *absence* of deliberation or intention in the former, in contrast to the latter.[18] But thinking and so also thoughtlessness are not only or necessarily psychological categories; we may infer them as well in the logical and moral structure of certain acts. And if deliberation or intention can ever be inferred, they appear here, in the abstractive process of conceiving, affirming, and then acting on a *principle* that claims a warrant, even an obligation, for group killing. Cain, when he first discovered or invented the possibility of individual murder, might have been thoughtless, simply enraged and thus striking out at Abel, who was near at hand as an immediate object. By contrast, it is in the *nature* of genocide that it requires deliberation, first in conceptualizing and generalizing its object—and then by intending and realizing a process of annihilation as a matter of principle.

Two systematic objections have yet to be considered in this account. The first of these concerns the claim of intentionality or deliberateness—and the evidence that for the corporate process of genocide, in any event of the *Nazi* genocide, such intentions may be fragmentary or unclear, not fully formed or deliberate at all. This indeed has sometimes been alleged to be a defining feature of totalitarianism: that it serves precisely to incapacitate individual and voluntary action. If this were the case, when that structure turns to waging war—however its opponents are defined—there would ensue "processes of destruction which, although massive, are so systematic and systemic, and . . . therefore appear so 'normal' that most individuals involved at some level of the process of destruction may never see the need to make an ethical decision or even reflect upon the consequences of their actions."[19] The process, in other words, moves itself, apart from or even in defiance of anything like an individual decision or intention.

But it is important to notice that this consideration presupposes a view of intentionality which is itself open to question, especially as juxtaposed to an alternative conception. Intention may be conceived as a mental "act" chronologically prior to what is intended and thus also physically separated from it; it is on this view that interpretation of the

18. Hannah Arendt, *Eichmann in Jerusalem: a Report on the Banality of Evil*, rev. ed. (New York: Penguin Books, 1980), 280–98.
19. Wallimann and Dobkowski, *Genocide*, xvi.

Nazi genocide as "unintended" largely depends. What would be required in this view would be explicit documentary evidence of a Hitler-order for the Final Solution, or at least the record of a public and collective statement by the Nazi hierarchy to the same effect—either of them prior to and thus setting in motion the Nazi genocide.

The failure to meet this requirement (no such Hitler-order has been found), however, may reflect as much on the requirement as on the facts of the matter; that failure, moreover, is to a great extent avoided in an alternative account according to which an intention "occurs" as an aspect of the act itself, not as independent and prior to it.[20] Since evidence of the presence or absence of intention often appears *only* in the shape of the event to which intentionality is ascribed (or denied); and since even when other external evidence exists, the shape of the event itself—that is, whether it *appears* to have been intended—is a crucial consideration, it seems at once more economical and coherent to link intention, the idea of the act, with the act itself rather than to define and locate the two separately. This does not mean that intention may not in *some* sense precede the act intended, but that both the evidence and existence of an intention is fully realized only in the outcome of the act itself. In this sense, then, where a corporate decision or act is in question, it is the intelligibility of the decision or act as purposive (and its unintelligibility otherwise) that is crucial to its identification as intentional. Individual or collective statements attesting to a role for intention are not irrelevant (such statements do in fact exist in respect to the plan for the Final Solution). But even when they are in evidence, such statements are not privileged; they must themselves be judged together with other aspects of the act itself. Only when all of these are joined is an intention constituted.

The second objection to be considered is that even given the conception of genocide as intentional, it does not follow that this deliberation is accompanied—for genocide as such or for the Nazi genocide in particular—by an intention to do evil. An act that turns out to be evil, in other words, may have been directed toward a specific end without having been intended *as* evil; and it seems clear, in fact, that many actions later judged to be evil initially have this character of innocence in the eyes of its agent. The issue occurs in a more general form in the traditional Platonic thesis that "no one does evil willingly"—that to do evil is always to act out of ignorance, since no one would knowingly choose to do wrong.

---

20. See, e.g., Ludwig Wittgenstein, *Philosophical Investigations*, trans. G. E. M. Anscombe (New York: Macmillan, 1953), paragraphs 638–49, and G. E. M. Anscombe, *Intentions* (Ithaca: Cornell University Press, 1957).

The general issue at stake here will be taken up in chapter 2, although, obviously, if it could be shown that the Nazis intended genocide knowing that it was wrong, this would also have implications for the general question. Admittedly, to show this would not imply that they intended the genocide against the Jews *because* it was wrong—but the first step in this direction would itself be significant.

Here, too, certain other general issues obtrude, for example, of how it is possible to prove that an act has been initiated "knowingly" (whether of good or evil). How, in other words, can it be demonstrated that someone has morally sufficient knowledge of what he is doing? One evident means of responding to this question would be to view the act in question in the context of other related acts; that is, in relation to other knowledge of the agent's conduct. And in this respect, other of the Nazis' acts, although themselves open to interpretation, are revealing. One preeminent feature of the Final Solution is that it was intended to be concealed from beginning to end by a cloak of secrecy. A detailed system of speech rules governed references to the Final Solution and what that "solution" entailed; the code words themselves were to be used sparingly. (This phenomenon is discussed further in chapter 4, "Language and Genocide".) At a different level, the operations of the six death camps which epitomized the genocidal intention—in four of them there was not even the pretense of "employing" the captive labor within them—were governed by rules of extraordinary secrecy, and required specific avowals of silence beyond the standard pledges of loyalty by all the members of the SS involved in their work. Great efforts were made (and were to some extent successful) to obliterate traces of the existence of the death camps: to erase traces of the gas chambers and crematoria that they employed; of the bodies or graves of their victims; and of the identities and the numbers of the victims.

In this sense, the fact that no documentary evidence has been located of an order issued by Hitler which set in motion the process of the Nazi genocide is not, as certain commentators have concluded, a problematic feature in identifying the genocide as intentional—let alone one that would exculpate Hitler as ignorant of the policy or imply that the process of genocide did not occur by design. So far as anything follows from this, it is that the absence of such evidence is consistent with a pattern of concealment that runs through the history of the planning and implementation of the Final Solution, at least from the time that its prospect came to be something more than a wistful fantasy. (It is also consistent with a pattern according to which Hitler sought to insulate himself from a number of the most morally portentous decisions made by the Third Reich.) This dedication to silence is compellingly formulated in Himmler's statement that appears at the beginning of this chapter (a statement originally made in a secret speech at Poznan): "I myself believe that it is better for us—us together—to have borne this for our people, that we have taken the responsibility for it on ourselves (the responsibility for an act, not just for an idea), and that we should now take this secret with us into the grave."

To be sure, there were official, even public references to certain of the individual events which together constituted the Final Solution; to conceal the presence of the fact itself would have been impossible, given the numbers and groups of people required for its implementation. But this is quite different from *announcing* a policy—and it is clear that an essential part of the policy of the Nazi genocide was precisely the opposite of this, that is, concealment (from the Germans themselves as well as from others). It was an ideal here that, in Himmler's words, the Jews should "disappear"—and the implication of this and the other evidence cited is that they should also *seem* to have disappeared, that is, impalpably and mysteriously to have dropped out of existence. (This was evidently also a premise on which the Nazi plan for building a Jewish museum in Prague was based: a museum that was being developed for the study of the history and ways of an extinct group at the same time—and by the same people—that the process of making that group extinct was being carried on.)

Admittedly, alternative explanations can be given for the fact that someone or group might wish to conceal its actions, even that it should go to great lengths to conceal them. The most obvious of these is that although Nazi officials were themselves convinced that the policy of genocide was warranted—justified, right—they knew also that many other people, within Germany as well as outside, would disagree. Thus, in order to prevent resistance (including, of course, resistance by the intended victims) and also to anticipate later retribution, it would be natural that they should build a wall of secrecy around the acts undertaken in order to implement the Final Solution.

There is no means, it seems clear, of proving conclusively that the phenomenon of concealment on the scale that it was practiced by the Nazis is a reflection of guilt rather than a calculation of prudence. (In any event, the former conclusion would not mean that the latter was not a motive, only that it was subordinate to the other.) But as the moral distance between the two explanations is evident, so, too, is their difference in plausibility. The many risks that the Nazis openly ran in order to plot and to implement the Final Solution; their acceptance of the need to sacrifice themselves for what they alleged to be the principle involved in the war against the Jews; their dedication to other aspects of the cause of

National Socialism and of the *Führerprinzip*, the source of authority that went beyond all other laws: these explicit commitments diminish the likelihood that the concurrent effort by the Nazis to conceal the details of the Final Solution was mainly the expression of a practical concern either for their own security or for the success of their plans. Certainly the probability that what appears here was a divided consciousness— bound on one side to the "principle" motivating the genocide against the Jews; on the other side, to an awareness of the moral enormity of that principle—is at least as likely as the prudential explanation. It would be on the basis of this consciousness that the affirmation given by the Nazis to the policy and act of genocide would also be an affirmation, at the very least an acknowledgment, of the evil which these entailed.

It should be mentioned that the efforts by the Nazis to conceal the Final Solution do not stand alone as evidence of their consciousness of its moral enormity. There are, for example, records of the kinds of medical and psychiatric care required for SS personnel assigned to the death camps and for those who had been members of the four Einsatzgruppen especially commissioned for massacre at the beginning of the Russian campaign.[21] There remain also fragmentary and isolated statements of certain officers in the Wehrmacht who protested aspects of the genocide; the fact that these protests were muted and had few practical consequences is less to the point than the indication in the protests themselves that they reflected a more widespread consciousness of the moral implications of the policy of genocide. There is the strangely parallel—and also secret—career of the program of "euthanasia" (known at T-4), which began at the time of the Nazi invasion of Poland and was officially ended not quite two years later, almost simultaneously with the invasion of Russia. (The conclusion of that program came most immediately in response to protests within Germany about the "mercy death" given to the approximately fifty thousand victims—mainly non-Jewish Germans—who were judged "unworthy of life." Its effect, however, was to allow a number of the doctors and other personnel involved in the euthanasia program to move on to the death camps in the East, where what they had learned about killing by means of gas was again put to use.)[22]

21. See on these consequences Robert J. Lifton, *The Nazi Doctors: Medical Killing and the Psychology of Genocide* (New York: Basic Books, 1986), 159, 437. For the emphasis on secrecy, see also Anna Pawelczynska, *Values and Violence in Auschwitz*, trans. Catherine Sleach (Berkeley: University of California Press, 1979), 83; and Fleming, *Hitler*, 19–20.

22. For accounts of the "euthanasia" policy, see Ernst Klee, *Euthanasie: Im NS-Staat* (Frankfurt A. M.: S. Fischer, 1983); Lifton, *Nazi Doctors;* Leni Yahil, *The Holocaust: The Fate of European Jewry 1932–1945* (Hebrew), (Tel Aviv: Schocken, 1987), 428–32. It is

There is thus substantial evidence, as inferred from the character of genocide in general and as visible in the course of the Nazi genocide against the Jews in particular, of the genocide's intentional character—intentional in respect both to the act of genocide and to the knowledge of its moral enormity. This conclusion may be more significant in its particularity than in any more general thesis on which it bears, but the challenge it represents to the traditional conception of evildoing as "unintentional" is unmistakable. There obviously are occasions when moral agents act in or out of ignorance, and there are rarer instances when such agents act out of a general moral blindness. In the tradition of philosophical rationalism, these explanations account for *all* acts of wrongdoing: there is no instance in which the wrongdoer has full or genuine knowledge that he ought not to do what he chooses to. There is no doubting the great power in this position, in the consistency of its view of knowledge and in its tribute to the faculty of reason. But the price paid for those advantages is evident in their clash with experience—experience which now includes, among less extreme events, the phenomenon of genocide. The levels of awareness required to move through the conceptual "moments" of genocide, the kinds of evidence and rationalization presupposed there, are such that if we still conclude that the Nazis were doing only what they *thought* to be right—with the implication that such error was based finally on ignorance—we give up all hope whatever of distinguishing moral judgment from what anybody, at any particular moment, does. Where the issues are significant, the conclusions reached by moral reasoning—like those of logical inference—are not self-evident; even their status as moral reasoning requires a decision which distinguishes them in those terms. And if, with the combination of historical and conceptual evidence disclosed by it, genocide were still denied as an instance of reason willing evil, we would also be forced to the conclusion that there is unlikely to be *any* act of wrongdoing for which the evidence would show that it had been done willfully. The very possibility of moral evaluation and the assignment of moral responsibility becomes problematic.

Admittedly, the more general question at issue here is whether evil is

---

evident that the chronological connections between first the "euthanasia" program and then the Final Solution, on the one hand, and the progressive expansion of the more general war, on the other hand, were not accidental. Even without the explicit statements made by Hitler in respect to this timing, coincidences of this sort would be very improbable; the timing is thus further evidence of the intentional design of the Final Solution (there has been little dispute about the deliberateness of the euthanasia policy). It is hardly a startling conclusion, but this chronology, like that of the Turkish genocide against the Armenians which consciously took advantage of the disruptions of World War I, points to the "cover" for genocide that wartime provides.

ever done knowingly or willfully, and it would hardly settle that question to say that if intended evil ever occurs it appears in the act of genocide, specifically in the Nazi genocide against the Jews. The alternative conclusion might be drawn that since it does not appear there, it does not appear anyplace. But the consequences of this response amount to a denial of the grounds for moral judgment of any kind whatever. Or again: the assignment to genocide of a decisive role in determining the question of whether evil can be intended might be considered impermissibly ad hoc. Is it not possible, on the basis of what has been claimed here for the place of genocide in the history of ethical "development," that another, still larger means of wrongdoing will be discovered or invented—one that would challenge the reference here to genocide as a "proof text" for the possibility of doing evil intentionally? Why not yet another stage in the progress of evil? But there is no need either to deny the point of such questions or to draw any conclusions from them about the character assigned here to genocide. That character means no more than that history is part of ethics, that historical paradigms—exemplary causes—are components of that history, as similar structures have otherwise, in other areas, also figured in the history of human ideas and acts. There is nothing surprising or problematic in the claim that we come to know what moral principle is—or, on its side, evil principle—by encountering it first in history, by seeing there, close up, its transformations and its consequences. It is, indeed, difficult to know what an alternative to this, as a basis for the history of ethics, could be.[23]

Genocide comes as close as any act of which humanity has experience to exemplifying the statement of Milton's Satan in *Paradise Lost:* "Evil, be thou my good." Historically, the figure of Satan has represented precisely this improbable conjunction: evil as a conscious and deliberate— intended—choice. We see in the phenomenon of genocide that Satan is not, after all, only a mythical figure, that also human beings can do evil voluntarily. That is, insofar as the concepts of good and evil, voluntary and involuntary, have applicability to human affairs at all. Genocide has undoubtedly not occurred as often as those using the term have claimed. But the fact that it has occurred at all, that we know it now always to be possible because it has been actual, discloses as much as is required in order to establish a relation between human intentions and the status of evil.

23. This is not to imply that the act of genocide or the judgment of it is *determined* by cultural norms, but only that such norms influence moral judgment. An apologia for slavery written in eighth-century B.C. Egypt *means* something different (and must then be judged differently) from an "identical" statement written in the United States today. Even moral blindness is thus not context-free; but this does not imply that there are no extra-situational ethical norms—only that history is a factor in shaping and applying them too.

2

The Knowledge of Evil and Good

Legal judgments may not coincide with moral judgments in the principles that underlie them or in the verdicts they reach. Both forms of judgment, however, set out from the fact that harm has been done or threatened, and most accounts of legal or moral responsibility hold that the "condition" of the person who does harm—his capacity or incapacity to know what he is doing—makes a difference in assessing it. A person who is judged insane is not accounted responsible (or at least is not punishable) for what he does, and a similar exception, on related grounds, is made for children or youths below a certain age (the age of "reason"). The incapacity of these agents to know what they are doing is what is at issue in such distinctions, not what they do or its consequences: the harm they cause is regarded as something apart from their condition or motives. The M'Naghton Rules, which since the mid-nineteenth century have influenced Anglo-American jurisprudence on the issue of legal responsibility, explicitly establish the criterion of a capacity to know as a requirement for culpability. According to those rules, a legal defense on grounds of insanity requires proof that the person judged did not know, *because* of a "defect of the mind," the "nature or quality of his act, or if he did know that, did not know that what he was doing was wrong." Someone who is unaware of the nature of his actions because he is unable to comprehend them is also not responsible or punishable for them.[1]

1. See the statement of M'Naghton (and a critical discussion) in Sheldon Glueck, *Law and Psychiatry* (Baltimore: Johns Hopkins University Press, 1962), 20–33; for analysis of

30

This account of the conditions of legal responsibility is significant for what it omits as well as for what it asserts. It does not stipulate, for example, that for a person to be held responsible for a crime, the person must have known that he was committing a crime at the time he did it; the requirement is that in order for him to be excused, his "not-knowing" must have been due to an incapacity beyond his control (in contrast to the possibility, for instance, that he was simply ignorant of the law). This implies that someone could in fact know what the law is but *nonetheless* choose to disobey it—an important principle which is presupposed, not only in the possibility of a legal defense on the grounds of insanity, but in the very notion of wrongdoing as such. If an incapacity to know what one is doing or to know that it violates the law removes the onus of responsibility, then it must be possible, in *other* instances, for a person both to be aware of violating the law and to violate it nonetheless. Characteristically, legal codes go still further than this, in the distinction they draw between acts committed with premeditation and those which are committed, perhaps still knowingly, but without premeditation. (Where ignorance of the law is appealed to, it is not an excuse; it may even be judged culpable in itself—but these consequences, too, assume the capacity for knowing what one is doing in the first place.)

There are obvious reasons why a legal code would, on the one hand, presuppose that an act *can* be committed in full knowledge that it violates the law but, on the other hand, not require that an agent should in fact have possessed that knowledge before he can be found guilty. If the latter requirement were in force, the agent's familiarity with the law would have to be demonstrated in addition to the evidence of its violation—the addition of a considerable weight to an already substantial burden of proof. The less restrictive requirement that a person must have the capacity to know the "quality" of his act but not necessarily know it in fact is more easily verified (although, of course, with difficulties of its own). That a person *could* have known the nature of his act but did not, does not, in these terms, affect the measure of culpability.

Even this broadened version of legal responsibility, however, fails to take into account the *moral* issue posed by the relation between wrongdoing and knowledge. It is one thing to admit the possibility that the laws of a state can be knowingly violated; it is a different matter to insist on the same possibility where the relation between moral knowledge and the personal decisions or acts based on such knowledge is at issue. It

---

M'Naghton in the general context of the concept of legal responsibility, Hyman Gross, *A Theory of Criminal Justice* (New York: Oxford University Press, 1979), chap. 7, esp. 297–310.

was this second relation that was the focus of discussion in chapter 1 about the concept of genocide and its exemplifications in the Nazi "Final Solution"—a focus only in part due to the fact that the legal concept of genocide applied only retroactively to the Final Solution. For quite aside from this consideration, the conclusion reached was that the Nazis indeed had the capacity to know the "nature and quality" of their acts in the genocide against the Jews; thus, that the Final Solution was not the result of individual or collective irrationality, but was deliberately and "reasonably" conceived—and also that the Nazis, substantively enough to have it influence their planning, recognized the policy and the acts constituting it as morally wrong. The additional conclusion was asserted, in fact, that the Nazis implemented the policy of genocide at least in part *because* it was wrong: wrongdoing had assumed for them the status of a principle.

The difference between the two claims referred to in these last statements should be noted: to act with the knowledge that what one does is wrong is not necessarily to do it because it is wrong. But even the conceptual possibility of the former, more limited assertion cannot be taken for granted. To be aware of what is legally obligatory or prohibited does not in itself constitute a commitment to obey the law; where the knowledge of *moral* obligation is concerned, however, the question of the relation between idea and act—of what space may exist between the two—is much more complex, and it has indeed been among the most persistent questions in the history of ethics. On the one hand, the phenomenon of wrongdoing committed with knowledge or deliberation seems a common—too common—occurrence; its possibility, even its likelihood, is assumed in virtually all the institutional structures of society and the moral exchanges of everyday life. On the other hand, because of the power conventionally ascribed to knowledge, when the knowledge—the *full* knowledge—of wrong or evil occurs, this knowledge is often viewed as so compelling as to make the decision to *do* wrong improbable or even impossible. However mistaken they may be, people characteristically believe that they are warranted in what they do; it has often been pointed out that the most notorious villains in history have, by their own lights, claimed justification for their actions. Evil, in this sense, is in the eye of the beholder and in any event not in the mind of the perpetrator (at least not at the time when he acts).

This theoretical and practical dilemma—on the one hand, that evil often seems to be committed knowingly; on the other hand, that the knowledge of evil as evil would preclude any such act—bears a more than accidental resemblance to the problem of evil for religious belief (that is, the question of how the existence of evil can be reconciled with the role of a beneficent and omnipotent God). In both antitheses, the harsh texture of contingent experience is opposed to a more abstract and unified power. The conceptual analogy extends, furthermore, to the resolution characteristically given to the two issues; like the religious traditions, philosophy, too, has often favored the second side of the dilemma—the conclusion, that is, that where there is genuine knowledge of good and evil, any moral decision that follows will act for the good. No one, in other words, would *knowingly* choose to do wrong—and by the same token, once the good or what ought to be done is known, subsequent decisions will follow that guidance. Where moral knowledge is concerned, the recognition of what ought to be done is on these terms held to entail the doing of it.

In his dialogues, Plato presents a sustained formulation of this view, asserting a close relation between knowledge and ethical choice and also tracing the consequences of that relation. So, for example, Plato recognizes that if the assumption is made that no one does evil knowingly, it would follow that anyone who does evil would then be acting out of ignorance—because he did not know better. And from this a theory of punishment also follows: that punishment ought to be rehabilitative or educational, not retributive. Since the wrongdoer does not know better, it is the lack of knowledge that must be treated and corrected. In this sense, given the causes of their actions, wrongdoers are not even culpable; they act out of ignorance both of what they do and of the alternatives open to them. In effect the "choices" or "decisions" of a wrongdoer are not authentic choices or decisions at all. And again, the basis for these conclusions is the concise premise of the ethical theory as a whole—that it is impossible to do evil when the knowledge is fully present that the act contemplated *is* evil.

This view of moral knowledge attributes to knowledge an unusual power, and Plato repeatedly calls attention to that power. So, for example, he asserts that "knowledge is a noble and commanding thing, which cannot be overcome, and will not allow a man, if he only knows the difference of good and evil, to do anything which is contrary to knowledge."[2] It is as though Plato argues here—as he also does elsewhere in relation to knowledge even when it involves no specific reference to ethics[3]—that genuine knowledge entails not only conceptualization but commitment; it occurs with the whole self. And of

2. *Protagoras* 352b.
3. See, e.g., *Republic* 510c ff.; *Theaetetus* 172c–177c.

course, if *that* were presupposed by knowledge, there could be no distance or discrepancy between idea and act: the act would already have been determined in the process of knowing.

One way of understanding this conception of the relation between knowledge and moral act is as a *definition* of knowledge. In these terms, the equation "To know the good is to do the good" would imply that if someone claims to know the good but then acts contrary to it, the outcome itself proves that the person did not *really* know the good. The assumption that if he did know the good he would do it implies that when he does not act in this way, this proves that he did not have genuine knowledge. But if *this* is the basis of the Platonic thesis, there could be no way of testing it at all; every counterexample proposed would be ruled out, and the only possible challenge would come, then, not from counterevidence but from another definition.

A second and more fundamental reason also suggests the importance of establishing the relation between knowledge and wrongdoing as contingent rather than as determined and a priori. If it were true that no one does evil knowingly and thus that no one *could* freely choose to do wrong, then it would also follow that the decision to do what is right or good (insofar as it originates in knowledge at all) is also "necessary," that is, not a matter of choice; at this point, too, there would be no alternative. The wrongdoer is thus denied a choice because he lacks knowledge of what he ought to do; the person who does what is right also does not choose—since the knowledge he has has determined the choice for him. In effect it is that knowledge, not a decision by the agent based on it that assures the act—as, on the other side, it is the lack of knowledge that would be the source of wrongdoing. And also analogously: as responsibility is diminished or removed when a wrong is committed out of or in ignorance, so, also, to do what is good or right will be to act without being responsible: there is no greater measure of choice here than in the other.

What is posed in this general issue, then, is the question of whether moral choice based on the knowledge of good and evil is at all possible. But it is the specific appearance of that issue in the question of whether wrongdoing or evil can be done deliberately, with knowledge, that is directly related to the subject of the Nazi genocide and which stands to affect the understanding and assessment of that corporate act. For a version of the Platonic thesis has often been cited in analyses of the genocide (almost none of them *intended* as apologias). So the argument is proposed that so far as ideas or beliefs were causally implicated in the Nazi genocide, it was Nazi ideology in its most literal form that served this function. This is to say that, however mistakenly, the Nazis them-

selves *believed* that the policies and decisions involved in the final
Solution were morally warranted; they, at least, believed that they were
justified in conceiving those policies and carrying them out. The Nazis
(on this account) acted in behalf of what they took to be the good, having found that conclusion to follow logically from the premises they first
laid down.

The link between this analysis and the Platonic thesis concerning the
relation between knowledge and moral decision thus emerges. For if indeed the Nazi policies were based on the beliefs (or "knowledge") they
repeatedly expressed that the Jews were less than human and that, as
such, they were innately and so unalterably a threat to the life of the German people as a nation and individually, then the conclusions that the
Nazis drew from these beliefs in the form of the Final Solution were arguably warranted or even obligatory—a matter of self-defense. On this
account, then, it is not the conclusions of the Nazi policy but the premises from which the conclusions emerge that are at fault—and these can
be objected to only in the way that mistaken beliefs or ignorance, not
malevolence, are ever at fault. And *this* conclusion in turn entails consequences that reflect the Platonic conception of wrongdoing and punishment as those have been outlined. However mistaken the beliefs that led
to the policy of the Final Solution—they might still be punishable on
grounds of culpable ignorance or negligence—it would follow more basically that since the Nazis did what they thought was right (however
guilty they were for not knowing other or better than they did, for ac-
cepting bizarre and discredited scientific concepts), they would still not
be guilty in the more radical sense of having done something that they
were aware of as wrong. Even to conclude that they *should* have been
aware of it as wrong would not add much force to the more basic contention that they nonetheless *were not* aware of it.

It is impossible to rule out a priori this analysis of moral culpability in
the Nazi genocide against the Jews, and there is some evidence to support it in the statements of Nazi ideology itself. That such an interpretation would necessarily mitigate the severity of any moral judgment on
the role of the Nazis, moreover, is not by itself an argument against it.
(The potentially mitigating force of this position is apparent in the defense on the grounds of ignorance that recurred in the Nazi war trials.
Industrial, government, and military officials sought to persuade the
courts that they were unaware of the policy of genocide, of which their
own actions were, in their terms, not only a small but an unrecognizable
part; the implication here was that if they *had* known, their guilt would
be substantially increased.) And yet if this account of the Nazi genocide
is based on the evidence of what was said or done, then it should also be

possible to show that the principle from which this conclusion of ex-culpation is drawn, whether in its general, Platonic conception or more specifically in relation to the Nazi genocide, may be mistaken; that is, that evil *can* be done knowingly, and, more specifically, that the Nazis were aware of the nature of the wrongs they were doing. At the very least it will be possible to find these claims true or false on the basis of the evidence; the test then must be in the assessment of what in fact occurred and in the conditions surrounding it.

The difficulties that such an assessment faces can be anticipated. The objection is predictable, against the contention that a particular act was done with the intent to do wrong, that, however mistakenly, the agents themselves believed that what they were doing was justified—and the fact that they did it is *itself* evidence of this. To refute this argument re-quires proof, then, that by their own lights, as this is evident in other of their acts and statements, the agents were indeed aware of doing wrong as they acted—and that this can be shown, perhaps not unequivocally or in the absence of contrary evidence, but sufficiently. To deny the legiti-macy of such a counterargument would be, as has been suggested, to deny the possibility of the moral judgment not only of evil but of good as well. It is unnecessary, however, to invoke this extreme consequence as a basis here—since evidence for the counterargument does indeed appear among the decisions and acts represented in the Nazi genocide. It is not the moral extremity of the genocide itself that establishes this counterar-gument. But more importantly it is also clear that its moral extremity does not, as might be supposed, block the counterargument. The evi-dence in fact reveals features of the genocide that underscore the degree of the enormity.

1. Contradiction, Shame, and Invention

How is it possible, in considering a wrongful act, to demonstrate that the person responsible for it "knew better"?—that the agent acted against ideals not merely as they were pronounced by others, but as the agent himself recognized them? The prima-facie evidence argues against this conclusion, since commission of the act may itself seem to imply that those responsible for it believed it to be warranted. The more compelling evidence, then, will not be found in the act alone but in its conjunction with what *else* was said or done that might disclose the intentions or motives behind it. Three groups of such features are distinguishable in the events of the Nazi genocide; these will be re-ferred to here under the headings of "Contradiction," "Shame," and "Invention." The appearances of these features are not slight or hidden among the events of the genocide; individually, they have often been noted. But the features have not usually been considered in terms of their connections to each other or as a group; viewed from this perspective, against the background of the general question of whether wrong can be done knowingly and the specific question of whether the wrong of the genocide was done knowingly, a pattern of evidence emerges that supports affirmative answers to both.

To be sure, the evidence of this pattern is not unequivocal; even if the interpretation given here were admitted as plausible, moreover, the conclusion might be reached that *on balance* the evidence nonetheless supports the contrary view that policies and decisions involved in the final solution were regarded in their Nazi sources as morally justified. But it should be noted that even on this conflicting interpretation, the terms of the original dispute would have altered. For what is contested now is the question of what the Nazis *really* thought or believed about what they did, in contrast to what the apparent or prima-facie evidence suggests that they believed. And with this distinction, a crucial premise of the present discussion would also be acknowledged: that the question of whether the Nazis acted with (even despite) knowledge of doing wrong is to be decided on the basis of the evidence of what they did, not as a matter of definition, not as deduced from even the act of genocide by itself, and not only on the basis of what they said (or denied) about what they did. Methodologically, the contention that they acted in the knowledge that what they did was wrong is now possible; the evidence available, furthermore, suggests that this contention is not only possible but warranted in fact.

In chapter 1 a number of contradictions were cited among statements made by the Nazis in their justification for the policy of the genocide against the Jews and also between such statements and certain actions by the Nazis in implementing that policy. These contradictions take a variety of forms, but they recur at such central junctures that the phenomenon of contradiction itself becomes expressive or symptomatic. What the phenomenon is expressive of can be seen first from examining the terms of the individual contradictions, and then from looking at the contradictions as a group.

The contradictions occur at a number of levels. So, for example, the point has been noted here that a recurrent theme in Nazi writings emphasizes the biological menace that the Jews represented as a race, comparable in danger and malignancy to disease (the main comparisons cited were to tuberculosis and cancer). The contention that the Jews were subhuman—a second, related claim—would not by itself support a genocidal response unless it were joined to a charge that the Jews posed a

threat of contamination or destruction. But—and here the contradiction—other features of the Nazi war against the Jews, both at the level
of idea and as practice, argue *against* these first claims. For example:
there is an obvious continuity historically between the Final Solution
directed against the Jews and the "ideals" and means of the"euthanasia"
campaign in Germany between 1939 and 1941. To be sure, the scale of
the latter was much smaller (estimates of its victims range from fifty
thousand to seventy thousand), but the evident continuity between the
two is pertinent to the issue raised here precisely because most of the
euthanasia victims were non-Jewish Germans. They included not only
people who were mentally retarded, but others suffering from degener-
ative diseases which even by the Nazis' standards did not deny their
status as human. The justifications for "granting" these people a "mercy
death" referred principally to the burden they imposed on society. (It
often goes unmentioned that the euthanasia program was continued on
the Russian front *after* having been terminated within Germany; its victims were German soldiers who had been severely wounded, and the
cadres responsible for their deaths, like those who at the same time were
organizing the killing in the death camps, included personnel from the
euthanasia centers.)[4]

That there were historical connections among these programs of
killing does not mean that their victims shared the same status. But it
suggests that reasons different from those actually cited for the genocide against the Jews might have led to that policy, certainly that it was
not *necessary* for the Nazis to believe that the Jews were an actual physical threat in order to move for their destruction. The differences of
circumstance among the various programs further underscore this possibility. The victims of the euthanasia program suffered from specific
physical or mental debilities; this was the justification given by the
Nazis for killing them. No such characteristics were required as justification for the extermination of the Jews. It was, in other words, neither
a necessary nor sufficient condition for the Final Solution that the Jews
should be believed to pose an actual physical threat against Germany
and the Germans. And although this means only that the metaphors of
pathology applied to the Jews *may* not have been the actual basis for
genocide, the opening provided by that possibility is significant when
joined to other evidence of contradiction.

If one asks why the Nazis, even on the assumption that they did believe the annihilation of the Jews was justified, made systematic humilia-

4. See references cited in chap. 1, nn. 21 and 22; and also Helmut Eberhardt, *Euthanasie
und die Vernichtung "lebensunwerten" Lebens* (Stuttgart: Ferdinand Enke Verlag, 1965).

tion and physical torture part of that process, the likely explanations are few. As has been noted, the one-time commandant of Treblinka, Franz Stangl, confronted with this question after the war, replied that this practice was necessary for inuring the camp personnel to their tasks, that is, to the process of killing.[5] Even this response, however, suggests that there were difficulties in sustaining the efforts of the guards and other functionaries in the camps—difficulties which would be hard to credit if the Jews had been recognized as a physical threat to the Nazis and to Germany more generally. Thus, on the one hand, the justification for the genocide against the Jews took the form of an argument based on self-defense; on the other hand, self-defense was not required by the Nazis as a justification for extermination—nor, as a matter of fact, was the process of extermination directed toward self-defense.

This last point has also been referred to previously in a somewhat different form but there, too, as an instance of contradiction. The evidence is clear that the Nazi genocide against the Jews proved costly to the Nazis in the more general war they were waging at the same time. It may be excessive and it is in any event unprovable to claim that the resources expended by the Nazis in the effort to annihilate the Jews were a decisive factor in their own defeat. But in a country facing the prospect of defeat (and certainly by mid-1943 this prospect was clear to virtually everyone in the Nazi hierarchy), it might be supposed that all the means available would be used to avert that defeat. There was, furthermore, no practical reason that this could not have been done—but it was not. Up until the last days of the war, in May 1945, the extermination of the Jews continued, with the diversion this entailed of material resources (trains, supplies) and of personnel.[6] The discussion in chapter 1 took this fact as evidence that the Final Solution was for the Nazis a matter of principle and an end in itself; the same fact is significant in the present context as it contradicts the justification proposed by the Nazis, that the Jews were a threat to the survival of Germany. For if that had been the real justification, German survival would have been the more basic—at the very least, a minimal—goal of the Nazis; the annihilation of the Jews would have been either a means to that end or at most a coordinate goal. But in fact the unwillingness to make use of the resources that would have become available if the deportations and the work of the death camps had ceased, and if the potential laborers killed in them had instead been ex-

5. In Sereny, *Into That Darkness* (see chap. 1, n. 17), 101.

6. See on this issue also Michael Marrus, *The Holocaust in History* (Hanover, N.H.: University Press of New England, 1987), 28–30; and Michael Musmanno, *The Eichmann Kommandos* (London: Peter Davies, 1962).

ploited in industries and elsewhere, suggest the contrary—that German survival was to be sacrificed or at least risked for the destruction of the Jews.

It can be argued that nothing follows even if such contradictions occur between the statements and practice of the Nazis. Ideologies are not typically bound by principles of consistency, and the history of anti-Semitism has been at least as much gripped by inconsistency as other ideologies: the Jews were excoriated because they were clannish and refused to assimilate, but also as cosmopolitans; because they were wealthy and powerful, but also as dependent and parasitic; because they represented a weightless modernity, but also because they were committed to an obdurate past. The explanations traditionally given for the capacity of anti-Semitism to encompass such contradictions (they often amount to restatements of the contradictions themselves) may to some extent apply as well to the contradictions in the Nazi justifications for the Final Solution, although it is clear that there is also a decisive break between Nazi anti-Semitism and that which preceded it. And there is, moreover, another possibility: that the contradictions are not the result of thoughtlessness but are themselves expressive. It seems likelier in fact that they attest here to an effort to find reasons for an idea and practice which themselves challenge the process of moral reason, reflecting a will that would violate even the principle of moral limits. On these terms, the contradictions are purposive, implying knowledge and an impulse to act that must be concealed from others but from oneself as well. The contradictions are between word and practice—and since practice includes words but much more as well, it is that which serves as a key for deciphering the contradiction. In any event, the price of contradiction would in this context seem to the Nazis not a very large price to pay; indeed it has its own expressive value, as the limits of logic as well as those of morality are impugned.

This interpretation of the phenomenon of contradiction in the Nazi justifications for their war of genocide as evidence of deliberation is supplemented by the two other features cited in the title of this section. It may seem improbable, given the enormity of their actions, that a sense of shame can be attributed to the Nazis in relation to those actions or indeed to any others. If shame had been possible, it could be argued, those acts would not have been committed. When this objection is joined to the unrepentant attitudes, virtually without exception, of the accused Nazis brought to trial since the end of World War II, the relevance of shame, with its implied admission of wrongdoing, seems still more improbable. Yet certain prominent aspects of Nazi conduct in the context of the genocide against the Jews suggest the presence of just this phenomenon: that the Nazis were aware not only of the practical consequences of their policies, but of their moral character as well—an awareness disclosed in the involuntary appearance of shame.[7] Some of these aspects have been referred to in chapter 1; others will be elaborated further in chapter 4, "Language and Genocide." There is a notable emphasis among these several features on secrecy or concealment, however, and it is this common element that is interpreted here as evidence of shame.

The planning and implementation of the Final Solution in its several phases were both formally and informally surrounded by a series of barriers meant to conceal that policy and the acts based on it, not only from the world outside Germany and from its intended victims, but also from the German people and even, in a strange but quite real sense, from the Nazi perpetrators themselves; these same measures also served the related purpose of impeding the assignment of responsibility for the Final Solution as a whole. Especially the latter fact has been the subject of an ongoing controversy between the "Functionalist" and the "Intentionalist" interpretations of the origins of the Final Solution. On the grounds that no specific "Hitler order" has been discovered that can be proved to have set the process of the Final Solution in motion, the Functionalists have argued that no such order was ever given; they infer from this that the Final Solution as it were "happened"—without intention and as the result of a series of independent decisions, taken by organizations competing with each other for control within the structure of the Nazi command. This contention has in turn been strongly disputed,[8] but the issue in this context is less a judgment of the argument than of the conditions underlying it. For it discloses a circumstance attested to

7. A distinction is commonly drawn between shame and guilt, with the former categorized as a response to external pressure, the latter, as reflecting internalized standards. (See, e.g., Helen Merrell Lynd, "The Concepts Shame and Guilt," in Lynd, *On Shame and the Search for Identity* (New York: Harcourt, Brace, and Co., 1958), 20–26; and Herbert Morris, "Guilt and Shame," in Morris, *On Guilt and Innocence* (Berkeley: University of California Press, 1976), 59–63.) The distinction in such accounts is directed to the origins of the two responses; in contrast, "shame" is used here to emphasize the external features of the two responses which would be *public* in both cases (even when the response was an attempt at public concealment).

8. For the terms of the dispute between the Functionalists and the Intentionalists, see also Fleming, *Hitler* (see chap. 1, n. 8); Saul Friedländer, "Historical Writing and the Memory of the Holocaust," in Berel Lang (ed.), *Writing and the Holocaust* (New York: Holmes & Meier, 1988); Michael Marrus, *Holocaust in History*, 40–46. See also the exchange between Martin Broszat and Saul Friedländer, "A Controversy about the Historization of National Socialism," in *New German Critique* (special issue on the *Historikerstreit*) 44 (1988), 81–126.

by other evidence as well: that Hitler went to great lengths to distance himself from connections which would associate him with the design or implementation of the Final Solution; and that the highest officials responsible to him for implementing the Final Solution (principally, Himmler) conspired in this effort at concealment, not only in respect to Hitler's role but also to their own and indeed to the existence of the Final Solution as such.

Some of the means of concealment employed have already been mentioned. These means include the set of "language rules" by which the killings of the Final Solution and the complex mechanism on which the process of genocide depended were disguised by a systematic nomenclature that—if the language rules had been capable of sustaining themselves—would have concealed the acts they referred to. This aspect of the general pattern of concealment will be discussed further in chapter 4; it may suffice here only to mention as an example that the term "Final Solution" (*Endlösung*), which was itself intended as a code word for the policy of genocide against the Jews, was in effect prohibited in documents intended for general circulation. Not only was it not to be used in public documents, but once the policy of annihilation was fixed, the term was not to be used, as a rule, even in official and secret documents. The code itself, in other words, was to be concealed—both the existence of the code (an awareness of which would naturally raise suspicions), and before that, the specific terms encoded, or at least this particular one. (Others, like the various synonyms for killing—e.g., *Sonderbehandlung*, or "special treatment"—could be used but even then circumspectly.) What appears here is an effort to conceal the phenomenon of the genocide within and by language.

For obvious reasons, however, the requirements for implementing the Final Solution could not be entirely subordinated to such restrictions. The process itself required organization and a command structure, and the principle of secrecy and concealment had to be extended accordingly. Thus, special oaths of secrecy would be required for SS personnel assigned to the death camps (the effort would be made within the camps, furthermore, to inculpate everyone assigned to them in the work of murder, in order to ensure that they would keep their vows of silence). Thus, too, extraordinary measures were taken to prevent the escape of anyone imprisoned within the camps and who so would have knowledge of them; as the possibility of discovery became increasingly likely, with the Nazi retreat from Russia and then from Poland, efforts were made to destroy the camps themselves and everything related to them—the machinery of the camps, the corpses of their victims, and the records of the process.[9] (It was the practice in the death camps that the victims "selected" for killing immediately on arrival at the camps would not be registered; even now, the number of victims at Belzec and Treblinka, for example, can be determined only by inference.) Thus, too, the highest ranks of the Nazi hierarchy, who felt impelled at times to refer to the duties required of their subordinates in implementing the Final Solution, would speak both in secret and *about* secrecy: The Poznan speeches by Himmler epitomize these purposes, and Himmler's proposal, in the speech cited in chapter 1, that they all—he himself, as well as the SS officers he was addressing—should take the secret of the Final Solution with them "into the grave" is only one, although among the starkest, reminder of a consciousness that would knowingly conceal itself.[10]

It is undeniable that these same items of evidence, like the evidence of the contradictions previously referred to, are also subject to a different interpretation. Concealment can be involuntary evidence of shame or guilt, but it can also be deliberate and directed toward a practical end. It is clear that in order to minimize resistance among their intended victims, the Nazis attempted to conceal the fate planned for them in the descriptions the Nazis gave out of "resettlement" and in the designs of the death camps themselves—the disguise of the entries to the camps and of the machinery within them (for example, representing the gas chambers as communal showers, even, at the next-to-last moment, sometimes providing the victims with pieces of soap). A practical motive for concealment appears here, then, together with a second one that extends beyond the possible resistance of the victims. For there is also a responsiveness in the Nazi hierarchy—erratic and unpredictable, but at times substantial—to public opinion both within Germany and in the Allied countries. In the light of what the Nazis ultimately proved capable of doing, it may seem difficult to credit this claim. But certainly before the Final Solution began and to some extent even afterward, there is convincing evidence of efforts made by the Nazis to anticipate public criticism, and as it occurred, to respond to it.

9. On the role of concealment, see chap. 1, n. 20; also Raul Hilberg, *The Destruction of the European Jews,* rev. ed. (New York: Holmes & Meier, 1985), 961–6, 979–80. In *The Terrible Secret* (London: Weidenfeld and Nicolson, 1980), Walter Laquer argues compellingly for the availability of information about the Final Solution before December 1942 (the point at which his study concludes). But that is not incompatible—in fact, it presupposes—the *attempt* at concealment, which continues past that date as well.

10. On these and the other Poznan speeches, see Bradley F. Smith, *Heinrich Himmler* (Stanford: Hoover Institution, 1971).

It seems clear, for example, that the "euthanasia" program was brought to an end by such pressure inside Germany; even earlier, the international boycott of German goods, initiated by Jewish organizations, in 1933, (although soon lifted) had immediate repercussions. Concealment would obviously be the most effective means of avoiding such pressures. (This fact weights more heavily the question of how the course of the Final Solution might have been affected had the reaction to its stages, inside Germany and internationally, been more explicit and determined than it was.) To this practical motive for attempting concealment, moreover, can be added a related prudential claim: that it was not the Nazis' own consciousness of wrongdoing that explains their emphasis on secrecy, but their recognition that others were likely to judge them harshly, for their individual actions and for those of Germany collectively.[11]

The question at issue, them, asks whether the Nazi attempts at concealment, viewed as a whole, can be accounted for by instrumental explanations to the exclusion of the phenomenon of shame and its implied recognition of wrongdoing (shame itself may be functional and expressive, but it is not deliberate and, in this sense, not instrumental). It is undoubtedly impossible to decide this issue conclusively without begging the question; this limitation seems in fact a characteristic feature of disputes in which exclusive claims are made for instrumental values (and perhaps of historical explanations in general). But it is also true that the evidence which is more than instrumental in the examples cited seems as compelling here as in other instances where the insufficiency of instrumental explanation is granted. It is possible to explain certain efforts at concealment by the Nazis on practical and prudential grounds; but not everything in those efforts, or the efforts viewed as a whole, can be accounted for in this way. The systematic pattern of secrecy and denial discloses more than simply prudential motives. The sense is conveyed here that the Nazis were not only aware of the judgment they knew would be passed on them by others for the act of genocide, but that they themselves—despite themselves—recognized the grounds for this judgment of opprobrium. There was at once a recognition and acknowledgment of the moral stigma attached to what they were doing. This recognition did not prevent them from going ahead with the Final Solution, but it meant that in doing so, they would attempt to conceal it from others and even from themselves. Such effort is one characteristic pat-

11. See Hilberg, *Destruction,* 521–23; also Konnilyn G. Feig, *Hitler's Death Camps* (New York: Holmes & Meier, 1985), 20–23.

tern expressed in the appearance of shame, and here, too, it reflects the awareness of wrongdoing.

Again: the claim of wrongdoing knowingly committed depends, in respect to the phenomenon of secrecy, on an interpretation of evidence which is equivocal; but here also, however, the claim is supported by evidence from the two other sources. Like the other evidence cited, the items that fall under the third heading, "Invention," have been noted individually. Also like the others, however, they have not usually been viewed in relation to each other or as a group—and from that perspective, they disclose a subtle aspect of the Nazi genocide which points once more to the role of evil knowingly intended. A number of specific moments or scenes or tendencies in the process of genocide reveal a striking connection to the imagination or the power of invention; associated with the idea of moral transgression, its imaginative elaborations represent that idea in a form that goes beyond anything that a practical or functional intention could realize; they depend for their efficacy on the recognition of the idea for what it is. These representations are freely conceived, even original; in this, they more closely resemble acts of the imagination in art than practical conclusions.[12] Like other acts of the imagination, these are set in a material and historical context which supplies an idiom and permits various degrees of generality or concreteness. But in all that variety, the idea represented—the principle that no moral limit or rule should go unviolated—is evident; in all its appearances, the elaboration of the idea exhibits the refinement of detail and the reflexive focus of artistic expression.

Undoubtedly, the phenomenon of brutality at times reflects a practical intention—the effort to intimidate, for example, or to punish. This individual motive may, furthermore, appear also corporately, when institutions or governments act in order to sustain or increase their

12. On the imagination of evil, see Philip L. Hallie, "Sade and the Music of Pain," in Hallie, *The Paradox of Cruelty* (Middletown: Wesleyan University Press, 1969), 37–62; Alan Macfarlane, "The Root of All Evil," in David Parken (ed.), *The Anthropology of Evil* (Oxford: Basil Blackwell, 1985), 57–76; Abigail Rosenthal, *A Good Look at Evil* (Philadelphia: Temple University Press, 1987); Elaine Scarry, "The Structure of Torture," in Scarry, *The Body in Pain* (New York: Oxford University Press, 1985), 27–59; Henry Shue, "Torture," *Philosophy and Public Affairs* 7 (1978), 124–143. See also, on the relation of the imagination of evil to the philosophy of history, Saul Friedländer, Gerald Holton, Leo Marx, and Eugene Skolnikoff (eds.), *Visions of Apocalypse* (New York: Holmes & Meier, 1985). Primo Levi refers to the phenomenon described here as "useless violence" (*The Damned and the Saved*, trans. Raymond Rosenthal; New York: Vintage, 1988, 105–26); but the phrase does not seem to me to give sufficient weight to the origins of the "uselessness."

control. The practice of torture sometimes occurs as one such "practical" means, for instance, when it is used to obtain information. But extreme as such instances of brutality are, another possibility open to them is more extreme still—when they occur with no specific end in view, when they become intrinsic to the system in which they appear. In this form, the victims are chosen indiscriminately; the means used are devised not for their "effectiveness" (since no specific purpose is being served) but because of a preversely aesthetic "fittingness" to the victims brutalized—the effort to fit the brutality to the victim. This is indeed the role that brutality and torture often took in the Nazi regime, most extremely but by no means exclusively in their work of genocide against the Jews. Such practices might (and did) claim anyone or everyone, appearing in forms that only an imagination focused on its own elaboration, not on utilitarian or extrinsic purpose, could account for.

Under the Nazis, the members of any group could be subjected to torture, whatever their status, whatever the magnitude of the "violations" they were suspected of, or even in the absence of such violations altogether: prisoners of war as well as guerrilla fighters; children as well as Wehrmacht officers; German civilians anonymously accused, as well as ministers or priests who spoke out in their pulpits. No one was immune, no one was in principle a less likely victim than others, no proportionality between "crime" and punishment was even conceived, no common or individual practical purpose was envisaged—torture itself took on the status of a purpose. It is in this sense that the practice of torture can be held to have been intrinsic to the system: in effect, a commitment in itself, not a measure taken in response to circumstance. It is from this perspective that Jean Amery suggested a contrast: that almost every twentieth-century regime, "white or red" and no matter how vicious, can be imagined without the role of torture—but for the Nazi regime, "No one can imagine it. It would have been impossible."[13]

The gratuitousness and inventiveness in respect to torture and brutality extend, beyond the selection of victims, also to the means of expression; these reflect even more pointedly the work of an imagination directed inward, to its own expression, rather than toward an external purpose. The evidence of this takes an unusual variety of forms (the variety itself underscoring the role of the imagination) of personal violation, including such gratuitous, but canny measures as forcing a pious Jew to spit on a Torah, or refusing to put waste buckets in the sealed cars of the "resettlement" trains (if they were provided, the

13. Jean Amery, *At the Mind's Limits*, trans. Sidney Rosenfeld and Stella P. Rosenfeld (Bloomington, Ind.: Indiana University Press, 1980), 31.

number was designed to be inadequate). Other examples are more elaborate and disclose an even more intense and knowing role for the imagination. One such example was the demand that captives in the concentration camps, starved and constantly on the margin of death, should sing together as they were marched out to the work that was part of the process of killing them. This was a requirement common in the concentration camps and, where there was an attached labor force, in the death camps as well. In Auschwitz, an orchestra was formed, the main part of whose duties was to accompany the singing of the "workers" as they left and returned to the compound; it would also play command performances for the guards and staff. (Orchestras were also organized at Belzec and Treblinka.) The practice, obviously, was not a disguise for bystanders: everyone involved knew quite precisely the extreme situation of the "workers." Was it meant then as an ironic joke? Perhaps in part it was this, although that, too, it should be noted, implies recognition of the terror of which the music was then part. More straightforwardly and simply, it was an elaboration of the consciousness of wrong: imposing what is commonly associated with well-being and civilization on a condition that was the opposite of both of these, and doing it in order to accentuate that fact.

Evidence for this phenomenon of imaginative evil hardly stops here. The sign over the entrance to Auschwitz read "Arbeit macht frei." But in Auschwitz, of course, proportionately few who entered survived even to work, and no one of these, much less of the others, would be free. Traditional German adages associate a variety of desirable consequences with work: "Arbeit macht reich" ("Work makes [one] rich"); "Arbeit bringt Ehr" ("Work brings honor"); "Arbeit erhalt das Leben" ("Work sustains life"); "Arbeit macht das Leben süss" ("Work makes life sweet"); and so on. The inversion of the reality at Auschwitz by the use of "Arbeit macht frei" is more extreme than it would have been even for these others, but a more fundamental question concerns the role of the motto as such. Once again, to explain it as an effort at deception, although not irrelevant, is insufficient. It is not necessary to assert the opposite of reality in order to disguise it; in fact when that is the option chosen, with so many other alternatives avoided, it seems clear that it is consciousness of the truth—not only the fact of the genocide but the moral violation it represented—that is inspiring the conception. "Work makes (one) free" at the entrance of Auschwitz is a tacit confession by the Nazis of their own recognition of what was happening in Auschwitz beyond the entrance—of the fact and of the "value."

The list of examples of evil as celebrated imaginatively and inventively does not stop here. There is, for example, the practice of having the canisters of Zyklon-B delivered to the death-camp gas chambers in lorries marked with the Red Cross; or the requirement that the beds of camp inmates—minimal, shared, and crowded, arranged in tiers with little space below or above, places not of rest but of disease and death—should be made up each day to extraordinary standards of neatness (on the usual threat of "most severe" punishment for failing these standards). For such projections as these, practical explanations are again not so much irrelevant as insufficient. The instances often work against utility rather than advance it; even where they do not work against utility, something more is required to explain the consistent theme of violation recognizable in them.

The principle that accounts for such acts of the imagination may be formulated variously, but it is difficult to avoid the evidence here of variations on a theme: the recognition of evil at work as it is elaborated inventively and creatively by an imagination which has not yet silenced the moral sensibility in its origins. Without this principle and its reiteration of the idea of evil, there might still have been murder and brutality, and with them moral culpability. But with the additional evidence of the knowing imagination, even murder and brutality reach a different order of moral significance.

It has already been mentioned that for the three groups of examples referred to—for each of them singly and for them all collectively—an alternative interpretation to the one proposed can be found. Even for the evidence of invention, it can be claimed that the imagination is not quite free, that a practical explanation is implicated in the work of the imagination; one might even conceive a practical basis for the imagination as such. But before invoking an all-purpose role for instrumentalism, it is necessary also to admit a form of experience in which act and idea have a place quite apart from considerations of use or function. In this form, knowledge—including moral knowledge, and so including knowledge of evil and good—is an attendant feature, even a motive of practice. The acts themselves are evidence of this source.

2. The Divided Self and the Unity of Evil and Good

A recurrent question in writings about the Nazi genocide asks, "How was it possible?" In part, this question is rhetorical, emphasizing the actuality of the events of the genocide by calling attention to their improbability. In this same manner of rhetorical indirection, the question also calls into doubt the principle discussed earlier in this chapter: the explicit and knowing design for wrongdoing that was required for the events of the genocide to have occurred as they did.

In addition to its rhetorical character, however, this question has a substantive, more literal intention that brings into view a test case, at the level of individual human agency, of what has been claimed here as the possibility of the willed knowledge of evil in practice. Such evidence is important because, however compelling the instances that have been cited as testimony in general, it is a matter of fact that few, if any, figures inculpated in the Final Solution individually professed or admitted a will for evil. Also retrospectively, it is not that central figures cannot be identified in the conception or acts of the Nazi genocide, but that even for the most obvious ones—Hitler himself, or Himmler—accusations of wrongdoing mingle with complicating factors of psychological or historical circumstance. Here, as constantly in its history, evil does not speak its own name.

This consistent self-justification even where the evidence of evildoing is overwhelming impedes and on some accounts mitigates claims of the possibility of the will-to-evil; it underlies the skepticism often directed against the conception of wrongdoing knowingly committed. (The best-known instance of this skepticism in reference to the Nazi genocide is the contrast Hannah Arendt draws between the "banality" of Nazi evil and the "radical" evil of pretotalitarian society.) One set of examples in particular suggests the unity rather than the dissociation of act and knowledge in evildoing; these revolve around the phenomenon of the "divided self" or the "doubling effect" attributed to certain figures in the Nazi genocide. The common descriptions of these figures point to the improbable conjunction in them of brutality and wrongdoing, on one side, and their apparent observance of a consistent and traditional moral code—in effect, the knowledge of good—on the other. Such people seem in effect to live two lives: the one of them involved with flagrant wrongdoing, the other bound by the restraints of a consistent and even self-conscious moral doctrine. Somehow—this then poses the issue—these two "lives" coexist in one actual life. The perplexity in the face of this phenomenon seems to mirror the perplexity in the face of the Nazi genocide as a whole: barbarism occurs here in the midst of civilization. How, again, could it be possible? That the occurrence of genocide may by its extremity have created or revealed this contradictory effect does not explain how it was possible—conceptually or psychologically or morally.

Robert J. Lifton, who introduced the term "doubling effect," based that concept mainly on the groups of Nazi doctors who carried out the process of selection, experimentation, and murder in the "euthanasia" program of 1939–41 and then subsequently, on a much larger scale, in the death camps—but who (allegedly) found no inconsistency between this "work" and their professional ideals as doctors and healers.[14] The doubling effect thus involved the contemporaneous expression of two conflicting moral identities—one of which not only sanctioned acts antithetical to the other but used the cover provided by the ideals of the one in order to accomplish the ends of the other. Lifton takes the apparent division between the two moral codes to hold quite literally; they contradict each other without meeting. The doubling effect is made possible psychologically, Lifton concludes, by a process in which one moral domain is blocked out or "numbed" when the other is present. The two parts of the single self do not interact with—question, criticize—each other, and this permits the persons who exhibit the doubling effect to act in each of the two domains without the intervention and in some sense without even the consciousness or memory of the other.

Examples of the divided self, although not always conceived in the same terms, have often been cited elsewhere in reference to the Nazi genocide.[15] So the phenomenon is remarked of the unusual proportion of higher academic degrees held among members of the four Einsatzgruppen—the SS groups who, at the time of the German invasion of Russia, initiated the killings which would then become the Final Solution. So also evidence is cited of commandants and guards in the concentration camps and the death camps who could move from murder and brutality in that world to roles as devoted family members or admirers of the arts in their "other" lives. That such examples are individual and in some measure anecdotal qualifies but does not refute the evidence—and the question arises here again, more pointedly than if the evil of the one world openly pervaded the other, of how such selves, divided by a moral schism, could inhabit what in a more immediate and obvious sense were single lives.

It is arguable that no general explanation can account for the varied instances of this phenomenon. Certain aspects of the doubling effect, moreover, are themselves open to question: even in settings where the pressure for conformity was less extreme than in Nazi Germany, academic degrees or the presence of an aesthetic sensibility have not been proof against acts of cruelty or brutality. Yet the features of the divided moral self seem quite real, even allowing for the exaggeration of those features

14. Lifton, *Nazi Doctors* (see chap. 1, n. 21), esp. 416–66.
15. For other formulations, see, e.g., Saul Friedländer, *Kurt Gerstein: The Ambiguity of Good* (New York: Knopf, 1969); Philip L. Hallie, *Lest Innocent Blood Be Shed: The Story of Chambon and How Good Happened There* (New York: Harper & Row, 1980); George M. Kren and Leon Rappaport, *The Holocaust and the Crisis of Human Behavior* (New York: Holmes & Meier, 1980); Eugen Kogon, *The Theory and Practice of Hell* (New York: Berkley Books, 1980).

by the enormity of the Nazi genocide as they appear there. In less extreme instances as well, the knowledge of evil and good appears divided
by a sharp line of demarcation and thus to represent incompatible ideals.
Where the two domains are thus distinguished,the divided self might be
admitted as possible and, in some cases, actual, even in the absence of an
explanation.

But the lack of an explanation when the phenomenon itself has such
large consequences for understanding moral conduct and the concept of
responsibility may, on the other hand, point to discrepancies in the description. Lifton's account suggests something like this not only because
it *is* a description (a reiteration of the evidence) rather than an explanation, but also because it ignores the possibility of an alternative description for which an explanation *is* available. The first part of this
contention is demonstrable; Lifton's claims for the phenomenon of the
doubling effect consist mainly of a reformulation of what he takes as evidence for it. The conduct of the Nazi doctors appear to Lifton as morally
contradictory, divided into two regular patterns. On the one hand, the
Nazi doctors in their earlier status and then in their roles in the camps—
in the process of "selection," in medical experimentation—conceived
themselves in their professional roles; on the other hand, they engaged
in acts which conflicted with the ideals of the profession, including the
fundamental medical precept of "do no harm." Thus, Lifton infers, the
doctors lived in two separate moral domains, blocking out each one in
turn as the other prevailed. But this conclusion does no more in effect
than repeat the evidence; and extraordinary as that evidence is, the question remains of how the claim of "doubling" can be sustained against the
conflicting conception of moral judgment which finds the knowledge of
good *and* evil joined in a single domain, the knowledge of each entailed
by knowledge of the other. Conscious or intentional moral contradiction
seems in these terms no less problematic than a willed logical contradiction: as there is no *logical* explanation for logical contradiction, so it is
unlikely that there should be a *moral* explanation for moral contradiction.

An alternative account of the morally divided self is possible, however, that disputes both the evidence and the conclusion of moral contradiction. This is based on the claim discussed earlier in this chapter that
evil or wrongdoing can be effected knowingly; from that basis, a conclusion diametrically opposed to Lifton's emerges which also brings into
question even his description of the evidence. Lifton's account proposes
for moral judgment a version of the general psychological phenomenon
of "split personality.": The mechanism at work in this general phenomenon, where the divisions between selves extend to the most
fundamental characteristics of individual personality (and where there

may be more than only two selves), has been variously described, but these versions agree that the selves or personalities which "inhabit" the single person appear independently of each other; there is no requirement of consistency among or between the selves, and indeed the inconsistencies—as in a Dr. Jekyll and Mr.Hyde—are the most striking features of the phenomenon.[16] On this conception, then, there is no reason why the different selves of a multiple personality should not exhibit *contradictory* qualities.

It is precisely on this issue, however, that a difference occurs between the general conception of the split personality and the doubling effect alleged to hold for moral judgment. For examined against the general background of moral judgment, the supposed division in the doubling effect differs fundamentally from the radical division characteristic of the split personality. Evil and good in the divided moral self turn out, in fact, not to be contradictory or even anomalous in respect to each other, but consistent; with this, they exemplify the process of moral judgment as it otherwise appears in its most common forms. The morally divided self, on these terms, emerges as nothing more than the traditional moral self, as facing the constant—sometimes extreme— moral choices between evil and good.

The doubling effect as an hypothesis assumes the existence of a sharp division between two moral domains to which a single person is simultaneously committed. The question is thus crucial of what evidence supports this premise and what conclusions that evidence supports. And here the argument—whether for or against the conception of the morally divided self—is forced to rely on certain inferences, rather than only on what is known directly from the evidence. It is possible, for instance, that the concentration-camp guards—or, more extremely, the Nazi doctors—cited as evidence of the divided self would not do outside the camps what they did as a matter of course within them; the testimony available, fragmentary as it is, suggests that this was often if not always the case. But this finding does not by itself prove that the guards lived in

16. Among accounts of "split" or "multiple" personality, see Henry B. Laughlin, *The Neuroses in Clinical Practice* (Philadelphia: W. B. Saunders, 1958), 355–58; C. E. Osgood, "A Blind Analysis of a Case of Multiple Personality Using the Semantic Differential," *Journal of Abnormal and Social Psychology* 49 (1954), 579–91; Otto Rank, *The Double: A Psychoanalytic Study* (Chapel Hill: University of North Carolina Press, 1971); Bert Rosenbaum and Harry Sonne, *The Language of Psychosis* (New York: New York University Press, 1986), 68–70, 99–104; Corbett H. Thigpen and Hervey Cleckley, *Three Faces of Eve* (New York: McGraw-Hill, 1957). In Jon Elster (ed.), *The Multiple Self* (Cambridge: Cambridge University Press, 1985), the emphasis of the most convincing accounts—e.g., by Donald Davidson and D. F. Pears—is on the patients' finding themselves returned to a unified self by way of the concepts of self-deception and *akrasia* ("weakness of will").

two independent moral worlds; an alternative conclusion is possible that requires fewer assumptions and accounts for a wider sweep of the evidence. This second view argues that it is not the *self* that is divided in the examples cited, but that a single self has turned its attention to what it conceives as two different—morally different—objects; and that this is effected within a single moral universe of discourse. The fact that the Nazi doctors or the camp guards might act differently in different "domains" does not mean, on this account, that they are following different principles; the principles could be consistent or even identical, entailing differences in conduct because their "objects" are judged to differ. Such differences are common in other contexts; for example, the legal and the moral status of adults is distinguished from that of children with no implication that the principles underlying the differences are contradictory or even that they differ.

The crucial question here then concerns the relation between the allegedly two domains—whether the two may in fact be consistent with each other or (more strongly still) whether they mutually entail each other. And on this issue the evidence seems quite different from what Lifton and other writers committed to a notion of the morally divided self have acknowledged. It cannot simply be assumed that the brutality of a Dr. Josef Mengele at Auschwitz or an "Ivan the Terrible" at Treblinka was left behind at the walls of the camps, that it would not also have been reflected in their lives outside the walls—still less that there was such a division in their actions within the camps. The burden of evidence, in fact, suggests the contrary. In Mengele, for instance, the claim for a morally divided self breaks down within the world of the camp itself, since his conduct in Auschwitz includes moments of apparent compunction interspersed with acts of violence and cruelty. On this evidence, it is more plausible to infer a single moral agent—one that granted greater conviction to evil than to good—than two independent moral domains that were constantly being traversed, and this is the case notwithstanding statements that the agent himself might have made in his own defense. Certainly it begs the question to hold that everything that Mengele—or Stangl, the Treblinka commandant, or Hoess, the Auschwitz commandant—did within the camp should be recognized as part of the one domain of the evil self, with a quite separate "good" self kept apart, as untouched by the other. That they acted differently at different times and in relation to different contexts is undoubtedly true— but it is also true of much human conduct that is held to be unexceptionable; that the specific differences at issue here were more extreme than they are ordinarily does not affect this conclusion. As the knowledge of evil and good is thus joined, the doubling effect also is unified.

What led to the appearance of the doubling effect may be something as extreme as the assertion that every limit may—even *should*–be violated; but this too would involve what has been referred to here as a knowing commitment to evil within the single domain of moral judgment.

The claim for this formulation of a single principle unifying the supposed distinction between the two worlds of the divided moral self is supported by the implication that the two worlds—as the "divided selves" of a Mengele or Ivan the Terrible themselves assert—are consistent, not contradictory or inconsistent at all. It is not, for example, that brutal medical experiments are conducted simply on *children* within the camp, but that the children who are the subjects of experiments have a designation which overrides their identity as children: they are Jews. This leaves the children who are not in the camp, the doctor's own children or others, as subject, not to the rules of a different moral world, but to the rules of the same one; they are treated differently not because of differences in the categories of two domains, but because children are categorized differently within the *same* domain. The doctors with their professional ideals and commitments are not other than the doctors who participate in the selections or process of murder; the doctors and principles are the same—but the "occasions" of their work are different, that is, they are *alleged* to be different. (How these arbitrary categorizations themselves arise will be further discussed in the account of moral universalization in chapter 7, "Genocide and Kant's Enlightenment.")

The drawing of distinctions among sources of obligation within a single moral universe, willful and malevolent in the example cited, is familiar and unexceptional elsewhere. People conceive their commitments to members of their families in different terms than their commitments to persons not related to them; friends often recognize obligations that they would not for strangers. The groups privileged in this way (and inversely, those on whom liabilities are imposed) acquire this status in no very systematic way, on the basis of varied ethnic and religious distinctions. The moral differences presupposed in these distinctions are not necessarily consciously defined or justified. But the distinctions themselves are clear and common; they are also more numerous than the number "two" cited in the doubling effect.

Admittedly, even the most common distinctions of this sort (the special obligations, for example, between parents and children) do not go without saying;[17] but more relevant to refuting the notion of the divid-

17. See, e.g., Alasdair MacIntyre, *After Virtue* (Notre Dame: University of Notre Dame Press, 220–25; Robert Nozick, *Philosophical Explanations* (Cambridge: Harvard University Press, 1981), 451–57; Christine Hoff Sommers, "Filial Morality," *Journal of Philosophy* 83 (1986), 439–56.

ed self is the fact that even in their own terms, such distinctions coexist with other obligations that cross the lines of the distinctions themselves. To admit that obligations vary in different relationships does not mean that *some* obligations do not apply in more than one relation or perhaps in them all. It may be that the special obligations depend at their foundation on the more general ones; but even without this assumption, it is evident that the claim for *differences* in obligation presupposes a form of justification similar to that implied in the claim for *any* obligation. The alleged distinction in moral worlds—or in the parts of a divided self—presupposes a contrast which is based on a standard applicable to both worlds or parts; but this could occur only within a single universe of discourse. Even if something like a divided moral self were to be posited on functional grounds, then, it presupposes a unified self—and so also, the single relation underlying them that links the superficially disparate wills for evil and good. In this sense, the doubling effect, with the contrast it alleges between one self committed to evil and a second self committed to good, does not differ essentially from the contrast, in *any* decision (or self), between the choices of evil and good; it is no more than what moral judgment confronts in its most common applications.

Obviously, the differences between certain decisions or acts are more extreme than those between others, and the contrast between evil and good in the enormity of the Nazi genocide understandably carries over into the differences alleged between those commitments among the agents of that collection of acts. The hypothesis of the morally divided self or of the doubling effect is intended to reflect such differences, but it has the effect of widening the division between evil and good in such a way as to leave each side of the division unintelligible to the other: the relation between them, which is fundamental—and necessary—for all moral judgment, becomes impossible. In the supposed examples of the divided self in the Nazi genocide, however, not only are the two sides of that self consistent with each other, but the knowledge presupposed on each side is also one and the same. Even if a single person *seems* to live in two different moral worlds, the definition of those worlds and the decision to distinguish them or to identify with one or the other at a particular time remains the responsibility of that one person, in the one world of which the several constructed worlds are only expressions. The disparities or "contradictions" that seem to occur among moral judgments as people apply them are more fully accounted for simply as moral wrongs or rights than by the assumption of two different moral universes of discourse.

That evil and good are unified and consistent in their different appearances implies that the knowledge of evil and good is unified and

consistent as well—and the very examples of wrongdoing appealed to as
evidence for the morally divided self provide evidence of this. Even dis-
regarding the likelihood that the figures who found their way into the
world of evil—the doctors, the academics, the good family men of the
Gestapo, the art-loving concentration-camp guards—brought that
same impulse to their other, "good" world as well, the consistency between the two domains, both alleged and real, remains; it is itself
evidence of an intentional pattern. In *their own terms*, the two worlds
were one, without contradiction—and although we need not (and
should not) accept those terms at face value, the supporting facts seem to
bear out this conclusion as well. The divided self, so far as one can speak
of it at all, is constructed by the self in order to avoid admitting what a
unified self would have to—that is, the knowledge of evil. That knowledge, however, is presupposed in the emergence of the divided self; it
remains ingredient in the two parts, furthermore, as they contrive to
know each other with sufficient force and clarity to remain distinct. Only
the knowledge of evil, it seems, would *require* a screen between the parts
of the morally divided self that blocked out what would otherwise be
openly present. The knowledge of evil and good and their unity in a single self are thus presupposed in the doubling effect; the effect itself is
evidence of their single existence.

3. Knowledge and Forgiveness, Knowledge and the Unforgivable

The discussion here has argued, from several directions, that in implementing the Final Solution, the Nazis acted with and despite an
awareness of the moral character of what they were doing; and that the
evidence of this is visible in what they did once this is placed in the contexts of their lives observed as wholes. It is undoubtedly a more common
feature in wrongdoing, however, that its agents act in or out of ignorance, mistakenly believing themselves justified in what they do rather
than doing wrong deliberately. Both the request for forgiveness and the
willingness to grant it apply more readily in the latter setting than in the
former, and the reasons for this can be seen in the conceptual features of
forgiveness.[18] If someone who has wronged another person asks that

---

18. Among the few philosophical analyses of forgiveness, see R. S. Downie, "Forgiveness," *Philosophical Quarterly* 15 (1965), 128–34; Aurel Kolnai, "Forgiveness," in
Kolnai, *Ethics, Value, and Reality* (London: Athlone, 1977); Hastings Rashdall, "The Ethics of Forgiveness," *Ethics* 10 (1900), 193–206; P. F. Strawson, "Freedom and Resentment," in Strawson, *Freedom and Resentment* (London: Methuen, 1974), 1–25. Martin
Golding, in "Forgiveness and Regret" (*Philosophical Forum* 16 [1985], 121–37), addresses
the issue of forgiveness specifically in relation to the Nazi genocide.

person to forgive him, acknowledging the wrong and indicating that he now understands his act in a way that he had not at the time, his request serves two purposes: it indicates that the person who committed the wrong had not acted in full knowledge at the time—that is, that his intentions were such that if he *had* had the knowledge he now has, he would not have done what he did—and it offers assurance of an effort to see that the wrong committed will not be repeated. The latter assurance may be stated explicitly, but even when this is not the case, it is implied in the wrongdoer's acknowledgment that he now more fully understands the wrong committed.

It has sometimes been held that forgiveness is possible even if the wrongdoer does not ask to be forgiven or, still more extremely, if he refuses even to admit that the act in question was wrong; in such instances, the wrongdoer would obviously offer no assurances that the act in question would not be repeated. But to "forgive" a person under these conditions seems as misplaced as it would be for someone to forgive a person for a wrong committed not against himself but against somebody else. At the very least, forgiveness in these circumstances is so attenuated that granting it has typically been associated with a divine, not a human source. Where God might forgive *any* human act—including a person's blindness to his own wrongdoing and his refusal to ask forgiveness—on the grounds of the frailty of human nature, it would itself be a moral violation for one person to assume this role in respect to another.[19]

What emerges here, then, are three conditions to be met for forgiveness. The agent acknowledges having done wrong and gives at least tacit assurance that, so far as it is in his power, the wrong will not be repeated. These comments are directed, with the request for forgiveness, to the person who has been wronged. The latter, then, has the power to forgive or to refuse to (a power which having been wronged confers). Certain other conditions of forgiveness are also sometimes cited, but with less certainty. These include such considerations as the relation between justice and forgiveness; for example, whether a wrongdoer has an obligation to ask forgiveness, or from the other side, whether the person wronged has an obligation to grant forgiveness when it is sought. They include the more severe question, applicable in

19. In *The Sunflower*, trans. H. A. Piehler (New York: Schocken, 1976), Simon Wiesenthal describes a request for forgiveness directed to him by a dying SS man who had participated in an atrocity against Jews. Wiesenthal left the hospital room without responding to the SS man. Following his account of this episode, Wiesenthal asks a group of historians, theologians, and writers what his response *should* have been. A number of these accounts criticize Wiesenthal's response; they thus presuppose that forgiveness *can* be given by someone other than the person who has been the victim of a wrong—but their formulation of this position remains largely unargued.

millions of instances to the Nazi genocide against the Jews, whether forgiveness is possible when, as a consequence of the wrong, the victims are
no longer alive to be addressed. They include as well a variation of *this*
question, directed in the context of the genocide at the wrongdoers who
are themselves no longer alive: can forgiveness be extended to them by
the survivors, insofar as the Nazis had not sought it and now cannot?

One issue in particular among these complexities extends to the
boundaries of the phenomenon of forgiveness. Here the question arises
of whether wrongs exist to which the concept of forgiveness does not
apply *in principle*—not because consequences of the wrong have made it
physically impossible for the person harmed to grant forgiveness or for
the wrongdoer to seek it, but because of the nature of the act itself. What
are the circumstances of an act that is, quite simply, unforgivable? Are
there such wrongs?

It seems apparent that there is no necessary connection between the
question of whether a particular act is forgivable or not and the magnitude of its consequences. The continued repetition of a wrong, for
example, sometimes bears more substantively on the possibility of forgiveness than does the extent of the wrong. Thus, a person who has
information that would bring about the release of someone wrongly imprisoned but who refuses to speak out repeats this wrong each moment
that the information is withheld; such repetition seems to make what
could be forgivable at an early moment increasingly less forgivable at
later ones—and this is the case even if the resultant injury is smaller than
that suffered in other acts which might nonetheless be forgivable.

This same example, moreover, can be interpreted in a way that associates it with the issue of evil knowingly committed. For it is arguable that
in this example it is the *knowledge* of what he is doing on the part of the
person who withholds the information rather than (or at least in addition to) his persistence that makes his act(s) unforgivable. One of the
conditions for forgiveness that have been cited is that the person asking
forgiveness should offer some assurance of a change within himself—of
an intention, at least, that the wrong will not be repeated. But when a
wrong is committed in the knowledge that it *is* wrong, the possibility of
such assurance is limited. If awareness of the wrong committed was present at the time, the subsequent admission that it was wrong adds nothing to what was recognized previously. Accordingly, assurance newly
given that the wrong will not be repeated lacks the principal evidence
that might make it credible: the prospect of change (at the very least, of
the attempt to change) on the part of the person who did the wrong. If
the knowledge of what he was doing did not deter the wrongdoer once,
what could he add now, either in speaking or in fact, that would point to
such a change?

To suggest that a wrong or evil may be unforgivable because it was committed with an awareness that it *was* wrong underscores a question that stands constantly at the periphery of the many references in this discussion to the "Nazi" genocide against the Jews. *Who* is it who had this knowledge and then acted on it? *Whose* acts, in the terms now presented, might be judged unforgivable—whether on the ground that the victims cannot be addressed or on grounds distinguished in the act itself? Is it certain individual Nazis? All members of the Nazi party? The German populace? Germany as a nation and thus also its future citizens, unborn at the time of the genocide? The issues concerning the relation between individual and corporate acts that are raised by such questions cannot be fully addressed here.[20] But it seems evident that if an act is judged unforgivable because it was committed with the knowledge that it was wrong, it is most immediately the individual persons who initiated or committed the act—those who "had" the knowledge—who are inculpated, irrespective of the groups of which they were members or representatives. To be sure, a single act or idea may be appropriated as the expression or representation of a group, and the role of groups in influencing individual acts is undeniable. But if there were no evidence of individuals meeting the conditions of moral responsibility, no charge could be made against the group. And, as has been amply shown in the record of the Nazi genocide, there *is* such evidence.

It can be argued that individual identity, and so also individual act and idea, are never quite separate from a social context which includes the identities of other persons and the relation among them. It is, furthermore, impossible to determine with certainty, in the context of the Nazi genocide, who "knew" and acted nonetheless, or who, on the other side, acted or failed to act without such knowledge. But these limitations are limitations in fact, not in principle; and even as limitations in fact they do not apply to the specific instances of wrongdoing knowingly committed that have been cited. The presence of knowl-

20. On the relation between individual and corporate responsibility, see Peter A. French, *Collective and Corporate Responsibility* (New York: Columbia University Press, 1984); Berel Lang, "The Pentagon Papers and the Problem of Corporate Responsibility," in Peter A. French (ed.), *Conscientious Action: The Revelation of the Pentagon Papers* (Boston: Schenkman, 1974), 110–34; Larry May, *The Morality of Groups* (Notre Dame: University of Notre Dame Press, 1988). In *The Question of German Guilt*, trans. E. B. Ashton (New York: Dial, 1948), Karl Jaspers warns against the appeal to "metaphysical guilt" as a means of excusing specific wrongdoing on the basis of general human fallibility (as in the doctrine of Original Sin). But the sharp distinction he draws between "political" and "moral" guilt—the former as implying collective responsibility for an abstract "state," the latter referring to individual responsibility—opens the way to just this basis for removing groups from moral accountability.

edge, of evil as an idea, is, for many individual acts committed in the genocide, unmistakable—evident to such an extent that it can also be inferred to hold for various groups and their collective awareness of what was common knowledge. Because of the individuals who are known to have shaped their policies, certain of these groups can be immediately named: the hierarchy of the chancellor's office, the SS virtually as a whole, the command structure of the Wehrmacht—and then, extending beyond this, the more attenuated groups whose members were linked, by association and then inevitably by knowledge, to these first ones: in the hospitals, the railroads, the churches, the universities. President Richard von Weizsäcker concluded in a remarkable address to the Bundestag on 5 May 1985 that only "the attempt . . . not to take note of what was happening" could account for the general claim of not having known. That attempt itself, of course, presupposed knowledge, of what was being done and of its moral quality.[21] "Common knowledge," used in this sense, does not deny the possibility of individual ignorance, but if in circumstances such as these the plea of ignorance is made, the burden of proof is on demonstrating that—not, as would more generally be the case, on the accuser to demonstrate its contrary.

Obviously, gradations of responsibility occur within the pattern of knowledge and act. Here as elsewhere, such gradations reflect the proportions between what individual persons actually knew and did (or failed to), and what was in their power to do (or to refuse to). In some contexts of moral judgment, the proportions between intention and consequence may affect and sometimes mitigate judgment of the acts constituted by those intentions and consequences. But where the possibility of forgiveness is at issue, the knowledge of evil in the act committed weighs more heavily even than the consequences to which it led. The professor who accepted promotion to the chair of a Jewish colleague who had been expelled from the university; the family that moved into the apartment left vacant when its Jewish inhabitants were "resettled": these were relatively negligible violations in proportion to the overall effect of genocide. But the knowledge of what was presupposed by such acts is not distinguishable in degree from the knowledge accompanying acts which were larger and more flagrant in consequence; particular knowledge, in each appearance, confirms the enormity of the whole.

Admittedly, on the analysis that has been presented, the issue of forgiveness is moot unless forgiveness has been sought. And a notable fea-

21. Reprinted in Geoffrey H. Hartman (ed.), *Bitburg in Moral and Political Perspective* (Bloomington, Ind.: Indiana University Press, 1986).

ture of the war trials held since 1945 of those charged with crimes related to the Nazi genocide is that in only a few instances, even after a verdict of guilt was reached, has forgiveness been asked by the persons convicted. This itself evidently is a form of repetition—a renewed affirmation of the original act, and thus an extension of it. Beyond this, moreover, the refusal to ask forgiveness establishes, with its reiteration, the value of forgiveness and the price exacted, beyond the wrongful act itself, by an act which is judged unforgivable. The loss incurred here affects the person wronged as well as the wrongdoer: to the latter, forgiveness offers the promise of renewal, of community with a person or group from which he had by his act cut himself off; for the former, when forgiveness is possible, it provides a means of healing, perhaps of forgetting the injury itself—thus also of revival for the future, and thus also a means of renewed community.

Forgiveness thus opens the possibilities of redeeming history from its past and of providing a shared existence in the future—and from this can be seen the extent of what is lost when the possibility of forgiveness is closed off. For those wronged, their loss, even in death, is compounded; for those who do wrong, the history of a contingent act becomes permanent. It is as though here, against the background of the Nazi genocide, in which evil was committed knowingly, a new principle of ethical obligation establishes itself, proportionate on its side to the unforgivable act of genocide as it was carried out: Do nothing, allow nothing to happen, for which forgiveness would be impossible. Like many more traditional ethical principles, the significance of this one became most evident with its violation; unlike those others, this one begins and ends with the meaning of violation itself.

3

The Decision Not to Decide

The history of philosophical ethics is a history of the will for generalization. Even to recognize individual judgments or acts *as* ethical requires a move to abstraction in order to catch sight of the principles that give them this character; and certainly, as writers on ethics offer recommendations for future decisions, with the many contingencies to be anticipated there, the impulse for generality is understandable. Thus, ethical discourse adopts the theoretical ideals of philosophy and with that, the requirement that its conclusions should be broad enough, not only to support this or that moment of ethical judgment, but to produce rules that bring consistency to the judgment of *all* such instances. "What is courage?" "What is piety?" "What is justice?" Socrates asks through the Platonic Dialogues—and we quickly recognize that those questions propel us well beyond the individual occasions of moral history which relate only how one person or group of persons has treated another at one time—not how they might have acted, much less how they or anyone else *ought* to have acted. So the great moral philosophers—Plato, Aristotle, Spinoza, Kant—reach an opening consensus about the requirement of generality in their work which impels them beyond the particular moral "facts" of ordinary experience, even if (as is usually true) they later return to and test themselves by those same facts.

The same impulse for abstraction is reflected even in the use of specific examples in ethical theory. For once again, as philosophers fix their attention on the *principles* of ethics, history has seemed beside the point. Certainly, insofar as examples are intended to engage the reader, the examples introduced by philosophers might as well be contrived or made up. To be sure, they are usually required to be plausible and relevant, and to this extent the world of experience or history is never far off. But fiction, too, is a variant of the common world, and thus plausibility turns out not to be much of a constraint—leaving the examples of philosophy free to exaggerate or invert fact with impunity. "Should I return a weapon to its owner, knowing that he intends to do someone harm with it? "Would I be justified in lying to a would-be assassin who asks where he can find his intended victim? So Plato and Kant bring testimony from examples which do not occur historically—at least not in *their* histories—but which by analogy, almost as metaphors, are intended to elaborate and to test ethical theories. What, we might ask, would a discovery that they were historical add to this?

It may be impossible to prove that the allegiance of philosophy to abstract or "mere" possibility explains the distance that has increasingly separated philosophical ethics from the world of ethical practice, but the fact of that disparity is itself unmistakable. Indeed, we find ourselves here addressing two apparently independent histories: on one hand, the history of philosophical ethics, which provides a number of theoretical and generalized perspectives from which ethical decisions and reasoning are to be judged; on the other hand, the history of moral practice itself, ethics in action, where there seem to be no general principles at all and where for every step forward we find another one backward: capital punishment declines and the incidence of torture increases; the benevolent disguise of feudalism breaks down, and the hypocrisies of nationalism replace it; slavery becomes objectionable, and genocide becomes inviting. Would anyone claim progress, in the diverse and otherwise often cumulative history of the West, for either the collective or individual conscience?

It may seem that to direct this criticism to the past of ethical discourse is also to raise doubts about its future and thus about its possibility. Certainly the minimal claim of a distinction between practical or ethical reasoning, on the one hand, and theoretical reasoning, on the other, has recently, after a long lapse, come to be acknowledged by philosophers, and this concession itself testifies, it seems, to the failure of theoretical ethics in the past. In certain respects, the evidence for that distinction seems as obvious as it is revealing. So, for example, theoretical or "scientific" knowledge is usually recognized as transferable and progressive: nobody now has to recreate the work of Newton or Copernicus in order to use their discoveries; grammar-school students start from the point at which the lifework of earlier scientific genius left off. By contrast, ethical or practical knowledge is dependent on the history and character of each person, continually to be renewed. For knowledge of this sort, individuals, if they do not have actually to traverse the history of culture, cannot simply assume its conclusions as their own: no one else can do the work of moral judgment for them.

But as soon as we put the contrast in these terms, we recognize that it may be overstated, that also ethics has a communal face, that social norms and expectations which are the main public and generalized expression of values have an influence, in fact and also by right, on individual decisions. And the question arises then, overriding the distinction between theory and practice, of how ethical theory and principle can affect the means by which ethical judgment and, before that, the ethical imagination constitute themselves. One obvious source to which one might turn in trying to get a grip on the contingencies of the ethical present is in the historical past, in events which are known to be possible because they have been actual and which might now reassert their significance if only we could determine—and experience—the point at which what had been possible and what was then made actual first met. The most characteristic and difficult feature of ethical decisions, after all, is that they occur in the present, that they *have* to be made. Not to make them is invariably also to make them, and it is always the individual person who is, in that present, compelled to act (even if only to accept someone else's earlier decision). The importance for ethics of historical examples does not diminish this emphasis on the present; here we see the deeper intention in Hegel's conclusion that the one thing we learn from history is that we have not learned anything from history. But if we do not, perhaps cannot, learn from history, we may yet learn something still more important—to place ourselves *in* history, to *imagine* historically, with the prospect that this will affect the way that we imagine and understand and then judge the present.

The Nazi genocide against the Jews may seem an unlikely basis from which to elaborate a conception of moral education. The features of that series of events are so extreme that we might predict that at best any conclusions drawn from them for ethical theory or practice would have no general implications, that at worst they would express only the partiality of moral hindsight or cant. But the other side of this is, of course, that the act of genocide was a moral phenomenon, the enormity of which continues to challenge the reasoned and balanced voice in which ethics has traditionally spoken. Hard cases may make bad law, but if ethics does not prove itself by extreme cases, its representation of simple ones becomes suspect. The most crucial practical issue in ethical judgment, moreover—the problem of making decisions where human life is at stake—recurs constantly in the events of the genocide, a challenge in every direction to which the genocide extended: to the German, non-Jewish citizens responding to the orders of a murderous government; to inhabitants of the occupied countries compelled to decide whether to resist or not; to the citizens of bystander countries who faced the decision of whether to intervene; and, of course, to the Jews, the principal object of the genocide, with the decision forced on them of reacting to a situation which offered them among its alternatives mainly different possibilities of destruction.

The last of these alternatives usually provided little that even resembled a choice; the knowledge of the few options that did appear, moreover, was often uncertain and limited, as was, still more surely, the power of action. Yet choices and decisions did nonetheless occur, and we are able, looking back, to recognize the form in which these choices appeared and what their consequences were. It is an easy temptation in such retrospection to infer from it a judgment on the past, as if such judgments had nothing to do with us in the present. But this would, also mistakenly, imply that those choices were now closed, completed—when in fact they serve as connectives which provide a means for the work of ethical imagination in the present. It is possible to place our own experience within the past, rather than the other, more usual way around, and it is valuable to do this, since the conclusions arrived at are quite unlike those reached by theoretical reason, which has no place for memory. A mathematical proof demonstrates no more in its second or third repetition than it did the first time—and moral judgment differs from theoretical reason in just this respect, that as it faces the "same" issue again, it may incorporate that new judgment into the past. To be sure, the ethical past often has a causal hold on the present by way of precedent or habit, and testimony from the past may serve as a continuing guide or standard. But it is also possible for the present, in imagining the past, to cross the temporal boundary that separates the one from the other and thus to confront the past in terms of the present (the more usual definition of the present is to see it narrowed rather than enlarged by the past). Time appears as an intrinsic element of moral judgment, in other words; there remains only the question of whether what has happened in the past will be viewed as inert in the present or whether it appears as still active, formative, itself dependent on the present.

The historical example to be considered here was undoubtedly the hardest, and harshest, instance of decision that faced the Jewish communities in the harsh period of the genocide. In most of the orders issued by the Nazis to the Jews, to be sure, there was no room for decision at all. That absence, in fact, is what in the last analysis distinguishes genocide as a phenomenon, distinguishes it from other types of murder and indeed from other varieties of evil: nothing the victim can do or choose (or could have chosen or could have done) makes any difference to the intention of which he is the object. But there were intermediate points in the Nazi genocide where a measure of autonomy remained for the Jewish communities and their members. The main one of these points, with the irony deliberately placed there by the Nazis themselves, occurred as the individual communities were ordered to choose between life and death for their own members—when, as the Nazis began to transport inhabitants of the ghettos to the death camps, they ordered that the selection of inhabitants for this "resettlement" should be made by the communities themselves, under the threat of punishment (implicitly or explicitly death) for members of the communities if these orders were not obeyed.

These orders were usually delivered by the Nazis to the Judenräte, the Jewish administrative councils of the cities and ghettos of Eastern Europe, which became objects of controversy almost from the date (21 September 1939) when Heydrich, the chief of the Nazi Security Police, gave instructions for their formation. It was these groups and their members, then, that were mainly confronted—at different times and in different ways but virtually without exception—by the decision of whether and how to decide on the basis of the orders they received. That role, it later turned out, had been anticipated for them from the beginning. In Heydrich's edict, the Judenräte were defined as administrative councils or bureaus, to be composed of up to twenty-four men in each of the Jewish communities in newly occupied Poland and in the ghettos which were soon established.[1] Since the ghettos themselves were conceived as an intermediate stage in the Nazi design of a Final Solution, this meant—and sooner or later was understood by everyone *to* mean—that the Councils would serve as instruments in *that* policy. They also, and this was a more immediate consideration for the members of the Councils, were responsible for civic arrangements that were left indeterminate by the Nazi orders for establishing the ghettos. Thus the Councils undertook to see that the Jews forced into the ghettos would, however minimally, be housed and fed; that opportunities for work should be arranged; and that medical facilities and other programs (educational, cultural) for which resources could be found were set up. (The dimensions of this task are evident in the fact that for Warsaw, the largest of the ghettos, this meant making arrangements for an average population, between September 1939 and August 1942, of about four hundred thousand.)

1. See Isaiah Trunk's standard work, *Judenrat* (New York: Stein and Day, 1972), and on this point, especially 7–16.

Even if the members appointed to the Councils in the early days of their existence did not know exactly what the function of the Councils was eventually to be, they knew enough to be wary. Few members of the Councils served eagerly; few served even willingly; many were simply appointed by the Nazis. Most of them, moreover, were eventually killed, and although there were important distinctions among the Councils and among certain leaders of the Councils (as, for example, between Adam Czerniakow of the Warsaw ghetto, who committed suicide when faced with the kind of decision discussed here, and Rumkowski, "King" of the Lodz ghetto, who used even such decisions for self-aggrandizement until he himself was sent to his death), it was the common function of all the Councils to formulate the responses of their respective communities to directives issued by the Nazis. Isaiah Trunk and other historians have concluded, in fact, that differences among the Councils (and indeed among the Jewish communities they administered) were so great that no generalizations about their comportment are possible.[2] But insofar as a common purpose of self-destruction was forced by the Nazis on all the communities, at least this one basis of comparison remains—and so, too, their responses to this one purpose as it became more and more explicit.

There persists, to be sure, a rather different, "boundary" question about the Councils in the claim, made prominent by Hannah Arendt but debated first in the beleaguered Jewish communities themselves, that the Councils should not have consented to function at all. It was Arendt's contention that the very *existence* of the Councils contributed to the Nazi goal of a Final Solution; that without the Councils, in the vacuum of disorder that would then have prevailed, many more Jews— perhaps half of those who were killed, that is, between two and a half and three million—would have survived.[3] Arendt's critics have disputed this prophecy, arguing that the Nazis would have acted even in the absence of the Councils, arguing also the need for *some* organization able to respond to communal needs.[4] Beyond these specific objections, it is worth noting that the radical disorganization which Arendt prescribes as an alternative presupposes in itself an extraordinary unanimity and strength of spirit; it would, in fact, have

2. Cf. Trunk's *Judenrat;* and also Yehuda Bauer, *The Jewish Emergence from Powerlessness* (Toronto: University of Toronto Press, 1979), 37 ff.
3. Arendt, *Eichmann* (see chap. 1, n. 18), 124–26.
4. See, e.g., Jacob Robinson, *And the Crooked Shall be Made Straight* (Philadelphia: Jewish Publication Society, 1965); Gertrude Ezorsky, "Hannah Arendt's View of Totalitarianism and the Holocaust," *Philosophical Forum* 11 (1984), 63–81; and Nathan Rotenstreich, "Can Evil Be Banal?" *Philosophical Forum* 11 (1984), 50–62.

represented a highly unusual form of collective resistance. Thus, the claim that the existence of the Councils contributed to the destruction of the Jews is not very far from saying that the existence of the Jews themselves did so. There was almost certainly no Council, no individual member of a Council, and even few Jews under the jurisdiction of the Councils, who did not at some point believe that the Councils' work might ameliorate conditions in the ghettos, that the Councils might buy time for members of the community, and that this time—any time—could turn into life. And although such beliefs were sometimes skewed by self-interested motives, at other times by what may seem now to have been confused or wistful thinking, the alternative to the existence of the Councils hardly promised anything more likely or more effective.

The questions that remain about the Councils, then, concern not the issue of their existence, but the decisions and actions which they initiated, and in particular the decision which at one time or other faced virtually all of them as they were ordered to select their fellow Jews for "resettlement" (*Umsiedlung*) or "evacuation" (*Aussiedlung*)—terms which under the Nazi "language rules" were figurative synonyms for "execution." (Genocide, the discussion in chapter 4 attempts to show, extended to the language as well as to people.) All the other decisions of the Councils are subordinate to their stand on this one issue. For if at the time that the Councils were first constituted, the Nazi goal of a Final Solution had not been fully defined, that definition was not long in coming, with the organization of the ghettos and the Judenräte very much part of it.[5] And although the Councils usually construed their own purpose to be that of preserving life, of making the ghettos as bearable as they could be given the violence that was a constant presence, this justification obviously became problematic just at the point where the Councils were themselves asked to make the decision between life and death for the members of their communities.

The term "problematic," with its connotation of uncertainty, is neces-

5. There is sufficient disagreement among historians about the exact date when this goal was determined to suggest that the search for exactness may itself be mistaken. See, e.g., Bauer, *Jewish Emergence,* 8 ff.; Hilberg, *Destruction,* 401–7. Part of the difficulty here is undoubtedly related to the problem of specifically locating a corporate decision, part to the difficulty—whether for a corporate *or* an individual decision—of assigning a "time" to an intention. Heydrich's order constituting the Judenräte, however, seems unmistakable at least in its portent, with the distinction it makes between "1) the final aim (which will require extended periods of time) and 2) the stages leading to the fulfillment of this final aim [which begins with the concentration of the Jews in the cities, the appointment of the Judenräte, etc.]"

sary even at that point, because then, too, the issues were not always clear. In some instances where the Councils faced such decisions, they could, in retrospect, justifiably have pleaded ignorance, that they did not *know* the fates to which they were sending the people who were selected (although this claim would at other times amount to no more than a refusal to credit the evidence). Moreover, the Councils would unavoidably have the task of drawing the line between this decision and other instances of "choosing" to which they had already assented. In the early days of the ghettos, for example, the Nazis often seized people off the street at random for forced labor, and the Councils in many of the ghettos agreed then to meet quotas for workers as a means of gaining a measure of control over this process. If the Councils were to have existed at all, *some* such instances of selection were probably unavoidable, although it could be argued that this made it all the more important that the Councils should have insisted on making distinctions among those instances.

There were in any event moments with none of these mitigating conditions, when it was quite clear to the members of the Councils what the consequences of a decision to decide would be, as well as what the refusal to do this would entail. This was the case on a sufficient number of occasions to bring into full view the stark features of the decision facing the various Councils, features that have not altered in retrospect. A captive population is ordered to give up for execution—again, called by any of the code names: resettlement, evacuation—a number of its members who are unnamed in the order and who thus have to be selected by the population or its representatives. Refusal to do this probably means punishment by death for perhaps as many or even more of the community as are referred to in the original order; obedience affords at least the momentary (and perhaps longer) reprieve for those not selected. The Councils then have to decide how to respond to the decree.

It might be expected that versions of this harsh dilemma can be found elsewhere in history—and that is the case, both in fact and in discussion, in Jewish history itself. One classic formulation of the issue, restating a number of its earlier appearances which date back to the second century, appears in Maimonides' *Mishneh Torah*. Maimonides describes there the demand made to a group of Israelites by a conquering enemy: "'Surrender one of your number to us, that we may put him to death; otherwise we will put you all to death.'" Maimonides then provides his response: "The [Israelites] should all suffer death rather than surrender a single Israelite to them. But if they [the enemy] specify an individual, saying 'Surrender that particular person to us, or else we will put all of

you to death,' they may give him up provided that he was guilty of a capital crime. . . . But this rule is not told them [the enemy] in advance."[6]

Certain aspects of this ruling by Maimonides warrant special consideration. For one thing, it is evident that the numerous qualifications
attached in Maimonides' account would make it virtually impossible
ever to justify turning over a member of the community in the face of
such a demand. For example, in order that a person should be turned
over requires not only that he be named but that he should have been
guilty of a capital crime (and, one supposes, found to be guilty by a duly
constituted Jewish court). And even then, as Maimonides later goes on
to say, he should not be turned over—*no one* should—if the demand to
do this is made as part of a systematic religious persecution. Maimonides' general attitude, in other words, is clear: that the community
should put itself at risk rather than to allow this to happen to the innocent individual. And although he does not provide a full account of the
reasoning which leads to this conclusion, we can infer much of that from
his statement of the conclusion itself, together with what he says elsewhere that bears on it.

The most telling feature in Maimonides' statement is his evident denial that numbers have a bearing on the decision to be made. He acknowledges, without commenting on it further, that rejection of the demand to hand over one or a number of victims may result in the death of
a larger number of people than would be killed if the order were
obeyed—all of them, the large number not less than the small number,
innocent. The basis on which he rejects the demand must then be something other than what is entailed in the most obvious *consequences* of that
decision. What this other basis might be is indicated in Maimonides' discussion, in the same chapter of the *Mishneh Torah*, of a number of absolute prohibitions—those biblical commandments that may not be violated even when the agent's own life is at stake.

Maimonides cites three such prohibitions, against idolatry, sexual
violation, murder; and it is evidently the last of these that directly impels
his rulings on the decision not to decide. The act of selecting and giving
over a member of the community would itself be inculpated in the
murder that follows; and the grounds for judging it in these terms, we
infer, are in part abstract—"Reason indicates that one human life ought
not to be destroyed to save another human life"—in part practical: how
would such a selection be made even if one believed that it was war-

6. Maimonides, *Mishneh Torah*, bk. 1, chap. 5. See also David Daube, *Collaboration with
Tyranny in Rabbinic Law* (London: Oxford University Press, 1965); and by the same author, *Civil Disobedience in Antiquity* (Manchester: University Press, 1972), 98–100.

ranted? For Maimonides, the act of selection extends to the community the responsibility that otherwise belongs solely to the murderer: by that act, they become his instruments. And the requirements implied by the *process* of selection verge on the same moral issue. Are there criteria commensurable with the stakes involved in such a decision? It is, as Maimonides seems to conceive it, life that is being measured against life—not a young life measured against an old one, not a talented life against an ordinary one, not even many lives against a lesser number: there is only equality here, and thus no grounds for preferment or selection.

The moral conviction and power in Maimonides' analysis are evident. But we also recognize that the conclusion he reaches and the prescriptions that follow from it are extraordinarily demanding. Not only do they require a community and its members to face the prospect of general destruction rather than to choose partial survival, but it also is clear that a different conclusion could be drawn from the same starting point, from what might arguably be the same value placed on life and the same prohibition against murder. This alternative conclusion does in fact appear in response to a demand which closely resembles the one that Maimonides described, formulated now, however, at the time of the Nazi genocide, and with an added issue at stake that Maimonides could hardly have anticipated: the threat of destruction not to one or another group of Jews, but to the Jewish people as a whole. In October 1941, the Judenrat of the Kovno ghetto, confronted by an order to bring the population of the ghetto together in order that a "selection" should be made among them for deportation, turned to the senior rabbi of Kovno, Avraham Duber Cahana Shapira, for a judgment on whether or not they should issue the order. Shapira's response was as follows—no less direct than Maimonides' had been but opposed in its terms:—"If a Jewish community (may God help it) has been condemned to physical destruction, and there are means of rescuing part of it, the leaders of the community should have the courage to assume the responsibility to act and to rescue what is possible."[7]

We should not suppose that this judgment by the Kovno rabbi was made without full consciousness of its divergence from the opinion of Maimonides, nor should we construe his rather oblique formulation in terms of "triage"—the necessity for deciding on a morally neutral order

---

7. Cf. Jacob Robinson, Introduction to Trunk, *Judenrat,* xxxi–xxxii. See also the Responsum by Rabbi Ephraim Oshry in Yitzhak Arad, Yisrael Gutman, and Abraham Margaliot (eds.), *Documents from the Holocaust* (Jerusalem: Yad Vashem, 1981), 402–3; and the account by David Kahana, *A Lvov-Ghetto Diary* (Hebrew) (Jerusalem: Yad Vashem, 1978), 62–65.

of priorities (as in allocating care to wounded soldiers under emergency conditions) where there is no question of complicity or guilt. The conclusion he reached, moreover, was not arrived at only in the Kovno ghetto—although it is also true that objections were at times raised elsewhere to the position he took. So far as generalization is possible, in the majority of instances where Councils faced the decision of whether to decide, their conclusions took the same form and relied on the same justification as did that of the Kovno rabbi. It is not difficult, moreover, to understand the grounds for this response.[8] Even before the tide of war had shifted against the Nazis, and still more so afterward, the possibility was evident that *some* members of the community might survive—and so the contention emerged that the sacrifice of some, as against the destruction of the entire group, would be justified if it made this possibility more likely. To decide *not* to do this, in fact, would itself impose a heavy moral burden, since by not rescuing those who might be saved, the Councils would open themselves to the charge that they were inculpated in the murderers' work. And if this were the case, if there must be moral violation *whatever* decision was made—either to decide, or with Maimonides, not to decide—should not the former alternative, with the possibility it held out of rescuing at least part of the community, settle the question?

Now it can be argued retrospectively that in fact the willingness to accept this line of reasoning did not work in favor of survival, that nobody was saved by the decisions of the Judenräte to decide. It has also been asserted more generally that whatever decision the Councils made on such questions, the outcome—the destruction of the ghettos and their inhabitants—would have been the same.[9] But even if these claims are true (neither is easily tested), they do not affect the moral issues in the decision itself, as those issues might occur in other contexts or as they did occur in the contradictory possibilities that have been described here. The question of what moral role should be assigned to practical consequences is, in fact, an important element in the disagreement between Maimonides and the Kovno rabbi. For although there is evident agree-

---

8. See I. J. Rosenbaum, *The Holocaust and Halakhah* (New York: Ktav, 1976), 17–46. The statement made in his own defense by Jacob Gens, head of the Vilna Judenrat, is a cogent summary of the position: "I take count of Jewish blood, not Jewish honor. When the Germans ask for a thousand persons, I hand them over, for if we Jews will not give them on our own, the Germans will come and take them by force. Then they will take not one thousand but thousands. With hundreds, I save a thousand, with the thousands I hand over, I save ten thousands." (See Philip Friedman, *Roads to Extinction* (Philadelphia: Jewish Publication Society, 1980), 370–71.

9. Robinson, *And the Crooked*, xxxiv.

ment between them on the importance of human life, the conclusion which Maimonides reaches suggests that the circumstances of the act by which life is preserved may weigh more heavily in moral terms than the results of the act itself; for Rabbi Shapira, that order of priority is reversed. Thus, on Maimonides' account, the number of lives involved in the decision does not weigh in the moral balance: it is not only one life that may not be balanced against any larger number, but that life itself is not to be distinguished where the means of comparison may ensue in the difference between life and death. In the view that opposes this, we infer that the consequences, the possibility of saving one group of persons, perhaps even one person—and thus of drawing distinctions among persons—might justify an act which by itself or in any other context must be reprehensible, forbidden. *Not* to engage in that act is also, on the latter account, a way of engaging in the act.

Unfortunately, the period of the Nazi genocide provides examples in which the difference in consequence between these positions is explicitly represented. The Lodz ghetto provides one such example, where the strategy of Rumkowski, the head of the Council, was from the very beginning to barter the survival of some members of the community against the destruction of others. So he urged the development of industries that would make the ghetto workers useful to the Nazi war effort; so he consented to the Nazi orders that the decision of life and death should be made among inhabitants of the ghetto, in order, he contended, to leave *some* of them for life.[10] And in July 1944 seventy miles separated the final destruction of the Lodz ghetto and the more than sixty thousand Jews still alive there from the advancing Russian army. Had the Russians continued that advance, those people—at least many of them—might well have survived, and we then look backward at the question of whether *that* would have justified Rumkowski's strategy. To maintain Maimonides' position consistently would be to conclude that even numbers like those would not provide a warrant for the decision by which the tens of thousands of other ghetto inhabitants had been selected for death; we thus understand the magnitude of what Maimonides' decision not to decide might entail.

An even more difficult example—more difficult because the attempt "succeeded" where the others referred to failed—occurs in Hungary, between August and December in 1944, where Rudolf Kasztner, negotiating a ransom arrangement with the Nazis for a number of Hungarian Jews, took on himself the responsibility for the decision to

10. See Solomon F. Bloom, "Dictator of the Lodz Ghetto," *Commentary* 7 (1949), 111–22.

decide and then for the deciding itself: "Once again we were confronted with the dilemma which we had been faced with throughout
our work: Should we leave selection to blind fate or should we try to
influence it? We convinced ourselves that—as sacred as every human
being has always been to the Jews—we nevertheless had to strive to
save at least those who . . .", and here Kasztner lists the criteria by
which he had chosen the seventeen hundred members of the community who were saved by this means; among the people saved were those
who had worked for the community, women whose husbands were in
the labor camps, orphans (and not, of course, very many of any of these
groups). That these people were chosen for life where usually, in the
process of selection, the choice was made for death does not alter the
moral issue at stake or the status of the decisions that Kasztner made
(and for which he was later tried—and, on appeal, acquitted—by an Israeli court).[11]

The suggestion has been made above that it should not be moral retrospection that is the main purpose of reflection on these examples and
the decisions on which they were based. This does not mean that there
are no judgments to be made on moral decisions of the past, these or
others, but only that one value of such retrospection is in exhibiting
rather than in judging the past, in revealing—even imagining—alternatives otherwise hidden from the present in the texture of that past.
Explication of this sort is especially important when, as for the conflicting judgments described here, the judgments themselves seem in certain
respects to reflect similar values, and in particular, for the instances cited,
the value attached to human life. Even the different emphases which
have been attributed above to the respective responses of Maimonides
and the Kovno rabbi—between the importance for moral judgment of
intentions or form, on the one hand, and of consequences, on the
other—may not be so sharply at variance as might be inferred. For
Maimonides, too, after all, the consequences of an act obviously matter:
whoever decides between life and death is inculpated only insofar as
something follows from that decision; for the Kovno rabbi, too, the act
and not only its consequences matter. Not to choose is also a way of
choosing—and that is, at least in part, why, on his account, it would be
wrong not to choose.

Is there then a fundamental difference between the two judgments?

11. The charges against Kasztner were in part motivated by the accusation that he had
not adhered to those criteria. The verdict for exoneration by the Israeli Supreme Court, on
appeal from an earlier judgment of guilt, came only after Kasztner himself had been assassi-
nated. See Dina Porat, *An Entangled Leadership: The Yishuv and the Holocaust, 1942–1945*
(Hebrew), (Tel Aviv: Am Oved, 1986), 388–91.

For it is obvious that *whatever* decision is made—to decide or not to decide—entails a loss; on either account the decision itself is wrenching.
And if indeed the values which are primary and so to be acted on are
shared between them, and if nothing in those values singly impels a decision in one direction rather than the other, then any judgment we could
now make, or, more importantly, any judgment that was made then by
the Councils, must be arbitrary—as arbitrary as the force was that compelled them in the first place to make an inhuman choice. It may be that
in this large sense, so far as the question of deciding whether to choose
was the issue, the issue should finally be viewed as an irresolvable conflict, with no possibility, on either side, of doing what is "right." But it is
also true that implied in the two accounts are divergent conceptions of
another issue which, although less immediately compelling, may nonetheless account for the apparent difference between them. This issue
involves not the specific decision to decide or not, but a more general
context—the structure or form of life invoked in the decision, and
specifically the relation between the individual and the community presupposed in it.

   It would be too much to claim that the two judgments of Maimonides
and Shapira simply contradict each other in their conceptions of this
more general relation, and that this contradiction accounts for the opposed courses of action they come to recommend. But their differences
at this more general level bear directly on the specific act of moral judgment at issue. Maimonides' conclusion that no member of the community should be turned away from it by the will of the community presupposes a conception of the individual life as tied intrinsically to that of the
community. As (according to this conception) no individual is allowed
to take the responsibility of choosing for others life or death, so he himself is not to be so chosen, even at the risk of life itself to other members
of the community. The life of the individual is thus identified with the
life of the community. As he may be persecuted for that identity, so also
it is that identity that persists (or in the event falls) with him: he can rely
on them both. It is in this vein that Maimonides proposes as a general
thesis in the *Guide of the Perplexed,* echoing Aristotle, that "man is political by nature, and it is his nature to live in society" (bk. 2, chap. 40)—a
thesis about human nature in general to which he soon adds a more specific one also emphasizing a common and collective identity: "All the
house of Israel are in duty bound to be united in one indivisible whole."

   There may, on the other hand, be a conception of the relation between the individual and the community which is as real but not as
strong as that of Maimonides; and the judgment provided by Rabbi
Avraham Duber Cahana Shapira offers such a view. Undoubtedly, the

justification for saving some lives at the sacrifice of others is meant also to include the purpose of saving the community, of maintaining continuity with future generations. But the relation between individuals—those who are sacrificed and even those who are chosen for life—and the community evidently has a different intensity here, with the emphasis on life *in* the individual. Those who are chosen for life are chosen as individuals; and this discrimination, however involuntary, will, it seems, be reflected in other relations that involve the individual under less extreme circumstances, as an implication of the general relation between the individual and the community. The latter account seems, then, to conceive of the community as constituted of individual lives, independent of each other and thus, in extreme but more often in ordinary situations, to be measured or judged or finally to be chosen against each other. There can be a community here, but it is evidently a community constituted of individual selves, rather than the other way around, where it is the community which only then makes the individual "possible."

The difference between the two accounts of the decision to decide or not may then be associated with two conflicting views of human nature: the one in which people are seen as essentially linked in their individual identities to the identities of others, a collective or communal self; the second in which the autonomy of the individual is recognizable and separable from the life of the community. Theories of human nature, we know from *their* history, are more than only empirical or inductive accounts, and so, when we consider the differences between two such representations, it is not only additional evidence that will bear on those differences but a recommendation—itself a decision made always in the present but whose basis will have been laid before that. And here, it seems, the implications of Maimonides' view have an unusual profundity, both psychologically and morally, in challenging the assumption of the autonomous but isolated individual which has been so constant a theme in twentieth-century thought and so constantly reinforced by the effects of a mass and technological society. The assertion of a common history and identity among persons and lives within a community is not an independent claim—but follows in Maimonides' account just because of the prior assumption that persons and lives would not be possible except as linked to others who have been similarly committed. The decision to accept this conception of the relation between the individual and the community would, it seems, in the situation in which the Judenräte found themselves, entail the decision not to decide.

To be sure, it is only too clear that nobody simply *chooses* a communal or even an individual identity; in that determination, history seems always one step, and often more than that, ahead of reflection or decision.

But it also seems evident that identity, individual or communal, is never confirmed or made actual *without* a choice. Any recommendation now of Maimonides' view even as a goal or ideal unavoidably sounds like a verdict on the past—but it is meant before that, more urgently, as a question put to the future, as an incentive rather than as a prescription. What (the question asks)—if we imagine the past as the future—would we hope for as an identity there?

There is a strong, a compelling ideal, perhaps one that is finally required for the possibility of social existence altogether, in the principle that no member of the community will be responsible for denying a place there to another member of the community, insofar as the demand to do so leaves the choice to the community itself. And this, irrespective of the consequences that are threatened. It would surely be desirable that no one should ever be faced by such a decision. But that such decisions may force themselves on us is something we now know. And we could then say—or hope—that with the decision forced on us of whom to select for turning away, for turning *over*, we would decide not to decide. If that point could be reached for the lives of anonymous members of the community, moreover, perhaps the will to persist might later appear even if they *were* named. This link between the life of the individual and the lives of other persons and, through them, the life of the community is not the only moral value—but without such a link, it seems clear, all other values must be diminished. It was in any event specifically this bond, between the self as the member of a group and the self as individual, that the Nazi genocide against the Jews set out to destroy, as it acted against both the group and the individual.

II

REPRESENTATIONS OF GENOCIDE

4

Language and Genocide

The explanation of an historical event inevitably bears the mark of artifice. If it did not omit or compress, it would be as extensive as the events it was intended to explain and would be no more coherent than they were individually. To be sure, it is not only because of the complexity of historical connections in general that even the most sustained attempts to identify the causes of the Nazi genocide against the Jews seem inadequate. The difficulties here add the extraordinary character of that occurrence to the problematic status of evil itself; even in less extreme appearances, evil seems always to leave a remainder after its apparent social, economic, or psychological "causes" have been named. Beyond these intrinsic constraints, moreover, we recognize the scale on which the Nazi genocide was set—crossing the boundaries of continents, involving as victims, agents, and bystanders scores of nations, tens of millions of people. Accounts of an event of this magnitude must be hard put even to distinguish between causes and effects, let alone to determine the exact points at which they met; it would be a considerable accomplishment, in fact, to establish a bare chronicle of the event—what *happened*—and this indeed remains the single most important task of all writing about that event.

Thus, too, the assertion which will be made here of a connection between language and the Nazi genocide may seem hardly to move beyond the claim that language was at once a victim of the genocide and one agent of many among its causes. But acknowledgment of even the connection itself is significant; the violence done to language in the geno-

81

cide—in a special sense, to the German language; in a larger sense, to language as such—provides a distinctive representation of what the intention to exterminate the Jews required of its perpetrators in the way of will and of artifice; it discloses how deeply set the design of genocide was and how fully developed a world view it became. The Nazi genocide, seen from the perspective of language, is unusual in another respect as well, inasmuch as from this perspective the victims are seen to include those who shaped or only used the language in addition to those against whom the work of genocide was directed. The distortion of language is in this sense a more generalized violation than others that have more obviously terrible consequences and in which the distinction between agents and victims is explicit and constant. To escape the consequences of language, for worse or for better, would require an impossible step outside history for its speakers or writers no less than for its audience— and it has been a principal theme of the preceding pages that whatever else can be known the Nazi genocide, the evidence is only too clear of its place *within* history, as motivated and embodied in historical cause as well as in effect.

The background to this claim is broader than the specific evidence of the role of language in the Nazi genocide. The existence of a causal relation between language and history, between linguistic practice and events in the social context, would be disputed only on the view of language as a neutral and transparent medium, perhaps following certain formal rules of development but even then serving as an incidental means for more "real" intentions of its speakers or writers. On this view, the capacity of language is independent of its objects; thus the moral character of the events of which language provides a representation is of no consequence for the detail of syntax and vocabulary on the basis of which the representation is formulated. In the terms made current by de Saussure, the "signifier" and the "signified" which constitute the linguistic transaction are arbitrarily related to each other—and also, beyond that, to the historical events which they are then, however mysteriously, understood to denote. On this view, neither natural nor historical causality influences the structure or stylistic patterns of language; nor, conversely, do the forms of language, whether in actual usage or in formal structure, reflect what is said by their means. *What* is said is thus held to be independent of *how* it is said; the same "thing" can be expressed in quite different ways and across what appear as quite different linguistic structures. It is linguistic content that has consequences—the descriptions or commands given, the purposes that are announced, and the evidence which is credited—but not, in any event, the variations in form of their expressions.

The narrowness of this view of language would be demonstrable even without the unusual evidence provided by the linguistic embodiment of the intentions directing the Nazi genocide. Testimony comes from many different sources of the history of language as "real" history, evolving in direct relation to features of the historical and social context. Those features extend from the constraints imposed by human physiology to the effects of specific technological developments such as the alphabet or the printing press—and then also to the consequences of radical political change that may affect not only specific linguistic usage but the concept of language as such. So de Maistre would write that "every individual or national degradation is immediately heralded by a strictly proportional degradation in the language itself," and his words here, one infers, bear not only on "degradation" but, more generally, on all significant change.

The relation between linguistic practice and the causes that affect it, moreover, includes among those causes the content of specific linguistic expressions as well as social history external to language. Thus, a central issue in the history of literature has focused on the problem of genres— the relation between literary forms or means and the content of the texts that have those forms. The difficulty evident from such analysis of sustaining a sharp distinction between form and content would itself suggest their interrelation, and this conclusion is further supported as instances of supposedly formal stylistic analysis revert, as they constantly do, to the question of content: what the literary text is "about" or "of." As the corporate forms of expression—art, legal institutions, religious practice—reflect the varieties of purpose and oral agency at their origins, moreover, it is hardly surprising that this should also be the case for language, which is another such form: one, in fact, on which the others depend. Indeed, as soon as discourse is conceived as a means of agency on the part of a speaker, this connection is made: *some* understanding of origin and purpose becomes associated with meaning; as historical, those sources then affect the shape of expression.

On these general grounds, it is predictable that linguistic developments which occurred at the time of the Nazi genocide would disclose features resembling those of the process of genocide itself; it would be difficult to understand how that process might occur without corresponding changes in the language. The evidence that there was such a connection is the basis of the discussion here—a connection which extends, indeed, to the *idea* of language as well as to specific patterns of usage. As individual features of language (syntax, grammar, figures of speech) come to be viewed in the Nazi vocabulary as mere instruments, subordinated in rhetoric or art or theoretical discourse to political ends, so when language is applied to the work of genocide, language as a whole is conceived of as an instrument, also subordinated to ends determined independently of it. Language is in this process detached from history and nature and finally also from moral judgment—becoming a means only by which certain intentions, themselves independently defined and allegedly translinguistic, are to be implemented. It thus takes on the character of impersonal technique, to be applied to whatever ends its agents independently decide on and reflecting only as much of those ends as the agents determine that it should. Language, in other words, becomes entirely contrivance, mute with respect to its own voice, detached from any sense of its own origins or purposes.

This conception of language differs markedly from another and more traditional view according to which language is historically bound—caused by and expressive of the agent who speaks or writes it. On these terms, language is intrinsically linked to thought and social practice, reflecting or representing its agents and their purposes as well as the objects to which it refers. To be sure, extreme versions of this view, where a particular language was identified with nature or with a particular source of self-legitimating authority (civil or religious), could be as dogmatic in their conclusions as the opposed denial of any such connections; they were no less common, moreover, than were the visions of a "universal," artificial language such as that proposed by Leibnitz. What was historically decisive in the relation between genocide and language, however, was the displacement at the levels of both concept and practice of language as a form of disclosure and expression. In that displacement, we find the representation of language entirely as an instrument or means, together with the conditions presupposed by that change—the claim by political authority to control also over social memory and history; the reconstruction of language as ideological and thus as independent both of facts and of human agency; the assertion of political power to fill the space which is left by the denial to language of all authority of its own.

These summary comments about the general relation between language and history do not depend only on the consequences for language of the Nazi genocide against the Jews or even, at a more general level than that, on the technological and totalitarian aspects of the Nazi state which were conditions, and undoubtedly necessary conditions, of that genocide. It is evident, moreover, that aspects of what is alleged here to characterize the language of the Nazis can be found in other linguistic usage as well, often as a consequence of the Nazi precedent, but in some measure independent of it. Yet as in other respects the Nazis defined paradigmatically the act of genocide, so too, through their explicit and methodical elaboration of that act—the *constancy* of their intentions—they provided an extraordinary view of the role that language both had and suffered in the phenomenon of genocide.[1]

One does not have to look for a significant instance of such usage beyond the term by which the Nazis chose to designate their genocidal war against the Jews—that is, the *Endlösung*, or Final Solution, which after the Wannsee Conference of 20 January 1942 was adopted by Nazi officialdom as the code word meant at once to disguise and to refer to that plan of extermination. In this term appear the characteristic features of a complex inversion of language—a linguistic equivalent of the very phenomenon to which the term itself refers; in it, we also see the form of the general turn that the language of genocide was to take.

It is well to understand that *Endlösung* had a history prior to its adoption by the Nazis, not so much as a term of general usage (although it was so used, albeit infrequently) as in the sense that other terms, close in meaning, had been "tried out" before the choice of *Endlösung* itself was made. So, there is reference to *Endziel* ("final goal") in Heydrich's order to the Einsatzgruppen (21 September 1939), to *Gesamtlösung* ("total solution") by Göring in his directive to Heydrich of 31 July 1941 (Göring in this same statement *also* uses *Endlösung*), and to the *endgültige Lösung* ("conclusive solution") in a statement by Himmler concerning the "Gypsy question" (8 December 1939). We have mainly to speculate about the process by which these alternatives came to be rejected in favor of *Endlösung* (for which Eichmann, probably on the basis of the Wannsee Conference, was to claim pride of authorship)—although one reason might well be that the latter term avoids possible ambiguities in the others: *Ziel* ("goal") as something that may or may not be within reach, *gesamt* ("total" or "collective") re-

1. Among the accounts given of the Nazi use of language, see especially Nachman Blumenthal, "On the Nazi Vocabulary," *Yad Vashem Studies* 1 (1957), 49–66; and "From the Nazi Vocabulary," 6 (1967), 69–82; Gordon A. Craig, *The Germans* (New York: G. P. Putnam's Sons, 1982), 323–25; Shaul Esh, "Words and Their Meanings: Twenty-Five Examples of the Nazi-Idiom," *Yad Vashem Studies* 5 (1963), 133–67; Jean Pierre Faye, *Langages totalitaires* (Paris: Hermann, 1972); Henry Friedlander, "The Manipulation of Language," in Henry Friedlander and Sybil Milton (eds.), *The Holocaust: Ideology, Bureaucracy, and Genocide* (Millwood, N.Y.: Kraus International Publications, 1980), 103–14; Rolf Hochhuth, "Als Nachwort ein Blick auf Wörter," in *Die Hebamme* (Reinbek: Rowohlt, 1971), 287–302; Eugen Seidel and Ingeborg Seidel, *Sprachwandel im Dritten Reich: Eine critische Untersuchung faschischter Einflüsse* (Halle: VEB Berlag, 1961); George Steiner, *Language and Silence* (New York: Atheneum, 1974), 95–109.

ferring to all the parts of a problem at a given time but not necessarily to settling the problem once and for all.[2]

In any event, it seems evident that the Wannsee Conference at which the *Endlösung* was ratified in name and intention took for granted that term's implication of *other* "solutions" that had been proposed to the same "problem" or "question" as the one addressed at the Conference, but that were not, by contrast, "final." It was not the Nazis, moreover, who initiated the use of the complementary terms—"question," or "problem," on the one hand, and "solution," on the other—in connection with discussions of the status of the Jews. The "Jewish Question" to which various solutions or answers would be sought was in fact a conventional locution, used by non-Jewish—and anti-Jewish—writers, but also by Jewish and philo-Jewish writers, however differently the "question" or "problem" was understood by each group.[3]

The first part of the agglutinative noun *Endlösung* as applied by the Nazis to the Jewish Question does, of course, also refer to the prior efforts of the Nazis themselves—the earlier and less than final solutions which the Nazis had been proposing virtually from the moment they came to power in 1933. Those efforts included the sequence of racial legislation epitomized by the Nuremberg Laws of 1935 which, by imposing a combination of economic and social restrictions, had as their principal purposes to confiscate property and to coerce Jews to emigrate from Germany—a policy which persisted with some variations until the edict of 23 October 1941 prohibiting Jewish emigration. (This policy included the scheme for resettling the Jews in Madagascar, a plan which never came close to implementation but was the occasion of speculation mainly between 1938 and 1940, and was certainly consistent with the policy of forced emigration—mentioned, among other instances, in statements by Göring on 12 November 1938, by Hans Frank in January 1940, and by Hitler himself in February 1941.)[4] Proposals such as this,

2. Göring was to offer a version of this distinction in his own defense at Nuremberg. See Gerald Reitlinger, *The Final Solution* (South Brunswick, N.J.: Thomas Yoseloff, 1968), 85.

3. Perhaps the best-known use of the term is in Marx's *Zur Judenfrage* (1844), reprinted in *Karl Marx: Early Writings*, trans. Gregor Benton (New York: Vintage, 1975); but see, for other examples, Ahad Ha'am, "Medinat Ha-Yehudim Ve' Tsarat Ha-Yehudim" ("The Jewish State and the Jewish Problem," 1897), reprinted in *The Writings of Ahad Ha'am* (Hebrew) (Jerusalem: Ho'zeah Ivrith, 1947); Theodor Herzl, *Der Judenstaat: Versuch einer modernen Lösung der Judenfrage* (Vienna: M. Breitenstein, 1896); Louis Brandeis, "The Jewish Problem and How to Solve It" (1915), reprinted in Arthur Hertzberg (ed.), *The Zionist Idea* (Garden City, N.Y.: Doubleday, 1959).

4. See Hilberg, *Destruction* (cited in chap. 2, n. 9), 394–98; also Leni Yachil, *The Holocaust* (cited in chap. 1, n. 22), 356–60.

LANGUAGE AND GENOCIDE   87

directed in common to the goal of a "Judenrein" Germany, were not "final solutions" for reasons that are only too evident. These proposals, moreover, had become increasingly problematic for the Nazis by the time of the Wannsee Conference, in part because the Nazis were encouraged by the lack of resistance to their earlier, less radical policies, but also because of the results of their military conquests. The partition of Poland between Germany and Russia on 28 September 1939 had itself brought almost two million Jews under Nazi control—and such developments afforded new temptation and new opportunity, including, of course, the possibility that whatever the Nazis might think of doing to the Jews could now be done farther from the sight of the West (indeed farther from the sight of the Germans themselves) and with the aid of native populations whom the Einsatzgruppen discovered immediately after the invasion of Russia often to be willing collaborators. It was, then, in this context that the *Endlösung* was proposed—to solve the now larger Jewish Question in a plan of extermination that was to include *all* the Jews of Europe, those of Great Britain and of the neutral countries, Sweden and Switzerland, in addition to those in countries over which the Nazis already held power.[5]

The superficial intelligibility from the point of view of the Nazis that is in this way supplied by the historical background of the term *Endlösung* joins the persuasive connotation of the term itself. For viewed out of context, in its dictionary meaning, *Endlösung* may seem even more benign a concept than its partial root *Lösung*. Solutions are responses to problems which, by definition, are troublesome, hindering, matters which *should* be overcome or solved. The problems also carry with them, in fact, the implied possibility of solution: to acknowledge something *as* a problem suggests that it is capable of being solved. Thus, phrases such as "The Jewish Question" or "The Jewish Problem," even in formulations well disposed toward the "question," anticipate responses in the form of "solutions." Given the reasonable corollary, moreover, that if a problem is to be solved, it is best solved once and for all, an *Endlösung* is desirable in a way that provisional or incomplete solutions are not. Out of its historical context, then, the prospect of a Final Solution offers a

5. Such plans were not matters of fantasy. They were explicitly referred to in the protocol of the Wannsee Conference, and indeed Germany had at the end of June 1940 occupied England's Channel Islands. Soon after that, legislation followed requiring the registration of the few Jews who lived on Jersey and Guernsey and the sale of Jewish businesses to non-Jews; almost all the Jews identified were subsequently deported to concentration camps on the continent. (A concentration camp was also constructed on Alderney; a number of Jews transported from the continent were killed there.) See Charles Cruickshank, *The German Occupation of the Channel Islands* (Channel Islands: Guernsey Press, 1975).

welcome convergence of discursive and affective content: problems are meant to be solved—and the more fully or finally the better.

And yet, of course, in the Nazi vocabulary *Endlösung* stands for the extermination of a people—not their deportation or their enslavement (although these also, as it happened), but their annihilation; this is the literal act to which the opposed connotation of the term was joined in the Nazi vocabulary. The blatant disparity between the normal connotation of the word and its reference in that vocabulary amounts to what in the usual conventions of linguistic meaning or logic would be seen as a contradiction. Moreover, the fact that the Nazis themselves took the trouble to develop a set of "language rules" explicitly intended to conceal literal meaning—among which the rule for the use of *Endlösung* occupied an important place[6]—suggests that they were themselves well aware of this tension. Furthermore, it must not be supposed that the use of language rules or a code was intended entirely or only for an external audience, that the Nazis among themselves were ready to speak openly—i.e., literally—of what the code concealed. For there is substantial evidence that the use of *Endlösung* (and of some of, although not all, the other terms to be discussed) was meant also in internal use to disguise or misrepresent something which it would have been dangerous or morally wrong to address more directly. This was so intrinsic a feature of the term that its own use was severely restricted: the code word itself was for limited circulation. Like other attempts at concealment by the Nazis which lead naturally to the question of *why* they sought to conceal it, language rules provide important evidence of what the act of genocide represented in terms of Nazi beliefs—what, beyond what they *did*, they *thought* they were doing.

In selecting and using the term *Endlösung* in any event, the Nazis were attempting to add to the referential force of the word elements that go well beyond the purposes of reference. What results from this process is a term that has been "figured" or "turned" much in the way that figurative language of any kind originates, reflecting, as such usage characteristically does, the intention to make a word mean more than it would in its literal appearance. There are, of course, various ways in which figurative discourse adds to the meaning of words, and it may seem perverse to suggest that an understanding of these literary means will be informative about a word with the extraordinary history—much more im-

6. These included limitations on its use altogether. So, Martin Bormann writes, "on instructions from the Führer" (11 July 1943), that there is henceforth to be "no public reference" to the Total Solution (*Gesamtlösung*). (See Arad et al., *Documents* cited in chap. 3, n. 7), 324. ("It may however be mentioned," Bormann's order concludes, "that the Jews are taken in groups for appropriate labor purposes.")

mediately social and political, after all, than literary—that *Endlösung* has had. Yet the possibility that the turns of language should reflect also the turns of nonlinguistic history is too evident to be ignored. Beyond the issue of this particular example, moreover, is a general question of the relation between "normal" and "abnormal" discourse, and then of the historical status of language as such; it is an instance again—as for the act of genocide more generally—where extremity serves as a proof or test of the ordinary.

Considered then against the background of conventional figures of speech, *Endlösung* may seem to have been intended as ironical, implying, as irony characteristically does, the opposite or at least a reversal of what it superficially affirms: it denotes a solution to a problem by proposing the destruction of the problem. On this account, the term would be a form of gallows humor, initiated from the point of view of the builder of the gallows rather than from that of the victim—a joke meant to be added to the larger aggression.[7] But both internal and external evidence suggest that it was not irony that was intended by the Nazi choice of the term, not even the less pointed equivocation we find in *Endlösung* when we recognize through it that not only the problem "to be solved" but also the *solutions* to the problem would have come to an end; it would also, after all, be the *last* solution. The purpose of the Nazi language rules, however, was to *avoid* calling attention to themselves and to their applications; this policy was evident in the guarded references allowed even to the code words themselves. Furthermore, there is at least one more general reason for doubting that the Nazi purpose here was ironic. The characteristic feature in irony of "double vision," of language reiterating itself with a difference—and with a negation at that, to be supplied by the reader—makes irony an unlikely feature of totalitarian discourse at any time. In this role, irony underscores the possibility of nonliteral meaning and impels the reader beyond the apparent text (thus also beyond censorship)—both of these affording to the writer and to the reader a measure of freedom that would undoubtedly be seen by totalitarianism as subversive.

In addition to such prima-facie evidence, moreover, nothing in the appearances of *Endlösung* in Nazi documents hints at an intention to undermine its surface meaning. It is rather the literal denotation, the deli-

7. Hilberg cites a counterpart to the Nazi vocabulary in that of the victims (for example, the designation in Auschwitz of the crematorium as "the bakery"; see *Destruction* (cited in chap. 2, n. 9), 1041–2. But what might be irony from the point of view of the victim is something quite different in the Nazi vocabulary. (A more recent example: a "hitler" has become the colloquial name in Israeli Hebrew for a household device that kills or drives away flies by the fumes it gives off.)

berate assertion that through it the Jewish "problem" will be solved once and for all, that is intended; and although for most instances of figurative language (metaphor, for example) the absence of apparent intention from the figure itself may be irrelevant or even an advantage, this is not the case for irony. A statement or term which is read as metaphorical will never have a meaning simply contradictory to the meaning of the same statement or term read literally or nonmetaphorically. Irony alone has that feature, and for it intention is crucial; there is no irony that does not itself disclose the will responsible for it, let alone irony that is altogether unwilled.

For the audience who were in on the secret of the Nazi language rules, the term *Endlösung* denoted the extermination of the Jews—although even for them, it was meant at once to affirm and to obscure the referent: to focus attention on the goal and thus to draw attention away from the means. For the German public or for anyone outside Germany, as they might encounter the term and half know, half not know what it referred to, it would, on one level in any event, have the benign connotation of designating something that ought to be done—tautologically, the resolution of a problem that should be overcome *because* it was a problem, with the accompanying concealment that abstraction ("solution") always provides when it replaces the name or image of a concrete act ("extermination"). No space remains for irony at either end of this combination of contradictory meanings.

The question thus persists: if *Endlösung* is not irony, what figure or trope of speech is it? For the term is evidently contrived, turned, figurative in some way; certainly it is not innocent or straightforward, not matter of fact or literal in its overall force, despite—more accurately, because of—its own evident intention that it should be understood literally. This apparently academic question about figurative discourse is not at all academic in its results. For among the four classical literary figures under which varieties of the linguistic turn are often subsumed, irony has already been ruled out—and none of the other three provides a more adequate account: not metaphor (the "solution" is meant literally as a solution: tenor and vehicle are one); not metonymy (as "final," the solution is not a part substituted for a whole); not synecdoche (again, *Endlösung* is a *denial* of the part-whole relation). Related or similar objections block the appeal to more restricted figures of speech. The suggestion often made that *Endlösung* is an instance of euphemism, for example, although superficially plausible is no more adequate than would be the suggestion that it is hyperbole. To refer to someone as having "gone to sleep" rather than as having died is to intend a euphemism based on a metaphor. The literal and the euphemistic versions agree at least that the person referred to is motionless and unconscious; the euphemistic connotation of sleep adds the comforting possibility of peacefulness and even of a later awakening. But when the description of an act has a connotation that *reverses* the act, turning it not aside but into its opposite, we may reasonably conclude that the linguistic turn taken is not euphemism but a different figure altogether.

It seems hardly too much to claim here, in fact, that with *Endlösung* (and the related terms mentioned below) the language of genocide has contrived a distinctive literary figure. The characteristics of this figure are that the denotation of the term, although logically consistent with it (in principle, *any* act might be called a solution), substantively contradicts it; that the term itself is abstract and general but designates an event or object that is concrete and specific; and that the figurative term is meant to draw attention away from both this change and from the individual aspects of its referent, thus concealing what is denoted (and attempting to conceal the fact of concealment as well). The figure of speech thus constituted diverges in each of these three respects from the common purpose of figurative language, which is at once to bring into focus—to "figure"—certain concrete aspects of the referent *and* to call attention to itself (and even to itself as figurative).

I propose, quite simply, to call this new figure by an old name, one which more usually would not be associated with *figures* of speech at all—that is, the lie.[8] The reasons for invoking this term should, however, be clear: as the person who is a liar knowingly affirms what is false, so here a linguistic expression affirms what *it* "knows" to be false. Moral violation thus takes on the guise of literary form. Admittedly, one can anticipate objections to this (or any) claim for a linguistic version of ethical principle. For one thing, figurative language is usually viewed as distinguishable from the speaker's own—extralinguistic—purposes, which can be understood literally and as the proper object of moral judgment. Thus speakers or writers may use hyperbole and other literary figures for the *purpose* of lying but still avoid lying *within* those figures: it is the action which the words serve that is in these cases subject to moral assessment. Moreover, when figurative language associated with poetry or fictional discourse is meant to be ornamental, an imaginative heightening of aspects or objects which would otherwise have only a nonfigurative, "literal" existence, this is not usually judged to be a lie or instance of deception. "Achilles is a lion" is not

<hr/>

8. See for an anticipation of this conception of the linguistic lie, Harold Weinrich, *Linguistik der Lüge* (Heidelberg: Verlag Lambert Schneider, 1966), 34–41; see also Bertholt Brecht, "Fünf Schwierigkeiten beim Schreiben der Wahrheit," *Gesammelte Werke*, vol. 18 (Frankfurt a. M.: Suhrkamp Verlag, 1967), 222–39.

intended to be understood literally; if it were, the statement would be a
lie as well as false. On the other hand, the distinction between figurative and moral discourse seems inadequate for understanding the
figurative terms defined by the Nazi speech rules: their moral quality
(morally problematic, that is) is so fundamental as to be part of the expression itself, to be engaged in the *manner* of speaking. A person who
denies having done something he knowingly did is lying—but it is not
the language that then does the lying, it is the speaker. By contrast, calling genocide a Final Solution turns the phrase itself into a lie, in the
same sense that the representation of Achilles as a lion discloses the latter term as a metaphor to anyone who otherwise understands the literal
denotation of those two terms. The figurative lie links two contradictory literal references; it also attempts, in asserting the connection, both
to deny the contradiction and to conceal the denial. (Oxymoron, although it includes the former feature, that of the contradiction, does
not have the latter.) To be sure, a speaker or writer who employs the
figure of the lie will often, perhaps even necessarily, also be lying in the
moral sense: language does not, after all, speak itself. But there is still
the distinction to be made between the language and its user; as the
tropes or figures of speech belong to the language apart from any individual application, so now does the figure of the lie.

To focus discussion of the language of genocide on the term by which
the Nazis designated the act of genocide itself is to cite only one example
of many possible ones; there is, in fact, a general vocabulary that provides much broader evidence of the role of the figurative lie. An
important example among these is the lengthy list of words substituted
in the Nazi vocabulary for "killing" or "execution." *Sonderbehandlung*
("special treatment") comes closest among these terms to repeating the
linguistic conditions mentioned in connection with *Endlösung*,[9] but
other "synonyms" have much the same character. So, for example:
entsprechend behandelt ("treated appropriately"), *Aussiedlung* ("evacuation"), *Umsiedlung* ("resettlement"), *Auflockerung* ("thinning out"
—as in the removal of inhabitants from a ghetto), *Befriedungsaktion*
("pacification") and *A.B. Aktion,* i.e., *Ausserordentliche Befriedungsaktion* ("special pacification"), *Ausschaltung* ("removal"), *Abwanderung*
("having-been-migrated"), *Säuberung* ("cleansing"), *Sicherheitspolizeilich
durchgearbeitet* ("worked through or directed in a Security Police manner") were all used in place of standard terms for killing or execution.

9. The first use of "Sonderbehandlung" in this sense is attributed to Heydrich in a letter
of 20 September 1939—directed against Germans rather than Jews. (See Josef Wulf, *Aus
dem Lexikon der Mörder: "Sonderbehandlung" und verwandte Wörter in nationalsozialistischen
Dokumenten* [Gutersloh: Sigbert Mohn Verlag, 1963], 7.)

Such usage occurred, moreover, not only in communications issued to the Jewish public when the intention of those issuing the communications was to deceive the Jews in order to minimize the likelihood of resistance, but also in addresses to the outside world and, perhaps more significantly, in internal communications as well, among officials who unquestionably knew (who were themselves sometimes responsible for) the linguistic substitutions stipulated by the language rules. (At times, of course, standard, nonfigurative terms were used for each of these audiences, but the context then was usually an order announcing the execution of individuals who were named, or in warnings directed against specific acts; the orders for larger and more abstract plans of killing under the general aegis of the Final Solution were almost always couched in diffuse and abstract terms of the sort noted here.)

Furthermore, the list of such terms does not stop with those that refer to killing: the apparatus that would make that act possible also required figurative elaboration. So, *Hilfsmittel* ("auxiliary equipment") designated the vans that had been turned into the mobile gas chambers which killed their victims by recycling the carbon monoxide from the vans' engines; these continued to be used elsewhere even after the *Badeanstalten* ("bath arrangements" or sometimes "swimming pool"—i.e., gas chambers) had been constructed at Auschwitz. *Briefaktion* ("letter action") would refer to coercing new arrivals in the camps to write to relatives or friends in the ghettos or cities, reassuring them about the prospects of "resettlement." *Gleichschaltung* ("putting into the same gear") could range in meaning from the abolition of divergent political parties to the removal of individuals (although not usually their execution)—in effect the smoothing or "evening out" of impediments.

Such terms, moreover, were not left to the moment or to individual inventiveness; they were part of an official, although evolving code or set of rules (*Sprachregelungen*) which identified the words that should not be used and the terms intended to replace them. An explicit example of how these rules were laid down appears in a directive by which the use of *Sonderbehandlung* was announced. This order (dated 26 September 1939) reiterates "the stipulation of the rules in accordance with which the so-called delights of war are to be renamed;" it then goes on to designate the abbreviation "Sb" as a replacement for *Sonderbehandlung* (itself substituted for "killing").

To be sure, even the most resourceful planning of "speech rules" would not anticipate all contingencies, and the requirements of a vocabulary consistent with the act of genocide might well run out of terms insofar as it depended on language that had not yet conceived of the act. The extraordinary phenomenon of the Nazi genocide discloses itself then also in the fact that for some of its features there simply would be—perhaps *could* be—no satisfactory terms, whether in the language then available or by later contrivance. In order to arrive at such terms, the events themselves would first have to be conceived—and there were features of the genocide which evidently posed difficulties even for the imagination. An important example of such difficulty is represented in the term "genocide" itself, which, as has been described in chapter 1, was coined by Rafael Lemkin in the early 1940's in his effort to give a name as well as a definition to the phenomenon exemplified in the Final Solution. The term "genocide," to be sure, is in the context not a neutral one and would probably not have been assimilated into the Nazi vocabulary by the Nazis themselves (at least as applied to their war against the Jews). But other examples that are not "tendentious" in this way indicate the difficulty *in principle* of finding words for features of the Nazi genocide.

Especially noticeable among these examples are the terms designating the status of the Jews who had been brought to the death camps. The problem of giving a name to the Jews in this role exactly mirrors the extraordinary nature of that role itself. Again: the Jews collectively had been condemned to death by the order to implement the Final Solution. (No single and explicit written order to this effect has been found, a fact which has led to arguments about whether such an order was ever given, or if it was, whether Hitler issued it, or more bizarrely still, whether Hitler was himself aware that the final Solution was being implemented. Yet there can be no doubt that such an order *was* given, and with Hitler's authority behind it.)[10] However, it was evident that, for "practical" reasons, any such order or series of orders could not be carried out instantly but required organization and time; this together with such other "practical" reasons as the need for skilled labor that the Jews might provide, sometimes argued for delaying the implementation of the order. Thus, distinctions were made on occasion even within the death camps and more often in the concentration camps between those to be killed immediately and those whose execution would be delayed. When the genocidal sentence of death is combined with such gradations of treatment (however temporary), the problem of finding a specific name for the still-living "victims" of such a decree is evident. They were to be treated arbitrarily as a matter of principle, with death as the end, though not necessarily immediate; while they lived, they had no rights, not even the right to a specific "death sentence," although they might indeed receive such a sentence if they took some action that was not merely submissive.

10. For an assessment of these claims, see Fleming, *Hitler* (cited in chap. 1, n. 8); and Jäckel, *Hitler in History* (see chap. 1, n. 8), chap. 3; Friedländer, "Historical Writing" (see chap. 2, n. 8).

Kadavergehorsam ("cadaver obedience") was the ghoulish term—familiar from its use in the German army and not a code word at all—that designated *this* requirement. The Jews held in the camps in effect lacked the rights that even animals were assured in the Third Reich. What then could they be called? They were, obviously, "prisoners," but that term would not distinguish between them and people held and *maintained* in custody for a specified length of time and possibly, then, released. For some of the same reasons, they would not be "inmates"—a term which adds the sense of protective custody to the possibility that rehabilitative measures might be part of the design. In the spring of 1945, when the camps still in existence (for example, Buchenwald and Bergen-Belsen) were overrun by the Allied armies, newspapers in the United States (e.g., the *New York Times*, 18 and 19 April 1945) typically spoke about the "slaves" who were found there: the dead as well as the living. This locution was based on the erroneous assumption—which in almost any other circumstance would have been reasonable—that the main function of the camps was to provide slave labor. But this, too, of course, skews the description, since although Jews in the camps were sometimes used as slave labor and although, like slaves in extreme settings, they lacked legal rights of protection or care, the *main* purpose for which they were in the camps was not to work but to die.

"Victims" is sometimes used in reference to the Jews inside the camps (as well as to those killed outside them)—but again, although obviously accurate in one sense, the conventional association of the term with people killed in individual acts of violence or even in accidents or natural catastrophes does not touch the rationale behind the death camps. (Even the reference to individual "victims" of premeditated murder misses the essential features of deliberation and organization that characterize genocide.) Nor could they be termed "captives," which might suggest both that they had been caught after having been free and that the future awaiting them was contingent. Yet, although in the strict sense they were "condemned" to death, they were not exactly awaiting execution either, since this, again, suggests a definiteness about their status and the fate awaiting them that did not obtain except in the most general sense: starvation, disease, and overwork were officially expected to kill many of the Jews in the camps— but that is not what is meant ordinarily, in judicial terms, by a death sentence. The term *Häftling* that the Nazis themselves usually applied comes close to the sense of "captive" or "prisoner" and is thus also something of a euphemism. (To the extent that *Häftling* implies captivity as part of a specific sentence or as awaiting sentence, it was simply misleading; to *be* a Jew, as the Nazis had defined that, was itself to have sentence pronounced.) The Nazis had a variety of reasons, symbolic and psychological as well as practical, for tattooing numbers on the people in the camps, but one consequence of the practice was that the number itself would commonly serve as a means of direct address or reference. The people in the camps devised for themselves the term "KZ-etnik" from the letters of the *Konzentrationslager* ("concentration camp"), a neologism that suggested something novel in their situation but was not itself descriptive. (For those who died, the Nazis sometimes explicitly prohibited calling them "victims" or even "corpses," stipulating the term *Figuren*—"figures" or "pieces," as in chess.) There seems in fact to be *no* term that meets the specific conditions imposed by the act of genocide, as the Nazis conceived it, on those who were subjected to the act. Not surprisingly, this same lack seems to recur in respect to the verb(s) associated with the act: "killing," "execution," even "murder"—all miss the distinctive character of the act, although each, to be sure, is within limits accurate. Thus genocide as it evidently stretched the imagination in its own conception, forcing revision in the history of evildoing, also reaches the limits of language as it requires terms to describe *what* it intended and attempted.

It is evident, moreover, that the consequences of genocide for language were not confined to official documents or statements, nor even to explicit decisions about speech rules, although these, too, reached the public domain. (So, for example, Goebbels—13 December 1937— would stipulate that "from today the word *Völkerbund* [League of Nations] will no longer be used in the German press. This word no longer exists.") There was also, as might have been expected, a revealing linguistic "unconscious," the consequences of which appeared in standard usage even when it did not refer to the Final Solution or to military or political matters at all. The inversion of language that results in the figure of the lie may not be as graphic in these more commonplace appearances as it is in terms like *Endlösung,* but the pattern of a general style disclosed by them is in certain ways no less significant. For here it is the image of a general social and cultural order that we see, not only the conscious dictates of a political or military will. And here, too, there is evidence of the same general purpose at once to rationalize language and to subordinate it to authority, that is, to make it into a political instrument which in its own structure would incorporate the features of moral violation that otherwise constitute the lie.

The usage thus introduced reflects in language a genocidal society in its "everyday" life; the linguistic features that might be cited in this connection extend from some that apply to aspects of culture in general to others that are specific to linguistic usage. The features of repetition and exaggeration or monumentality have often been cited as characteristic of totalitarian "style"—and these were indeed persistent features of Nazi rhetoric (thus, Kenneth Burke's association of Hitler's hold on his audience with the "power of endless repetition")[11] as they were elsewhere also, for example, in Nazi architecture, drama, and in the giant Nazi rallies. Furthermore, those same features extended beyond the official language to common linguistic usage, in journalism and popular fiction as well as in school textbooks. In these media, too, the style of domination controls the expressive means; language appears as a technological instrument that may serve purposes quite apart from, even in conflict with, the direct representation of events or objects.

The specific means employed for this purpose cover a spectrum of changes that extends beyond the style of figurative discourse to semantic and syntactic alterations as well. Thus, for example, hyperbole is normalized with the common use of exaggerated terms like *einmalig* ("unique"), *historisch* ("historic"), *total* ("total"). *Fanatisch* ("fanatic"), which had the connotation of madness, would now in the Nazi vocabulary count as commendable (and expected, i.e., normal) dedication. The same pattern of repetition and hyperbole was further joined to a conscious effort at defamiliarization: archaic or "folk" words were revived—e.g., *Mädel* for *Mädchen* ("girl"), *Sippe* for *Familie* ("family")— and certain foreign words were adapted (e.g., *Aktion* for *Unternehmung*). It may seem that the two latter impulses conflict—one attempting to reach back to German history, the other reaching outside it, to alien sources—but in context the two are quite consistent. The former is impelled by a mystique of the German past that served as an important ideological element in Nazi doctrine; the latter provides an aura of technological rationality and irrefutability that the Nazis wished now to extend to language as well. Thus, on the one hand, the sources offer the lure of the unfamiliar and so of novelty and power; on the other hand, they conspire to turn a history of ethnic origin into a promise of national destiny (and once again, of power). Again, more generally we infer from this usage the intention to subordinate language itself to political authority, if only in order to demonstrate that this common medium of exchange, which often appears in the guise of nature itself, also will not escape political domination. The Nazis would not only contrive a language *of* domination, but they intended to demonstrate that language itself was subject to political authority.

The means by which the theme of domination is given a linguistic

11. Kenneth Burke, "The Rhetoric of Hitler's *Battle*," in Burke, *The Philosophy of Literary Form* (Berkeley: University of California Press, 1973), 217–18. See also Harold D. Lasswell, Nathan Leites, and Associates, *Language of Politics* (New York: G. W. Stewart, 1949), Introduction; and Saul Friedländer, *Reflections of Nazism*, trans. Thomas Weyer (New York: Harper & Row, 1984), 50–53.

form are designed in such a way as to leave an audience no option except submission to the spoken or written words that address it. The use of puns and alliteration in Nazi political slogans, for example, forcibly joins words and phrases that have little to do with each other except for the process of assertion itself. Thus: "Die Liebe der SS das Leben des Führers umgürtet." ("The love of the SS protects the life of the Führer.") Or "Das Leben des Führers bleibt nicht eine Wirklichkeit sondern wird zu einer Wahrheit." ("The life of the Führer does not remain a reality but becomes a truth.") An analogous example is the use of conjunctive phrases in contexts the purpose of which is to assert the conjunction rather than to identify related meanings—in such redundant transitions, for instance, as *und damit* and *und mit diesem* ("and thereby" and "and therewith"). It is not only the *act* of conjunction that is intended in such usage, moreover, but the whole that is then constituted (*organisch*, or "organic," is itself a favorite term): the reader or listener was to see *himself* as part of the whole. Thus, as the conjunctions lead to larger and larger units, the alternatives left to the audience turn out to be those either of full acceptance or of an equally complete denial—the latter, from the point of view of language, tantamount to an acceptance of silence and nonexistence. There are no gaps left in the discourse that might be claimed by the listener or reader for questions or objections, or for the proposal of an alternative; the writer or speaker anticipates all the questions that arise or, more characteristically, denies their possibility: the implied audience is to be of one mind with the author.

The implication that things or events are not determinate or accessible unless they are brought together in a discursive whole is also emphasized by the practice of adding suffixes to nouns that attach a *state* of being to references which otherwise might be specific and active, not merely potentialities for action: so, for example, *Volkheit* ("peopleness") or *Wehrheit* ("defenseness"). These suffixes identify the thing named as itself indeterminate or tentative—and thus as requiring for "real" existence a state or condition shared with other would-be individuals and provided by a more general and abstract source of being. Thus, what superficially might seem to be a single and independent noun, standing for an individual referent or thing, turns out, more basically, to be part of a larger—by implication, of a single—whole. It requires no great imaginative leap to see in that whole the totalitarian will or its political embodiment in the state.

Again, the features thus identified recurred in popular and informal writing as well as in official documents. (To be sure, given the increasing control of censorship, virtually anything published in Germany—textbooks, newspapers, etc.—after the first years of the Nazi regime would have to be considered an official document.) Admittedly, sustained analysis of stylistic change at this level would require the study of personal correspondence and other informal writing that was not intended to be published, as well as of fiction or poetry that (for literary, not political reasons) moved as far as any publications officially sanctioned could from "normative" usage. The study of these sources is not undertaken here, but even viewed superficially the stylistic representations of the Nazi vocabulary seem also to recur in these unofficial sources—in academic and literary prose and in personal and casual communications that were not intended for public inspection at all, in what might be called the "private" style. This correlation is predictable if not inevitable: the distinctions that language makes or avoids would be likely to reflect the more general social context in which the distinctions had themselves arisen.

To be sure, like other figures of speech, the literary figure of the lie is accessible to analysis and even before that to the self-consciousness that enables a reader or listener to place it historically in a context of motives, intentions, and consequences. There is also the sense in which all expression, however figurative, is nonetheless literal and truthful; willingly or not, it discloses its own means, art not quite concealing all of art. The "style" of common linguistic usage under the Nazis is subject to this disclosure no less than are the language rules officially commanded: one thing that the will to domination cannot control is the appearance of the will to dominate as seen from the outside—if only an "outside" remains. Viewed from that perspective, the language of genocide, even in its many and complex facets, reveals the intention to turn language itself into an instrument of domination and deceit, enabling in practice and in principle an act that controverts the ideals of moral life by the denial of the social reality of language and of human relations beyond that. This is, as has been suggested earlier in these pages, exactly what the physical fact of genocide itself intends and accomplishes: the willing of evil for its own sake quite apart from the consideration of practical consequences. Language itself, we now see, may become a part of that intention, even one of its agents. Certainly it is no less revealing of the mind that conceives of and intends genocide than were those other, more obvious instruments of which the will for genocide made use.

The assertion made here of a relation between genocide and language does not claim that violence done to language, even on the scale of violence realized by the Nazis, leads inevitably to genocide. Nor does it claim that genocide would only be possible in a setting for which the inversion of values had been so complete as to include language—the currency of thought—as a whole. An alteration in language of the sort described is thus neither necessary nor sufficient as a cause—but again, there would be nothing unusual in such a limitation on tracing historical causality in general or on attempting to identify the sources of the Nazi genocide in particular; indeed these limitations would be more plausible for an aspect of culture as subtle and diffuse as language than elsewhere. It might be argued that the way we become aware of the role of language as a feature of genocide at all is through being confronted *first* with the physical act of genocide—although as soon as we hear this, we recognize that even this prior awareness may include the violation of language. It is the mind, together with bodies, that genocide acts to destroy; and as language is an essential element of mind, it would be extraordinary if an attack on bodies did not also threaten the mind, if the genocidal destruction of a people, directed against every level of its existence, could be envisioned without an accompanying assault on what is thought and said. Like all other action, evildoing requires a means—and the more elaborate and profound the action, so too the means required for it. The fact that it was the German language that most immediately suffered this violence is an irony of the Nazi genocide, although one that bears on another more general and more familiar irony—that evildoing claims among its victims the evildoer as well as those whom he had intended to harm.

Then, too, the claim is not made here that the role which language assumes in the Nazi genocide is uniquely located either there or in the phenomenon of genocide as such. The forces contributing to the deformation of language did not begin or end with the Nazi genocide, although there is a connection, causal as well as conceptual, between the two. And both the conception and practice of language that emerged to such coercive effect in the Nazi genocide seem to have taken on a strange life of their own subsequently. Evidence of that development is as close at hand as almost any newspaper report of political rhetoric in the years since World War II: so the view of language as a technological and impersonal instrument, a view which at the level of political reality was not long ago a radical innovation, now becomes naturalized and familiar, something virtually assumed as native to political language and discourse, even for institutions professedly opposed to and in other basic respects removed in intent from that of the Nazis.

It hardly needs to be said that compared to other aspects of the moral enormity constituted by the Nazi genocide, the inversion of language described here, in the elevation of the lie to a principle of discourse, does not constitute the most immediate or the greatest harm that was done. But since it does not appear by itself but as part of an effort at total de-

struction, there can be little comfort in this. As people live by representations in the present and by memory in the past, moreover, the role of
language in the genocide remains a cogent representation of that event
more generally. We find it, in this role, replete with evidence of the will to
do evil, the power of the imagination to enlarge on that will, and the
capacity for violence which such impulses nourish, inside language or
out. These effects can be understood in the character of genocide itself
and the requirements imposed by it on those who conceive and "do" it.
If it is true that genocide implies the deliberate choice of evil as an end,
assuming in the act of killing a conceptualization of a group and the
choice of that group as its object, the violation of language in the act of
genocide represents something more than a simple analogy between language and genocide. It is not only, then, that language becomes morally
culpable by its figurative device of the lie—but that elements of the lie
are also themselves effective causes in the deliberate act of genocide.
There is in these elements the denial of both truth and history—a denial,
we learn by way of the Nazi language rules, of which the Nazis themselves were aware. Furthermore, the objects of genocide—people and
language—which are denied the right to exist are closely related to each
other in their group or social character. For language as for people, it is
not only individual parts or functions that are violated, but language as
such, a corporate entity much like the corporate object, the *genos*, of genocide itself.

This is not meant to suggest that all evildoing turns out to be one, that
any single act entails all others and also the guilt for those others—or
more specifically, that genocide and the violation of language are intrinsically related. But it does mean that as evildoing involves always human
agents and almost always human victims, there will undoubtedly be
more at issue in any single act than what the act itself explicitly designates. Especially in language do we recognize the moral status of its
source; there is little to distinguish linguistic representation itself from
what it is a representation of or from the agent who intends it as a representation. Thus also, the language of genocide, long after the conditions
that initially produced it, persists still, as a challenge to the present as
well as to the past. It would be a mistake to imagine that the history of
the language of genocide, any more than other consequences of the
genocide, ended with the conclusion of the physical act.

The relation between character—whether in the individual or in the
group—and language becomes further evident in what began in the discussion here as analogy but has disclosed itself as more than that: in the
common feature of domination that in the name of principle engendered
both the act of genocide and the instrumental role ascribed to language.

On both sides of that analogy, distinctions based on evidence and moral principle are obliterated; categories and distinctions devised and willed by the agent are made to seem natural and necessary, and this is itself part of the intention. Not only language but logic is brought inside history by these efforts, moreover; and not only the cultural appearances of these domains are brought into history, but so also are the "objects" they ostensively refer to. There is nothing in language, or in humanity more generally, that is exempt from the controlling intention. The will to do evil through the medium of genocide is in fact the will to transcend *all* limits or restrictions, and this intention, which includes language among its objects, produces a lie of even a larger order than does the use of language specifically tied to the act of genocide. In this generalized consequence, the moral lie comes close to being absolute, denying the figurative representation of truth in all its forms and even the possibility of truth itself; the moral lie chooses evil as its good on grounds of principle, and this means that no subordinate purpose which is not evil is acknowledged or chosen by the agent of genocide. For the *language* of genocide, the change is smaller but hardly less noticeable. In it, the lie becomes a figure of speech, when it had been the native purpose of figurative language, arguably of *all* language, to disclose and to enlarge, not to conceal or to diminish, much less to destroy, still less to destroy completely.

5

Jabès and the Measure of History

Edmond Jabès is right but for the wrong reasons. Jewish life and history *are* tied to the life and history of the letter, the word, the book—but not because of the alien and driven presence he claims in common for those histories, challenged wherever they would settle, contingent, permanently in exile. For them each—Jew and Writing—the will to exist follows a different and direct route, much less tenuous than the one Jabès traces and then exemplifies in his own writing. The convergence between the history of a people and the life of discourse is still there: this much of Jabès' claim, startling, ironic as it is, survives. But the convergence is in affirmation and assertion, in a common and extraordinary will to exist—not in hesitation or doubt or anxiety. One would never recognize this order of history from what Jabès discloses to his reader; and the reason for the failure, first of author and then, as he submits, of reader, attends one question that is not uttered in *The Book of Questions*[1] but must have been presupposed for *The Book* to exist at all. It is thus, unhappily, repressed—this question of whether writing centered in the Nazi genocide against the Jews, is even possible: literarily and morally *possible*.

---

1. *Le Livre des Questions* (3 vols.) (Paris: Gallimard, 1963, 1964, 1965). Quotations cited here are in the translation of Rosemarie Waldrop (Middletown: Wesleyan University Press, 1976, 1983).

To direct that question at Jabès of the many writers to whom it could be addressed may seem mischievous: *The Book of Questions* is so unremittingly self-conscious, so deliberate, so firmly attuned to the principle of equity and to the reasons of language and of history. And surely one part of the answer implied by Jabès to the question is worth holding to: that far from being an instrument, a neutral means, writing is itself an action with moral design—and that thus, as other persons are obliged to take responsibility for such acts, the writer, too, will stand moral inspection for the relation between what he does and what he does it *to:* his writing is a judgment on the *character* of his subject as well as a portrayal of it. What writing is about, in other words, ought to make a difference in the writing itself, on moral no less than on aesthetic grounds; here, indeed, is a point at which those two categories, usually separated by literary taboos, converge. Why *not* write a traditional novel with the Nazi genocide as subject? And we learn, in response from *The Book of Questions*—from its repeated disruption of the narrative texture, the continuing dislocation and relocation of anything like the authorial point of view, the incessant putting of questions that remain unrequited—that the steady temper and domestication of family history that traditionally govern the novel will not suffice. A genre committed to life or even to death in the bosom of the nineteenth-century middle class would simply fail as the vehicle for a subject that challenged the very possibility of social existence.

One consequence of this infringement by ethics on literary convention is to make explicit the possibility of potential literary subjects that cannot be written about at all. For if the subject of discourse is to have a voice in determining the character of that discourse, then there may be subjects that prove intractable for *any* of the available literary forms—indeed, if "literariness" is intrinsically bound to the doubling and thus mediating effect of representation, that cannot be embodied in any *possible* form. An example of the mediating effect is indeed quickly evident, fixed in the question that Jabès represses. For if an ostensive subject of literary discourse demanded to "speak for itself"—like "the facts"—then to interpose another, even artistic voice would inevitably be to mute that first one, to blunt or avert its force and so to diminish it. This is in fact very much the objection that Theodor Adorno was to direct at the possibility of Holocaust poetry; for him Paul Celan's "Todesfuge" would be immoral in what it *attempted* to do, not for its failure or success in the attempt.

To be sure, Jabès has decided this same issue differently: Holocaust writing, for him, *is* possible. But the question of justification, the necessity of a defense for the word against the alternative of silence, is none-

theless real enough. Moreover: Jabès acknowledges the unusual requirements posed by the Nazi genocide as a literary subject, not only through
the unsettled genre of *The Book of Questions* but through structural per-
plexities within that means. The continuing indirection and obliqueness
in his writing is identifiable by none of the standard literary figures of
indirection such as allegory or irony; these, we infer, are not sufficiently
indirect or oblique. He seems, in fact, to devise here a new literary figure
by which the Unspeakable or Unwritable is hinted at, alluded to, implied—supported by a premise which asserts that for any Unmention-
able nothing *could* be spoken or written that did more than ascribe the
"name." The Nazi genocide against the Jews, disclosing itself in the lives
of the two main characters, Sarah and Yukel, provides a frame for *The
Book of Questions*. The "questions" asked or implied within the text, the
events related, the knots resolved or retied by aphorism, verge continually on this background; it is itself one of the personae dramatis. But
never is the Nazi genocide or any of the pieces of history that make it up
given by name or identified in those terms. This is true for quite specific
items as well as for the framework within which they appear. The SS
man, the number tattooed on an arm, the yellow star: each of these appears in Jabès' text, but without preface and without elaboration. The
reader who did not already know what they were or did not otherwise
have a lexicon available would find no understanding in Jabès' words; he
would recognize only that he was meant to be pained by them (the words
and the things). If anything more than this monitory sense is required in
his response, the reader must supply it himself; it is he, the reader, then,
who must write the circumstances within which the questions of *The
Book* are raised, the circumstances not only of fact but of the emotional
and moral force that the facts carry with them.

Jabès' strategy here may be surmised. The enormity of the Nazi genocide against the Jews is evident, goes without saying. Because of this, it
cannot be represented by the usual poetic or fictional devices that would,
if they worked as they usually do, "epitomize" it, exhibit features by
which the reader might more fully imagine or realize it. At best, the writer would here only labor the obvious: what artifices could more fully
"realize" the facts of such events? At worst, what he wrote would fail
even to match the intensity of those facts themselves. Let us then write in
the assumed presence of the events, take the existence and enormity for
granted—even if this means that the reader will be left to provide on his
own the texture of historical detail and evocation of imagined responses
that the representations of the text, individually or together, do not. In
one sense, to be sure, there is nothing unusual in this strategy of Jabès':
the reader is always required to bring *something* to a text, even if this is

only an understanding of grammar and vocabulary. But once we move beyond such commonplace requirements, the question of literary propriety—of when the writer is requiring the reader to do the *writer's* work—becomes more pressing. Is there not a warranted division of labor between writer and reader? Or is the reader obliged to supply *whatever* the author chooses (for whatever reasons) to leave out? We can reasonably doubt that if an author fails to give a literary account of the character—in literary fact, emotion, value—of events that have significant consequences within his work, the burden of doing so is simply transferred to the reader.

We understand here the dilemma that Jabès—and any writer who takes the Nazi genocide against the Jews as subject—confronts. On the one hand, it is difficult, perhaps impossible, for a writer to meet that historical act face to face, to re-present it. The events themselves are too large for the selective mirror of fiction, too transparent for the conceits of literary figuration; linguistic representation is in any case redundant—thus an impediment—when the events that converge on a subject speak directly and clearly for themselves. On the other hand, to write about those events obliquely, by assumption, leaves the task that had been declined by the author to the reader, who can hardly—if the *writer* will not—hope to find a passage from personal emotion and imagery to artifice. Where then is the work of literary representation to be done?

This dilemma, as has been noted, does not affect Jabès alone; it has in fact affected and been acknowledged, tacitly or explicitly and in much the same terms, by other serious writers on the Nazi genocide, many of whom also, as it happens, choose the alternative within the dilemma that Jabès himself follows—the way of indirection, of assumption. D. M. Thomas, Aharon Appelfeld, Jakov Lind: each demands that the reader provide a supporting ground and literary frame of fact and expression—detailing the face and aura of horror—that more usually, for less extravagant and painful subjects, the writer himself would accept responsibility for enacting. And the converse also seems to hold: that among the writers on the Nazi genocide who fail, many fail precisely because they would directly impose an artistic hand—fictionalize, epitomize, give figures to the events of the Holocaust, as they might write any other subject, heedful only of literary conventions and techniques remembered from another and easier life. Authors like Elie Wiesel, William Styron, Leslie Epstein come to mind here.

It might be objected against the formulation of this dilemma that it obtains its force only by begging an important question; this is the question of whether Holocaust writing (or, for that matter, any writing) is, or need be, representational—whether it is characteristically "about" something at all. For if that archaism (as the objection has gone), that "nostalgia for a presence," could be avoided, the dilemma it serves as a presupposition would also disappear. If writing were not, or did not need to be, representational, the issue of commensurability between literary appearance and historical or even moral reality would not arise. There would no doubt be other obstacles that a writer would have to face: the standard literary problem of persuasion, for example, of the author's need to overcome the will of the reader. But the context then would be between will and will—not between them (singly or together) and an external means of measurement.

This objection, it may be recalled, marks the beginning of a recent theory of writing that was first proposed in a context broader than that encountered in the writing of extreme situations; and when Jabès attempts in *The Book of Questions* to revise the conventions of literary balance or equity, it is evidently the germ of this recent theory that moves the design of his work, that is meant to impel the reader away from the possible worlds of fictional artifice to an insistence on a single and unmediated reality. The conclusion drawn by this theory—for example, in Roland Barthes's conception of "intransitive" writing, according to which the writer does not represent or reflect on an object but "writes-himself"—is directed specifically against the theory of writing that fosters the dilemma of the Holocaust writer.[2] For intransitive writing means precisely writing that is nonreferential, nonrepresentational; not even the existence of a world external to the literary work, let alone the properties of that world, are to affect the writing about it (or, then, its reading). Thus, the subject of discourse is problematic even in its existence—and here we also see the price exacted by this first step in the reaction against representationalism. For if the reference of discourse is now internalized in the writer himself, it is reasonable to wonder what happens to the event—or subsequently, the fact—that would otherwise have existed independently as the reference of discourse. The most evident possibility here, of course, is that event and fact, together with the words of discourse, should simply be bracketed, suspended: that the facts of history should be denied their usual privilege of reference. This possibility, obviously, is more than an exercise in abstraction; it means that the items otherwise assumed to constitute history are liable to suspension—and this, by implication, means for Holocaust writing a suspension or bracketing of the events of the Nazi genocide itself.

Any such consequence might be viewed as refuting the theory from

2. Roland Barthes, "Style and Its Image," in Seymour Chatman (ed.), *Literary Style: A Symposium* (New York: Oxford University Press, 1971).

which it follows, although this has not seemed to hinder the appearances of the theory. The need to consider this objection, however, is itself muted because of the appearance of a *third* formulation of the relation between writing and representation. In this new alternative, Jabès evidently means to go beyond the second account—of writing as intransitive—and the difference here is important even if it does not quite succeed. The systematic progression here is itself a narrative. For if representational writing is incommensurable with the events of the Nazi genocide; and if the step beyond that, intransitive writing, escapes the tyranny of representation only at the expense of denying historical reference, still another step remains that is also not relational, not "about" something, but one-sidedly *with* or *in* the events: thus, not writing *about* the Holocaust, and not, beyond that, writing the writer—but Writing-the-Holocaust. Here, in contrast to intransitive writing, the subject, not the author, is written: in effect the subject writes itself. The narrative voice—so far as we refer at all to what is now quite clearly an anthropomorphism—is the voice of history; the object itself takes over, construing the form and means in addition to the literary content.

Like the two other conceptions of writing, this one revises the relation among the syntactical elements of a text; thus, in *The Book of Questions,* Jabès, writing now not *about* a subject but writing-the-subject, proposes to the reader that substantive issues—moral, cognitive—turn into, *are,* literary form; thus, for Jabès, writing is not detachable from what is written about, but an immediate function or appearance of it. Only so, it seems, could we understand the strain that Jabès' writing puts on the conventions of the text and then on the expectations of the reader; only so does the indirection, the constant blurring of a "subject" come into focus for the reader: there *is* no subject distinct from the medium, there is only the event, the span of history itself.

This turn or trope has important consequences at the level of the theory of discourse, but its more immediate consequences are also more dramatic, at least for the claim that it is at this juncture that Jabès himself seems to go astray. For if Jabès—the author now as medium or vehicle—means to have his subject write itself, to have the "voice" of the event speak, then the reader is entitled, even obliged, to measure the discourse he hears as he would any voice that claims reality for itself, without allowances for the insulation or distancing that "fiction" commonly claims in pleading the case for its divergence from fact. If it is the Nazi genocide that allegedly speaks (and behind it, the character of Jewish history), in other words, then the reader is responsible on *his* side for deciding whether the voice is authentic. And if Jewish history as it expresses itself is linked in *The Book of Questions* to a conception or even a theory of the word that *provides* the voice, then the two of them together, not simply the analogy but its content as well, must also be recognizable, must persuade the reader that it is indeed they who are present. And it is here that *The Book of Questions*—now the event of Writing the Holocaust—misleads the reader; and that Jabès, as medium, if not as author, bears the scrutiny of history.

On the evidence of his writing, we infer that the Nazi genocide came as no surprise to Jabès, that it only confirmed what he had already, perhaps always, known. It was, after all, another moment, larger but not otherwise distinguished, in the persistent counterpoint of Jewish history: the threat of an imminent end to that history. "Being Jewish," *The Book of Questions* answers itself, "means having to justify your existence. It means having the same sleepless nights in common, suffering the same insults. It means desperately looking for the same buoy, the same helping hand. It means swimming, swimming, swimming, in order not to sink." Genocide, in other words, was for the Jew no twentieth-century invention. He had long lived under its shadow; it had in fact been part of his original conception of self, a measure of the way he defined and saw himself. To take these stipulations at face value is also to infer that "the Holocaust" is no more than an instance of "holocaust"—with holocaust the pattern that has given shape to Jewish history as a whole. We know then why *The Book of Questions* moves so freely between events of the mid-twentieth century and the centuries of Jewish history before it: together they occupy a single, virtual present.

Nor, again, is it accidental that it is the Jews, as Jabès asserts, whom history has embedded in language and books; that with the Jews, the Word becomes something more than a mere instrument or means, revealing itself as physiognomic, as the spirit and ethos of the speaker. For language, too, we are supposed to understand, is symptomatic—an *instance*—of holocaust, of life on the abyss. "The world exists because the book exists," Jabès first notes, placing reality inside language, and then: "The wings of the word are questions." And so to the conclusion: "Judaism and writing are but the same waiting, the same hope, the same wearing out." It is absence, privation, from which language sets out and which then constantly shapes—and threatens—it. Language starts with the question, the recognition of incompleteness; why otherwise (Jabès might with this question hope to provide evidence for his own claim) would language have come into existence at all?

Even read as fiction, this remarkable conjunction of the history of a people and the nature of language—is it symbol? metaphor? a *literal* joining?—might well move Jabès' reader to silence. That two independently evolved artifacts should turn out to be mirror images of each other would be startling even if the two were small and rudimentary; and here, where it is the extraordinary human invention of language and the causally overdetermined history of the Jews that are matched, the effect is stunning, an intimation of the possibility that history, even as a *whole*, may turn out to represent in its apparently innumerable pieces, traces, reversals, only one thing, a single character.

But a striking possibility is all, in the end, the Jabès can make of his analogy, since the content of that analogy is what he would have it judged by—and what finally is also open to question and, beyond that, to objection. The reader's questions here may well in fact usurp the questions of the text: *Is* there reason to admit the description of the Jew as alien, as outsider, as continually beset—what the historian Salo Baron titled, with a noticeable edge, the "lachrymose conception of Jewish history"? Is there evidence for thinking of language itself as a divisive or alien presence, as intrinsically endangered? To be sure, Jabès is not alone in entering these claims. In his view of the Jew as wanderer, in fact, he may speak with the voice of the majority, at least of a recent majority. One important line of such thinking, for example, ironically opposed to Jabès in its conclusions, is evident in Zionist writers who take as their starting point the role of the Jew as exile, deracinated, estranged. For these writers, the redemption of Jewish history—a latter-day messianism—will come only as that historical exile is brought to an end, when the Jew "finds himself." Even the remarkable analogy between Jew and Writing, moreover, has echoes elsewhere; Jacques Derrida epitomizes this background by locating the "differance" in writing at the juncture between the Jew and the Letter: "The situation of the Jew," Derrida compliments Jabès on his theme, "is exemplary of the situation of the poet, the man of speech, and of writing."[3]

But corroboration requires more than repetition, and in the end the analogy thus asserted is historically disproportioned; it may, beyond this, be simply mistaken. The dissonance here comes from several directions—historical, moral, and, not least, psychological. If, for instance, we ask in respect to its conceptual development from whose point of view the designation of alien or outsider is *first* made, at least one account would find that title first ascribed from a point of view that is not *itself* alien. It is the person who is at home and is then obtruded on who reacts most immediately to the stranger, to whatever or whoever disturbs the familiar network of relations and expectations within which he

    3. Jacques Derrida, "Edmond Jabès and the Question of the Book," in *Writing and Difference*, trans. Alan Bass (Chicago: University of Chicago Press, 1978), 65.

lives. As self-consciousness assumes a consciousness of others, so too, the consciousness of self-as-alien will follow the consciousness of other-as-alien. Certainly this genealogy offers no less plausible an account than its alternative; and according to it, the representation of the Jew as alien would not, could not, have come from the Jew himself but from the outside, joining itself to whatever identity the Jew had first chosen—or found—for himself. But the *latter* identity, by implication, would then initially not have the character of alienation or estrangement at all.

Even the possibility of this order of development has, however, been ignored in the many accounts according to which Jewish identity is engendered primarily by conflict, by the antagonism of anti-Semitism, by the imposed awareness of the contingency of Jewish existence—in short, by the premonition of genocide. In these, the threat of extinction from the outside is held responsible for the internal will to survive, and even before that for the will to exist. This is a premise, we recall, of Sartre's *The Anti-Semite and the Jew*, in which the designation of "Jew"—exactly like the designation "Dirty Jew"—is alleged to come mainly from without; once remove the external pressure exerted by either of these and the *internal* commitment to Jewish identity also disappears.[4]

To be sure, Jews writing about themselves have often repeated a similar view; but even this proves only that it is possible that persons may come to know no more about themselves than what is imposed from the outside. No one doubts that an external view can be adopted as his own by the person viewed, but such assimilation is usually no more than a matter of individual biography; certainly it does not—*could* not—account for the persistence of the Jews as a community or group. The designation of outsider or alien may be a *consequence* of survival—it can hardly be its motive or purpose. The contradiction threatened here, moreover, is finally as much logical as it is psychological: can one first deny (oneself or anybody else) in order to affirm? The role of alien or exile could not disclose itself first as assertion or affirmation—and it is to the latter that we must look for explanation of first the life and then the persistence of Jewish history.

The measure of confidence required here is at once as basic and as general as that expressed by Spinoza—met on all sides as an alien, cut off from non-Jew and Jew alike—who would write in the *Ethics* that "the effort by which each thing endeavors to persevere in its own being is nothing but the actual essence of the thing itself" (bk. 3, prop. 7). For

4. Jean-Paul Sartre, *Anti-Semite and Jew*, trans. George J. Becker (New York: Schocken Books, 1948). So, for example, Sartre's contention that "the Jew is one whom other people consider a Jew" (69).

surely, if one feature stands out in Jewish history that might account first for the origins of the Jew and then later for his continuing history (even in opposition), we find it intimated here, in the singular desire of the Jew to exist, and to exist *as* Jew. This impulse, moreover, is not the familiar but secondary version of desire as inspired by anxiety or fear, by the sense of mortality; it is rather the desire for an object where the object is known and directly willed. Is it so difficult for the modern consciousness to admit that the idea of the divided self, of a spirit alienated from itself, is a recent artifact—that the image of the Jew as congenitally alien is not *itself* congenital but rather an historical contrivance, nourished conscientiously in the Romantic notion of alienation by volunteer poets and philosophers from Germany, France, England in the nineteenth century? As Zionism was moved by the nationalism of that century, so the conception of the Jew as wanderer and alien was also nourished externally, by the same currents, at the same time; it is itself, in good measure, alien.

The contrast between the instructions of this overheated and recent past and those of older—and longer—periods of Jewish history makes the parochialism of the recent view evident. Even searched randomly, the pages of the Hebrew Bible disclose not simply the absence of an alienated consciousness—of self or others—but its opposite. Certainly we can not think of the Psalmist as estranged when he sings "The earth is the Lord's, and the fullness thereof." Nor is Amos divided in himself when, scolding Israel, he holds out to them a future in which they will yet "walk humbly with their God." Job, in anger and despair, still "knows that his redeemer liveth"—and the Hebrews at Sinai, as a people and with one voice, respond confidently, willingly, that they "shall do and they shall listen." From Abraham to Koheleth, there is assurance, not doubt, resolve rather than temporizing. When Israel backslides or sins, it is not even then because of inner torment or doubt; its sins are those of self-assertion, pride, appetite: these are, after all, a "stiff-necked" people. The prose style of the Hebrew Bible is itself as far removed from tentativeness or the anxiety of a contingent existence (and from Jabès' prose) as any text in the history of writing.

To be sure, the biblical Jew is, even if central, not the only indicator of a long history: exile begins as the biblical narrative ends—and with it a new factor of physical distance and separation. But to say even then that it is this later phenomenon of estrangement that becomes the moving force for the Jew, that it is the physical separation, internalized, turned into consciousness, that then dominates the subsequent history and work of the Jews is so partial a view as, by itself, to be false. Rabbinic Judaism and the Talmud, the migrations and settlement in North Africa and France, even the walls set up around the medieval ghetto: the sense of dislocation and separation that undoubtedly accompanies these institutions does not impede even then the purposeful and unproblematic consciousness required (and forthcoming) to maintain the strong and live communities that express themselves here. In the literature of the Jews, the most explicit formulation of the idea of alienation, of the spirit in exile, comes in the Kabbalist and later the Hasidic writings; but it is important to remember that when these traditions emphasize the doctrines of loss and separation, of *Zimzum,* they are speaking finally of *mankind and the world* as alien from God, not restrictively about the Jew. And again, more than this: these traditions are themselves contested from within, eddies in a broader and more potent—and quite differently directed—stream. When Jabès writes that "every Jew drags behind himself a scrap of the ghetto," he openly concedes that he does not speak of Jewish history *before* the ghetto; he fails to suggest altogether what else the Jew may be "dragging" behind him.

What is it then that Jabès is right about but for the wrong reasons? There remains the form of the analogy between the Jew and language— an analogy that can stand on grounds other than, even opposed to, those that he offers. If we think, for example, of the requirements of affirmation, in persons as with language: is it too much to claim that with the covenant that first linked the Jews and the one God, defining the Jews as Jews, language, too, took on a new identity? We do not know historically when language first found itself adequate to the making of promises; difficult as it is to know what the logical and then the moral requirements for the act of promising are, it is clear that both these norms are tied closely to the verbal expression of the promise itself. But it also seems clear that at the moment when promises become possible—simultaneously with the negative counterpart of that event, in the discovery of the lie: the *un*making of the past or present—language and the consciousness it represents assume an identity they had not had before. Nietzsche's version of this change cannot be ignored: that promise-making nourishes *ressentiment,* placing the will in thrall to the future. But on the latter account not less than on the former, the promise or covenant transforms language as a whole, turns it from mere description or expression—the response to a stimulus—to a claim on time, embodying not only expectation but the will. Language itself here becomes self-conscious.

The biblical God is only heard, never seen; he challenges everything palpable. The written word is the one graven image that is exempt from the many biblical interdictions against idolatry; as an image, it too has a principal appearance, but what matters even so is the part of it that does not appear at all. Language is also, after all, a way of dispelling the alien, of opening passages among persons and between them and the world. Admittedly, there is a risk in the venture of a word, even a menace—as the speaker or writer chances himself, substitutes assertion for privation. The word itself, moreover, is mute: once spoken or written, it cannot answer *for* itself—it too becomes an historical object. And if we were to look only at these dangers, then we might indeed think first of the precariousness of language, of its contingency, of the challenge it offers to silence with the odds of success heavily against it. (The fact of language, John Dewey remarked, is a miracle beside which the wonder of transubstantiation pales.) But all these threats seem slight indeed when we compare them to the menace of a world *without* language: surely it is there, in silence, that isolation and contingency—the truly alien existence—would be met. Thus, the bonds among the word, its utterer, and its witness together shape an affirmation, in the identity of the Jew and in the character of language. The connections also bring the two together in what is itself a covenant, one that marks them commonly in history.

But against such a view of Writing and Jew, *The Book of Questions* insists that The Book—every book—*is* questions, tacitly if not openly, in its origins if not in the present: language and the word, we are supposed to understand, begin life as interrogatives. This version of linguistic origins is undoubtedly a useful corrective, morally and historically, to the pseudoanthropology that for so long represented those origins as exclamatory or phatic. But should not history itself be observed here, meager and fragmentary though its evidence is? The oldest writings of which there is record are more prosaic than either exclamations or interrogatives. They consist mainly of items that are not often subsumed under a grammatical category or literary genre at all; they constitute rather catalogues or lists: of supplies, possessions, battles, anecdotes. The List is in fact a revealing literary "kind": more openly than almost any other, it reveals the elements of writing, its natural history, recreating the act of memory, with one foot in the past and the other in the present. The List, moreover, becomes likely—even possible—only in a moment not of privation but of surfeit: that together with everything else that the speaker or writer has, sees, knows (these are the items *on* the list), there is also room for a list (this is not itself on the list). Abundant, even self-indulgent, the list is a means of creating a home, of being at home. And that, it turns out, is only a prelude or intimation of what language can do in the way of affirmation, of securing a foothold where there was none before. None of these features, to be sure, solves the possible objection that the list, so far as concerns literary invention, is a primitive device, that we learn nothing from it about discourse, about tense and connective, about form. But there is nothing natural or necessary about narrative form; it is itself an invention. And one might in fact, looking backward, see the list as a premonition of literary structure as well—as narration manqué: it is only the connectives that remain to be, and later would be, supplied.

Is it enough to say, then, of Jabès' contrary view of character in the Jew and in language that it is simply mistaken? The matter seems more one of inequity than of error. Jabès, a Jew in exile himself, sees all Jews as exiles. (He would himself, forced in adult life to find a new homeland, choose France, not the State of Israel; he could imagine no resolution in Israel, since exile for him was ontological not geographical. Would this choice also reflect the alien *language* of Israel? Thus, alien beyond the already alien . . .) And even then, the language *he* uses—in his own terms, necessarily a stepmother tongue—becomes chancy, problematic, also in exile, never at home with the norms of representation or with an affirmation of the present: writing, following life itself, turns into question. The plea cannot be made here that we owe Jabès, like other writers and artists, the "benefit of clergy"—the license of poetry and art to imagine their own worlds, to be tested only by their own premises, by the quality of their individual invitations to suspend disbelief. There cannot be too literal a reading of Jabès, for, in proposing to write-the-Holocaust, he has himself agreed—stipulated—that no distinction should be made between facts and literary facts, between facts and fiction. Moral discourse—and it is this character that he would realize in his writing—has only one face; unlike aesthetic discourse, there are no disguises by which it can conceal itself.

We might say then that we learn from *The Book of Questions* more about Jabès than we do about the Jew, more about Jabès' life as a Jew than about the Jew's life as Jew. And this brings us back, a long way around, to the problem of the writer in the aftermath of the Nazi genocide. The author for whom memory forces attentiveness, it turns out, cannot simply assume the existence of the events of the genocide in his writing; nor, with the history of domestication which has shaped the instrument of writing, can he simply write *about* those events. He may perhaps, as the attempt appears in Jabès, write-the-Holocaust—but that possibility makes extraordinary demands on the writer: in serving as medium, calling his subject to speak for itself, the author himself must then be willing to be measured by that subject. And it is there, as the Nazi genocide turns out for Jabès to be not one event or set of events but a universal history, that the genocide *fails* to write itself, with the responsibility for that failure falling then on Jabès, if only as scribe.

Jabès, in a way that few writers of "imagined literature" have dared to, takes as a subject for literature the life and consciousness of the Jew. He thus ventures much more than do the many writers for whom the Jew provides an idiom or dialect (the *parole*), with life itself and its universal moments—loves, partings, sorrows, pleasures—supplying the *langue*. His boldness here reflects an unusual will for literary particularity; it might deservedly remain a standard and a challenge for writers and writing, whatever the direction they turn in. But this artistic daring does not itself guard Jabès from the danger of historical misrepresentation. In this sense, *The Book of Questions* is evidence that even at the extreme, where a writer would efface himself by looking to his subject to write itself, there is no escape from the grasp and measure of history.

One objection to the very possibility of writing about the Nazi genocide is that where the facts speak for themselves, anything a writer might then add through artifice or literary figuration will appear as a conceit, an obtrusion. There might well be agreement, moreover, that only distortion can result when a writer "enlarges" on the Nazi genocide by generalization, in making it a symbol for others. But this in the end is what Jabès does—and although he writes always on principle, effecting what he views as a convergence of moral justice and literary means, the intention by itself does not vindicate his account of the Nazi genocide as exemplifying the general pattern of holocaust in Jewish history. Because his claim for the general pattern is exaggerated, also his view of the Nazi genocide as an instance results in misrepresentation: not arbitrarily or willfully, but nonetheless. Thus Jabès is right: the history of the Jew and the life of language *are* closely linked. But to see the one or the other as symbolized in the Nazi genocide is not only to connect but to replace history with art—an exchange in which both lose.

6

The Representation of Evil: Ethical Content as Literary Form

Since Plato, in the *Republic*, first attacked the poets for their falsification of both truth and moral value, an argument has persisted in philosophy and in social and critical analysis as well about the relation between ethics and the forms of expression now subsumed under the heading of art. Painting, music, but mainly literature have been repeatedly indicted and as often defended for their alleged failings, and the twentieth century could be the sixteenth century or Plato's own for all the differences that history has made in settling these claims and counterclaims. Plato himself was evidently reacting against a popular belief in the moral authority of art; but his objection to admitting that role for art was soon countered by Aristotle's defense of poetry, also based in part on moral grounds—and the same disagreement, although not always in the same terms, has continued to reappear in the convergence of social and intellectual history and the history of art.[1]

At a first level in this dispute, the process of literary representation is

1. See, e.g., Plato, *Republic*, bks. 2 and 10, and Aristotle, *Poetics*, 1448a–1449a, 1451b–1451c. For discussion of the relation between art and moral judgment in this historical context, see also Gerald Else, *Aristotle's Poetics* (Cambridge: Harvard University Press, 1957); Paul Friedlander, *Plato* (vol. 3), trans. Hans Meyerhoff (Princeton: Princeton University Press, 1969); Eric Havelock, *A Preface to Plato* (New York: Grosset and Dunlap, 1967), esp. chaps. 1, 13, 14; Iris Murdoch, *The Fire and the Sun: Why Plato Banished the Poets* (Oxford: Clarendon, 1977), and *Acastos* (New York: Penguin, 1986).

viewed as itself constituting a moral act. In this formulation, since literature has significant moral consequences, it deserves to be judged in the same way that other such "acts" are. Literary themes and images reflect the author's treatment of the subjects represented in them; they also affect the thought and life of their readers. On both these counts, the literary work and its author are morally accountable. That the act of writing presupposes a role for the imagination might seem to insulate that act from moral judgment of its consequences; but so far as the question of responsibility is concerned, the imagination figures as only one among other elements of human agency. The writer is responsible also for what the imagination does, and this is true even if the directions in which it moves are not the results of deliberation in its usual sense.

To be sure, recognition that literary representation is subject to moral judgment does not imply that its consequences are morally harmful or bad, as Plato goes on to assert. In the distinction between those two claims, it is the former that underlies the discussion here of the relation between literary and moral structure in writings for which the Nazi genocide against the Jews is a subject. As earlier references in these pages have shown for specific forms of discourse in respect to the Nazi genocide, the more rudimentary act of *writing* about that event—whether in "imaginative" or in discursive or scholarly writing; that is, in writing *as* writing—is also obliged to represent in its own means the measure of that moral enormity. In all writing about the Nazi genocide, then, it is not only that subject which has morally distinctive features; the writing itself is distinctive in its conceptual, literary, and, finally, in its moral features.

This thesis bears in significant ways on the general relation between moral "content" and literary "form." By its emphasis on the connection between historical fact and literary representation, it also calls attention to certain features of its nonliterary subject, that is, the Nazi genocide. Even without these reasons, however, the importance of considering the literary representations of that event *as writing* should be evident. No one who now reflects on the Nazi war against the Jews can avoid relying in that effort on the writings in which it appears as a subject—whether writings from within the war itself or the continuously increasing number that have appeared since then. These writings are, in effect, lenses through which all present knowledge and judgment—indeed, all that can be imagined—of the Nazi genocide are made possible; without their provision of evidence and a community of discourse, even personal experience or memory would be insufficient. To gain access by way of this source to the facts of the genocide, however, requires an understanding of the effect the lenses have on the representations seen through them, a grasp of how the lenses shape or articulate the subject itself. The act of writing, it is evident, is an essential part of literary representation and of what is disclosed or implied there. In this sense, writings about the Nazi genocide have two subjects, not one, and readers of those writings cannot avoid considering the one in order to judge what they know of the other.

1. The Contents of Form

Despite their other differences, the principal views in the long-standing dispute on the ethical status of literary representation—views that extend from Plato's indictment of the poets to the elevation of art in the Kantian distinction between aesthetic and moral judgment and in the subsequent lines of nineteenth-century Romantic thought—have drawn in common mainly on the evidence of literary content. For these accounts, it is the themes or ideas in literary texts that determine their moral significance; such significance is thus centered on the literary "meaning" inferred by readers and critics from the intentions displayed in or underlying texts and from the later consequences of those texts in the lives of their readers. The reliance on this type of evidence is based on accounts of moral judgment and linguistic meaning *outside* of literature—since in these other, more common cases, intentions or consequences are typically held to be the main and sometimes the only source of evidence.[2] Given that precedent, it is not surprising that the moral status of literature should be addressed in similar terms, transposed now into a literary version of questions which ask what a text is "about" and what it does to or with that subject.

But this starting point, however plausible, ignores the possibility that moral meaning may also be linked to the formal or specifically literary features of a text—that the literary means may themselves be a function of literary content and thus of what the text asserts or implies. The past failure of literary history to recognize this possibility has not been accidental; it reflects a prior commitment to the distinction between content—or "matter"—and form, a distinction that has been commonly assumed in the analysis not only of the varieties of literary and artistic representation but of other kinds of social and cultural expression as well. In the literary application of this distinction, it is the content of a

2. Philosophical paradigms of these two conceptions of ethical judgment can be found in Kant (e.g., *Foundations of the Metaphysics of Morals*) and J. S. Mill (e.g., *Utilitarianism*) respectively. On the role of the form-content distinction in art and aesthetics, see Monroe Beardsley, *Aesthetics: Problems in the Philosophy of Criticism* (New York: Harcourt, Brace and Co., 1958), chaps. 4 and 5.

text that defines any truth claims associated with it. As the general distinction is presupposed, ethical values, like the other elements of literary meaning, are viewed as part of its content. It follows, then, that whether represented tacitly (e.g., symbolically) or stated explicitly, the moral point of view ascribed to a text is considered to be itself nonliterary, an imposition on literary effect from the world outside art. In extreme versions which appear under the rubric of "aestheticism," this imposition gives rise to an objection: that since what essentially distinguishes art are its formal features, moral judgment—whether inside the work or the part of the reader or viewer—is at best irrelevant, at worst a defect.

If the sharp distinction between form and content is rejected, however, the way is open to regarding also the formal or stylistic features of a text as elements of its "content," including whatever moral implications may be associated with the latter. The literary *structure*, in other words, becomes an assertion or idea, an element of its subject: conversely, no longer alien to the "literariness" of the text, moral meaning becomes part of it. It is this conception of the relation between ethical content and literary form that stands in the background of the discussion here of the imaginative representations of the Nazi genocide. Once again, the moral extremity of that set of events is fundamental—since for writing, too, this extremity unavoidably affects the process of representation. The "content" of such writings, in other words, is implicated in their literary structure, not only as it happens or by an author's deliberate choice but intrinsically.[3] The constraints and possibilities of literary representation, on the one hand, and the historical and then the moral character of what the representations are "of," on the other hand, converge.

To identify the moral features of literature in formalist terms does not mean that the same end could not be reached by an analysis which focused on literary content. The results of this more traditional approach have, however, remained problematic—a fact nowhere more evident than in the elementary questions that persist about the moral consequences of literature. What difference does reading the "classical" works of literature make in the life of a reader? Is the reading of "bad" literature, in any of the latter's many senses, actually harmful? What are

3. For discussion of the issues involved in determining the "content of form," the writers related to Russian Formalism are especially important. See, e.g., Boris Eichenbaum, *Aufsätze zur Theorie und Geschichte der Literatur*, trans. A. Kaemfe (Frankfurt: Suhrkamp, 1965); Victor Erlich, *Russian Formalism* (The Hague: Mouton, 1955); Jan Mukarovsky, "The Esthetics of Language," in Paul L. Gervin (ed.), *A Prague School Reader* (Washington, D.C.: Georgetown University Press, 1964); Valentin N. Volosinov, *Marxism and the Philosophy of Language*, trans. Ladislav Matejka and I. R. Titunik (New York: Seminar Press, 1973).

the effects on people who do not read at all? Rudimentary as they are, such questions remain largely unanswered and even unasked.[4] To be sure, the inconclusiveness of the evidence has not prevented partisans from taking sides. Governments and educators continue to make decisions on censorship or school curricula as though the basis for doing so were clear. But their decisions have disclosed less the intentions and consequences of literature than the traditional commitments or prejudices of social practice; the question of evidence, even of what should *count* as evidence, remains open.

Again, the failure in studies of the moral status of literature to include its formal features in their account is understandable historically. As moral judgments outside literature characteristically focus on the content of what is done—that is, on the explicit "act" and its intentions and consequences—it is predictable that the ethical status of literary texts would be analyzed in those same terms. One consequence of the form-content distinction in particular, however, indicates why the inadequacy of that distinction as a basis for literary analysis would also be likely to obstruct moral judgment. This is the implication that since the content of literary representation is independent of its form, a single content can in principle be inscribed in many, perhaps in any, forms; and, conversely, that the same literary form can be applied to many (or any) contents. On these premises, the ethical status of a text's content—irrespective of the nature of its moral claims—would have no bearing on its literary form; the one (the literary subject) is quite independent of the other (for example, the literary genre or style). *Any* content, in other words, can be represented in *any* literary form; the significance or meaning of a text, including its moral import, is of no consequence for its structure.[5]

Admittedly, this assumption of a sharp distinction between literary form and ethical content clashes with what is no less commonly acknowledged as a connection between form and content: it is usually taken for granted that differences in literary genre (for example, between the short story and the novel) are related to the complexity of the themes that those genres can accommodate. But this recognition has not led to the parallel but more difficult conclusion that formal consequences can be inferred from the ethical content of literary themes or, conversely, that ethical judgment itself depends on a text's formal features. The aura

4. Among writers who *have* addressed these questions are Raymond Williams, *Culture and Society 1780–1950* (New York: Harper and Row, 1966); and Richard Hoggart, *The Uses of Literacy* (New York: Oxford University Press, 1970).

5. For the issues involved in stylistic synonymy, see Berel Lang, "Towards a Poetics of Philosophical Discourse," in Lang, *Philosophy and the Art of Writing* (Lewisburg: Bucknell University Press, 1983).

of a moral presence in literature has been outweighed by fear of the charges of philistinism, of a failure to recognize the distinctive claims of art. Most theorists and critics have been unwilling to consider whether a moral index of literary or stylistic features is even possible.[6]

It is worth noting that Plato himself, as he emphasizes the dissonance between moral value and literary representation, finds the basis of that dissonance reflected in literature's formal characteristics no less than in its content. Not only are the effects of poetry morally harmful in Plato's account, but the source of those effects is evident in the poetic structure itself. Literature, like other artistic representations, stands at a second remove from reality, imitating what is already an imitation (the visible world). The fact of this falsification, furthermore, appears *in* the representation: as "true" knowledge is self-verifying, not requiring an independent criterion, so "knowledge" that turns out to be false also discloses itself as a feature of the representation. Such falsity may at times be mistaken for truth, but the source of error is then not in the literary object but in the viewer; the content of the object is present in its form.

To be sure, Plato's sweeping verdict *against* literature is not entailed by the recognition that literature is liable to moral assessment (which could be positive rather than negative). It is, again, this second, more general premise that underlies the discussion here of the relation between ethical content and literary form in writings about the Nazi genocide against the Jews. The specific thesis which will be defended asserts that certain limitations, literary and moral, are intrinsic to "imaginative" literature—novels, drama, poetry—about the Nazi genocide. This thesis itself has two parts, both of them based on a distinction between historical or documentary writings about the genocide, on the one hand, and figurative or "imaginative" writings about that subject, on the other.[7] In its first part, the thesis applies this distinc-

6. The major exception to this claim has been in Marxist aesthetics and criticism. See, e.g., Terry Eagleton, *Criticism and Ideology* (London: Verso, 1978); Lucien Goldmann, *Towards a Sociology of the Novel,* trans. Alan Sheridan (London: Tavistock, 1977); Frederic Jameson, *The Political Unconscious* (Ithaca, N.Y.: Cornell University Press, 1981). The reaction recently against the ahistoricism of Deconstruction (a reaction within as well as outside it) has also moved in this direction—see J. Hillis Miller, *The Ethics of Reading* (New York: Columbia University Press, 1987); and Tobin Siebers, *The Ethics of Criticism* (Ithaca, N.Y.: Cornell University Press, 1988).

7. The strong distinction asserted between historical and figurative or imaginative discourse runs against the current of much contemporary literary theory and historiography (see, e. g., Hayden White, *Metahistory: The Historical Imagination in Nineteenth-Century Europe* (Baltimore, Md.: Johns Hopkins Press, 1973), and *Tropics of Discourse* (Baltimore, Md.: Johns Hopkins Press, 1978); Dominic LaCapra, *History and Criticism* (Ithaca, N.Y.: Cornell University Press, 1985). The issues raised by that line of argument cannot be addressed fully here, but the crucial point of difference between it and the position defended here is discussed in section 4 of this chapter.

tion descriptively; the claim argued is that the values and methods of historical writing have held a disproportionately large and symptomatic role even among the *non*historical writings about the Nazi genocide (as in the novel and in drama). A dominant feature in such imaginative writing, the claim goes, is its commitment to the ideals of historical authenticity and truthfulness, and consequently to the literary means for realizing those ideals.

The second part of the thesis, based on the same distinction, is evaluative. It asserts that the most significant and compelling—the most valuable—writings about the Nazi genocide appear in the forms of historical discourse, not in those of fictional prose or drama or poetry. What accounts for the differences between those two modes of writing, in this part of the thesis, are "moral correlatives"—the points within a text at which moral and literary values intersect as the moral character of the literary subject imposes constraints on the formal features of the text. On this basis, the conclusion emerges that the literary difference between imaginative and historical writings about the Nazi genocide is grounded in the moral features that also, and more basically, distinguish those two literary forms.

The two parts of the thesis, taken together, thus assert a connection between literary structure and moral content; they also, by implication, pose a requirement of moral justification for the literary text, most immediately for writings about the Nazi genocide although, as the argument might be extended, for other writings as well. Sections 2 and 3 in this chapter present evidence, respectively, for the two parts of the thesis, but some aspects of that evidence may serve as a useful anticipation. One such aspect reflects on the "psychology" of the text: this is the sense of doubt or precariousness that writings about the Nazi genocide often convey about themselves, the sense that the very act of writing about that subject is open to challenge. This self-consciousness appears in certain stylistic features, for example, as those writings reject the standard literary conventions—a rejection that suggests either the need for conventions more adequate to the extraordinary subject or a challenge to the use of such conventions altogether. Other evidence is more explicit—for example, when authors include in their texts statements of justification, claiming the truthfulness or authenticity of their accounts, as though to anticipate a presumption to the contrary.

What underlies such evidence and then reappears in its literary representation is the moral status of the Nazi genocide as an historical, *nonliterary* subject. Admittedly, ethically significant features of literary representation are in certain respects quite independent of any particular subject. Simply as an act, writing entails judgments by the author both on what is written about and on his readers. Where the moral implications of a literary subject are extreme, moreover, it would hardly be surprising that the features of its representation should include elements of ethical judgment (although the justification for that inclusion would still remain to be argued). In one sense, the *fact* of writing reflects a moral judgment, through its implied claim that writing will usefully add something to what the subject otherwise, *un*written, would fail to disclose of itself. For many literary subjects, this claim, even if tacitly present, seems hardly worth noting or challenging. But where the literary subject involves moral extremity, every element in its representation, including the act of representation itself, becomes morally significant. At a theoretical level, then, the thesis proposed here at once assumes and tests the assertion that the standard categories applied in literary analysis, such as those of genre, point of view, or tropes and figures of speech, have moral as well as stylistic significance—indeed, that those two aspects of representation, often held to be independent of each other, are intrinsically related.

Admittedly, even if these several parts of the overall thesis were granted—including the invidious distinction it asserts between imaginative and historical writings about the Nazi genocide—it might still be objected that the thesis applies only contingently or incidentally. It is arguable that imaginative writing requires more time for the assimilation of a subject than does historical writing, and if this were the case, it would still be too early to lay down distinctions among writings about the Nazi genocide. Or again, it could be held that certain social conditions—thus the background from which writing emerges, rather than the nature of a particular subject—have tended recently to emphasize historical rather than imaginative genres of writing. According to these explanations, the liabilities ascribed here to the nonhistorical genres of writing might be remedied either as external conditions change or simply with the passage of time.

The rejection of the distinction between formal literary categories and the ethical content of literary works can concede these objections, however, without giving up its own claims. The contention that among representations of the Nazi genocide, documentary and other forms of historical writing are more significant—more compelling morally *and* literarily—than other modes of writing draws, beyond the evidence of practical criticism, on certain intrinsic features of writing and figurative discourse. The issues thus raised concerning the representation of the Nazi genocide disclose what might be called a "boundary question" directed to that writing in principle as well as in fact. When Theodor Adorno refers, in his much-quoted phrase, to the "barbarism" of writing lyric poetry after Auschwitz (all the more, by implication, for writing poetry *about* Auschwitz),[8] or when Elie Wiesel asserts that a "Holocaust literature" is a "contradiction" in terms,[9] they call into question the moral and aesthetic justification for the very act of writing about the Nazi genocide, whatever the genre or other literary means. What warrant is there for "re-presenting" it *at all* is the question raised here—and tacitly or explicitly, this boundary question has been a constant presence in much that has been written about the Nazi genocide (no less significantly, in virtually everything that has been written about that writing). The status of this boundary question is itself the subject of the concluding section of the present chapter. But in order to understand how literary fact turns into value—how an historical emphasis in literary practice is symptomatic of a privileged position for historical writing in principle—it is important to see first what that emphasis in practice involves. Analyzing the strategies of historical writing which recur in imaginative writing about the Nazi genocide is thus a first step in explaining the convergence of ethical judgment and literary form that is so constant and distinctive—and unavoidable—a feature of both those types of writing

2. Historical Truth in the Literary Imagination

The descriptive thesis proposed asserts that the imaginative writings about the Nazi genocide have "aspired to the condition" of history—that even allowing for their historical subject, their adaptation of the means of historical discourse to "literary" representation attaches to those means a role of exceptional importance. In addition to the unusual reliance among these writings on literary genres which explicitly invoke historical conventions (the diary and the memoir), strategies used in the more traditionally central genres (the novel, drama, and poetry) reflect the same tendency. The considerable number and variety of these strategies is itself symptomatic of the importance attached to their goal. These literary means include the revision of generic conventions in the direction of historical discourse; authorial statements, within and outside the texts, claiming historical grounds for their "imaginative"

8. Theodor W. Adorno, "Engagement," in *Gesammelte Schriften* (Frankfurt A. M.: Suhrkamp, 1974), 422. Adorno quickly enlarges the issue to cover *Kunst überhaupt*—"art in general" (423). Less often noticed has been Adorno's qualification of this statement: "Perennial suffering has as much right to expression as a tortured man has to scream; hence it may have been wrong to say that after Auschwitz you could no longer write poems." (*Negative Dialectics*, trans. E. B. Ashton [New York: Seabury, 1973], 362.)

9. Elie Wiesel, *A Jew Today*, trans. M. Wiesel (New York: Random House, 1978), 197. See also Gila Ramras-Rauch, Introduction to Gila Ramras-Rauch and Joseph Michman-Melkner (eds.), *Facing the Holocaust* (Philadelphia: Jewish Publication Society, 1985), 3–5.

representations; and assumptions in the texts of both specific historical knowledge and a nonfigurative moral point of view on the part of the "implied reader."[10] Means such as these, it seems, can have only one purpose: to convey the authority—and presumably the reality—of historical truth.

It will be recognized that appeals to historical authenticity as a literary device have not been uncommon in the history of imaginative literature. Such references, moreover, have appeared, not only in the diary or the memoir, but in the novel and in drama, which are not commonly identified as genres of historical discourse. So, for example, novels otherwise as different as Defoe's *The Journal of the Plague Year*, Goethe's *The Sorrows of the Young Werther*, and Hawthorne's *The Scarlet Letter* employ historical conventions which are, however, and would be known to their readers as, fictional. Again, as the genre of autobiography spans the line between fact and fiction, the narrative "I" of the autobiographical novel (as in Dickens's *David Copperfield*) attempts to convey the "truth" of historical narration in imaginative writing. It is arguable that the very distinction between fiction and nonfiction evolved mainly within the traditions of imaginative—fictional—literature; but even more conservative views of literary history acknowledge the continuing interdependence in the claims of imaginative and historical writing.[11]

Even allowing for this pattern of development, however, the importance attached to truthfulness and historical authenticity in imaginative writings about the Nazi genocide has been unusual—to an extent that points to the subject itself as the cause of the emphasis. As further testimony to this, a question has been raised in relation to these writings that does not (although it obviously could) occur for other literary subjects: Why, it has been asked, in light of their claims of historical authenticity, have the writers of novels, dramas, or poetry about the Nazi genocide not more directly chosen to write history itself? This question has sometimes been posed by the writers themselves: Leslie Epstein, whose *King*

10. Versions of this thesis have appeared elsewhere, although without being related to the contrast found here between figurative and historical discourse. See, e.g., Sidra Ezrahi, *By Words Alone: The Holocaust in Literature* (Chicago: University of Chicago Press, 1980), 25 ff.; Irving Howe, "Writing and the Holocaust," *The New Republic* (27 October 1986), 27–39 (reprinted in Lang, *Writing*—see chap. 2, n. 8); Alvin Rosenfeld, *A Double Dying: Reflections on Holocaust Literature* (Bloomington, Ind.: Indiana University Press, 1980), chap. 3; James E. Young, *Writing and Rewriting the Holocaust* (Bloomington, Ind.: Indiana University Press, 1988).

11. On the historical background of the relation between fiction and nonfiction, see, e.g., Lennard J. Davis, *Factual Fictions: The Origins of the English Novel* (New York: Columbia University Press, 1983), chaps. 1 and 6.

of the Jews is a fictional representation of Rumkowski and the Lodz ghetto, concluded (at the same time that he was writing his novel) that "almost any eyewitness testimony of the Holocaust is more moving and more successful at creating a sense of what it must have been like in the ghettos and the camps than almost any fictional account of the same events";[12] and similarly, Cynthia Ozick spoke in favor of historical discourse as a means of representing the Nazi genocide—even as measured by her own commitment to imaginative writing.[13] Admittedly, both these authors—and also Adorno, in respect to his more radical claim—later qualified these invidious comparisons. But the fact that they were made at all anticipates the grounds for the thesis posed here.

An emphasis on historical authenticity is most obvious in the literary genres which themselves profess an historical role and which, partly as a consequence of this, stand on the borderline between historical and imaginative discourse. The diary, the chronicle, and the memoir are the principal genres of this sort, and the large place occupied by these forms among writings on the Nazi genocide is itself significant. That prominence is explained only in part by the availability of these forms to the writer (the diary and journal as written within the historical events themselves, the memoir with a substantial part of its content accessible in memory); the subject addressed *within* the genres is also responsible. Admittedly, it is not only for their evocation of history that the diaries and memoirs from the Nazi genocide have gained their large readership; even the sparest, most "objective" texts within these genres also disclose the expressive and figurative elaboration of imaginative literature.

The diary, because of its unusual position exactly at the point where the lines of historical and literary representation converge, can serve as a standard by which to judge the relation between those forms of representation in other genres of writing. Diaries may, on the one hand, be read as sources for the historical record (so, for example, the important group of diaries written from the Warsaw ghetto);[14] moreover, virtually all the diaries written from within the Nazi genocide that have survived were *intended* by their authors to serve this purpose. But the interest that these works continue to attract even when their historical importance

12. Leslie Epstein, "The Reality of Evil," *Partisan Review* 43 (1976), 639–40.

13. Cynthia Ozick, "Concluding Discussion," in Lang, *Writing* (see chap. 2, n. 8), 284.

14. E.g., *The Warsaw Diary of Chaim A. Kaplan,* trans. and ed. Abraham I. Katsch (New York: Collier, 1973); *Notes from the Warsaw Ghetto: The Journal of Emmanual Ringelbaum,* trans. Jacob Sloan (New York: Schocken, 1974); *The Warsaw Diary of Adam Czerniakow,* ed. Raul Hilberg, Stanislaw Staron, and Josef Kermisz (New York: Stein and Day, 1979).

has been superseded by more systematic scholarship suggest a role for them that is literary as much as historical. It is important, then, to consider how this combination of factors shapes the genre.

Since the diary is written at the same time that the events of which it takes note occur, it combines an unmediated connection to those events with the individual and expressive point of view of the author. In no other genre, literary *or* historical, do the historical moment of the events recounted and the expressive process of writing coincide in this way. Public records (laws, proclamations, church registries, railroad timetables) are often more important than diaries as a basis for systematic historical accounts—but they are not, except incidentally, expressive responses. Scholarly histories provide a more comprehensive and detailed view than diaries, but they are not themselves *in* the history. The diarist writes from day to day, unknowing of what will ensue in respect to the events described or for his own future—and of course with a conscious uncertainty of whether the diary being written will even survive, let alone be read. In the context of the Nazi genocide, moreover, not only individual but group survival stood in the balance. The urgency of these several contingencies is integral to the role of the diary first as written and then also, more complexly, as read. The literary representation of the diary, furthermore, allows for no revision. Where such retrospection occurs (as with the disclosure of an earlier draft for "the" diary of Anne Frank), the status of the diary itself is radically altered. Even when the diarist goes beyond the recording of specific events or feelings—for example, in generalizing about them or in making predictions about the future—the status of the diary as the record of immediate response is not affected. These, too, define a relation between the historical moment and the writer's view of it.

The diary, in other words, is historically and expressively incorrigible; it is a representation of the diarist's experience, and about this the diarist-author will always have the last word. The force of this authenticity is accentuated, furthermore, by the framework of retrospective knowledge within which diaries are typically read. Certainly it is an important factor in any reading *now* of diaries from the Nazi genocide that the reader knows the outcome of the events they refer to, and, usually, the diarist's own fate. Such knowledge frames the act of reading, intensifying the text's historical claims by the contrast between the contingency of the events represented and the finality of their outcome as the reader is aware of that.

In this sense, the framework in which diaries from the Nazi genocide now appear suggests an analogy to the relation in classical tragedy between individual character and the framework of cosmic fate, a relation

THE REPRESENTATION OF EVIL

which imposes on the reader the characteristic double vision of irony. (In *The Ghost Writer,* Philip Roth requires his reader to imagine that Anne Frank had survived Bergen-Belsen; concealing her identity, she reappears as an aspiring writer in the United States. The effect here depends on the *contrary* presuppositions usually assumed in the reading of her diary.)[15] For the genre of the diary, however, in contrast to classical tragedy, the irony imposed is entirely the reader's contribution—impelled by the "naive" commitments of the diary's own words. For the diary itself enters a claim, beyond historical representation, of absolute truth—not in the sense that the events reported "actually" happened as recounted, but in that the diarist's assertions are self-verifying. Even if it could be demonstrated that the diarist was factually mistaken in a particular statement (or, at an extreme, that the diarist had lied), the diary itself remains beyond dispute as recording the writer's view. In this sense, the reader is not asked to "imagine" the events of the diary; all that is demanded is an understanding of the words themselves as they establish contact with the events they mention. The second "eye" of the double vision of irony, then, is added by the reader in the form of historical knowledge: the diary is ironic as read but not as written, insofar as it is sustained by historical—and extraliterary—reference.

Again, the diary and the closely related genres of the journal and the chronicle have all been assimilated to the tradition of "imaginative" literature (so, for example, Samuel Pepys's *Diary* and Boswell's *Journals*). But examples such as these, in their detachment from the original contexts, only underscore the unusual emphasis on historical reference in the response to those genres among writings with the Nazi genocide as their subject. It is possible that the prominence of the diary or journal among these writings will diminish as the distance in time from that event increases and as other forms of writing provide more sustained and complex views of it. Even if such a decline should occur, however, it would still leave the present emphasis to be explained.

The memoir, which also occupies an unusually large place among writings about the Nazi genocide, is, although structurally distinct, analogous to the diary in the importance it attaches to the authenticity of historical representation. Unlike the diary, the memoir is written retrospectively and at a single "moment," not sequentially. For it, too, how-

15. Philip Roth, *The Ghost Writer* (New York: Farrar, Straus and Giroux, 1979). This contrast itself raises moral questions in respect to Roth's text. The line between irony and perversity may not be clear, but this does not mean that certain "literary ideas" cannot be distinguished in those terms. On the different versions of Anne Frank's diary, see *The Diary of Anne Frank: The Critical Edition,* prepared by the Netherlands State Institute for War Documentation (New York: Doubleday, 1989), 61ff.

ever, the literal reference to events independent of the discourse serves as
a fulcrum. The writer is a larger, more cohesive presence in the memoir
than he is in the diary, since the events recounted there are shaped by a
point of view asserted at the single "moment" of writing. (For memoirs
from the Nazi genocide, the author's own survival is obviously a central
part of that point of view.) But this perspective from the writer's "present" nonetheless depends on the causality of the past events that led up
to it. The author of a memoir need not claim to make those events themselves intelligible, but the intention in recounting them is at least to
make intelligible his present view of them, to show how the self which
speaks or writes now was constituted in the past. The distinction between the memoir and the more extended genre of the autobiography is
itself based on the literary role of historical boundaries: where the former considers a limited group of events in the writer's life, the latter
reflects on the life as a whole. So, for example, Primo Levi, in *Survival in
Auschwitz*, writes about his experiences from the time of his capture to
his liberation; in *The Reawakening*, he describes the period between his
liberation and his return home. In these memoirs, the historical
causality of the chronological boundaries is itself an effective part of the
narrative structure.[16]

Even when the author's experience of the war and its aftermath coincide with the dates of the author's lifetime (as it does in Saul Friedländer's *When Memory Comes*),[17] the particular historical center rather
than the life as a whole is the focus around which the narrative revolves:
whatever happens happens because of that center or at least in light of it.
The author relates the past to the present as a—the—condition of the
latter. In contrast to the diary, the "present" of the memoir's author is
distinct from the past that is his subject; in calling attention at once to
the distinction between them and then to the convergence of these two
chronologically separated points of view, the writer underscores the importance of historical reference in the memoir's narrative.

These characterizations of the diary and the memoir may suggest no
special relevance for those genres to the context of the Nazi genocide.
But this is in part due to the resistance of the two genres to structural
variation—a resistance which is itself due to their basic historical commitment. The features that distinguish the diaries of the Nazi genocide

16. Primo Levi, *Survival in Auschwitz*, trans. Stuart Woolf (New York: Collier, 1959);
The Reawakening, trans. Stuart Woolf (New York: Collier, 1986). When Levi, still addressing the same subject, moves away from the conventions of this historical ground—as in the
novel *If Not Now, When?*, trans. William Weaver (New York: Penguin, 1986)—the writing
is very different and much less compelling.

17. Saul Friedländer, *When Memory Comes*, trans. Helen R. Lane (New York: Avon,
1980).

from other diaries are thematic: first, through the heightened sense of contingency and precariousness in respect to the events recorded, and second, through the author's concern that the diaries should survive. It might seem that these factors must have other substantive or formal consequences for the genre—for instance, that these diaries should be more reticent than others about recording personal feelings or, correspondingly, that they should place more emphasis on public events. But any such shift in proportions seems limited in fact. (This is evident, for example, in *The Chronicle of the Lodz Ghetto*, to which various authors contributed. Even here, with an effort made to minimize the individual differences among the authors, and in a sparer genre than the diary, private impression mingles with descriptions of public fact.)[18]

Again, there are undoubtedly reasons in addition to the one proposed for the unusual attention accorded the diaries, journals, and memoirs based on the events of the Nazi genocide. Not only were the forms of the diary and journal more immediately available for the writers (they could be written at odd moments, in snatches), but they were also "complete" once the war ended; many of them, accordingly, were among the earliest published writings after the Nazis' defeat. The memoir, too, because its content was immediately accessible to the author, lent itself early to writing and publication. But such considerations do not account for the disproportionate role which those genres have maintained among the writings—and readings—about the Nazi genocide; to explain *that*, one comes back to their subject and to the impulse for historical representation evoked by it.

This impulse becomes more notable literarily as it appears in genres less dependent than the diary or memoir on conventions of historical representation—in drama, for example, which has yielded fewer individual works about the Nazi genocide than the other major literary forms.[19] The latter fact itself warrants consideration, and one likely reason is the role of "spectacle" in dramatic representation—the visual representation of events which, given the extraordinary character of the Nazi genocide, could be sustained only obliquely or by understatement. In this respect, written texts, in contrast to visual representation, provide a distancing or insulating medium (even film, by the intervention of the camera, affords for the viewer the sense of a mediating control absent from the stage). To be sure, intensity of emotion and the spectacle of

18. Lucjan Dobroszycki (ed.), *The Chronicle of the Lodz Ghetto, 1941–1944* (New Haven: Yale University Press, 1984).

19. See Alvin Goldfarb, "A Selected Bibliography of Plays of the Holocaust," in Elinor Fuchs (ed.), *Plays of the Holocaust* (New York: Theatre Communications Group, 1987), 303–10.

horror have been important in the dramatic tradition. But their most
compelling examples—in *Medea* or *Oedipus Rex* or *King Lear*—also suggest why the subject of the Nazi genocide would resist dramatic
representation. As drama does not have available the distancing device
of authorial intervention, its action is characteristically motivated by the
thought or will of individual characters—and the difficulty of representing the events of the Final Solution as a relation between perpetrator and
victim seriously limits these possibilities. The causality initiated by the
"principled" commitment to evil of an individual Iago or Richard III
would not be adequate as a dramatic ground for events of the sort exemplified in the Nazi genocide. Unlike their decisions and the consequences which followed from them, the origins of the Nazi genocide
combined individual choice with collective and often only tacit decisions
in a way that virtually blocks its attribution to any particular agent: as
was suggested earlier in this volume, the corporate victim of genocide
has an analogue in the corporate agent. Obviously, certain figures in the
Nazi hierarchy were more directly responsible for the act of genocide
than others. But to name the central figure of Hitler as by himself
accountable for it would misrepresent history and skew its literary representation as well. It is noteworthy that few accounts of the Nazi
genocide, imaginative *or* historical, have ventured any such claim.

The motivating force of dramatic representation would then have to
reflect in its own means the dispersion of causality that occurred historically. It is not surprising, then, that the two most compelling dramas
yet written about the Nazi genocide should focus their "plots" in characters who are either off center from the main causal origins of that
event or who, more directly implicated, nonetheless, constitute a virtually nameless group of historical agents. These sets of dramatic
characters, moreover, are in one version literally (that is, juridically), in
the other, symbolically "on trial"—an immediate means of assuring
historical presence in the representation since representation depends
on the testimony of defendants and witnesses, both of which groups
are defined historically. So Rolf Hochhuth's *The Deputy* gathers the evidence (cited in an "historical appendix" as it might be in a straightforward historical account) against the Catholic Church, in particular
against Pope Pius XII, for its calculated indifference to the fate of the
Jews at the hands of the Nazis. The play itself "as far as possible adhered to the facts"[20] in Hochhuth's terms; it was thus *meant* to evoke
the response of historical representation, and Hochhuth was obviously

20. Rolf Hochhuth, *The Deputy,* trans. Richard and Clara Winston (New York: Grove
Press, 1964), 287.

successful in this. The controversies that have recurred in relation to the play's performances have pitted against each other conflicting judgments based on the *historical* claims made or implied in it—on one side, from defenders of the Church; on the other, from viewers supporting Hochhuth in his criticism. In this dispute, as in the dramatic action of the play itself, the events of the Nazi genocide constitute an assumed background and text, with the addition only of certain parts of the dialogue subsequently invented or (in Hochhuth's own term) "imagined" (so, for example, the conversations in which Pius XII takes part and in most of the words attributed to Kurt Gerstein). It is historical reference, then, that establishes both the "pre-text" and the text of the drama.

Peter Weiss's *The Investigation* goes to a further extreme even than *The Deputy* in the extent of its historical implication. With few exceptions, the dialogue of the play draws directly on the court records of the Frankfurt trial in 1963–65 of twenty-one guards and functionaries at Auschwitz.[21] Weiss rearranges and elides parts of the court record, but the words spoken in court are nonetheless mainly the words spoken by his characters. Here, too, moreover, the dramatic issue is made corporate rather than individual by the institutional framework of a trial in which the defendants appear as a group (finally, as Weiss enlarges on *this*, as exemplary of mankind in general).[22] That Weiss turns to the court record as material for his play is itself acknowledgment, beyond the potential effectiveness of law and the courtroom as drama, of the need for history to speak in respect to the specific events represented. The tradition of "historical drama" as a genre extends from Greek tragedy through Shakespeare's histories to the work of contemporary writers such as Shaw, Brecht, and Giradoux. But the relative importance of the events of the Nazi genocide is greater for the plays by Hochhuth and Weiss than are the historical backgrounds in such other works—a fact which once again reflects on the subject itself.

For the purposes of understanding the unusual emphasis on historical authenticity in literary representations of the Nazi genocide, the evidence provided by the genres of the novel and poetry is crucial. Unlike the diary and the memoir, the novel is not usually conceived as a form

21. Peter Weiss, *The Investigation,* trans. Jan Swan and Ulu Grosbard (Chicago: Dramatic Publishing Co., 1966).

22. So, Weiss's statement that "I see Auschwitz as a scientific instrument that could have been used by anyone to exterminate anyone. For that matter, given a different deal, the Jews could have been on the side of the Nazis. . . . *The Investigation* is a universal human problem." Interview with Oliver Clausen, "Weiss/Propagandist and Weiss/Playwright," *New York Times Magazine,* 2 October 1966, 132.

primarily of historical writing; it is, furthermore, a more flexible genre than the diary or memoir in its openness to variation (e.g., in its more diverse possibilities of authorial point of view and of plot and character). It is the more significant, then, that in many novels about the Nazi genocide this potential for diversity is also constrained by the ideal of historical authenticity—a fact which is further accentuated in novels that otherwise closely follow the conventions of the genre. Here, if anywhere, it might be expected that the emphasis on historical authenticity would be minimal, but precisely the opposite turns out to be the case. There are other objections to which these novels are open because of their reliance on the traditional conventions of the novel. But in such works as Jakob Presser's *Breaking Point*, Leslie Epstein's *The King of the Jews*, or William Styron's *Sophie's Choice*, the concern of the authors for historical truth is nonetheless constantly demonstrated, both in external claims by the authors of their attentiveness to the "facts" and as stated or implied within the works themselves. So, for example, Presser insists on the purpose in his novel of disclosing the "whole truth," and Epstein has asserted of his expressionistic novel that each episode in it has a "realistic" source (even if not exclusively from events in the Lodz ghetto).[23] It is as though the writers here are impatient with history for not being "historical" enough; they thus intend by their "fiction" to fill out the historical record—but for the sake of history, not of fiction.

The disproportionate role of historical implication which is most obvious in the conventional novels about the Nazi genocide also figures in works where historical reference more subtly and imaginatively shapes the literary structure. So, for example, a considerable number of novels about the events of genocide appear in the fictional guise of diaries, memoirs, autobiographies, or "objective" historical studies.[24] Richard

23. Jakob Presser, *Breaking Point*, trans. Barrows Mussey (Cleveland: World, 1958), 21; Leslie Epstein, "Writing about the Holocaust," in Lang, *Writing* (see chap. 2, n. 8).

24. Richard Elman, *The Twenty-eighth Day of Ellul* (New York: Scribner, 1968), *Lilo's Diary* (New York: Scribner, 1969), *The Reckoning* (New York: Scribner, 1967); Elie Wiesel, *Night*, trans. Stella Rodway (New York: Hill and Wang, 1960); Marguerite Duras, *The War*, trans. Barbara Bray (New York: Pantheon, 1986); John Hersey, *The Wall* (New York: Knopf, 1950); Jean-Francois Steiner, *Treblinka*, trans. Helen Weaver (New York: Simon and Schuster, 1967); Anna Langfus, *The Lost Shore*, trans. Peter Wiles (New York: Pantheon, 1963), *Saute, Barbara* (Paris: Gallimard, 1965), *The Whole World Brimstone*, trans. Peter Wiles (New York: Pantheon, 1962); Zdena Berger, *Tell Me Another Morning* (New York: Harper, 1961); Lore Segal, *Other People's Houses* (New York: New American Library, 1964); D. M. Thomas, *The White Hotel* (New York: Viking, 1981); and Anatoly Kuznetzov, *Babi Yar: A Documentary Novel*, trans. Jacob Guralsky (New York: Dial Press, 1967). On the controversial relation between *The White Hotel* and *Babi Yar*, see James E. Young, "Holocaust Documentary Fiction: Novelist as Eyewitness," in Lang, *Writing* (see chap. 2, n. 8).

Elman's trilogy—*The Twenty-eighth Day of Ellul, Lilo's Diary*, and *The Reckoning*—takes the forms respectively of a correspondence, a journal, and a ledger. Elie Wiesel's *Night* and Marguerite Duras's *The War* are written in the genre of the memoir, and John Hersey's *The Wall* in the genre of the diary. In his afterword to *Treblinka*, Jean-François Steiner cites his research and his interviews with survivors as evidence for the historical reliability of his account; he maintains this although substantial evidence, including details internal to the text, underscores its "imaginative" character. Such autobiographical novels as Anna Langfuss's trilogy (*The Lost Shore, Saute, Barbara*, and *The Whole World Brimstone*), Zdena Berger's *Tell Me Another Morning*, and Lore Segal's *Other People's Houses* draw on the self-verifying effect of a first-person narrator to underscore what is meant to be evident in the content: the authenticity of historical memory in the presentation of self and as a response to the nature of the events narrated. D. M. Thomas, in *The White Hotel*, introduces historical documentation within his fiction (he borrows some of this material from Anatoly Kuznetzov's *Babi Yar*—a "Document in the Form of a Novel"—another instance of the same usage) in order to sustain the reader's conviction for the figurative aspects of his own novel. Thomas Keneally's *Schindler's List* appears as what, in literary convention, would be a biography; but the reader is made aware by the author both that the work is fictional and yet that it is not *only* this. So Keneally writes in his preface that he has used "the texture and devices of a novel to tell a true story"; in doing this, he has wished "to avoid all fiction, since fiction would debase the record."[25] In these varied examples, then, what is crucial is not so much their *success* in achieving historical authenticity as their acknowledgment of that as a goal—their deference to the conventions of historical discourse as a literary means.

One of the most compelling examples of such imaginative writing remains Tadeusz Borowski's sequence of stories *This Way for the Gas, Ladies and Gentlemen*,[26] which is effective in large measure because its claim for historical authenticity is, although tacit, unmistakable. The status of the discourse in the volume is ambiguous, with clues balanced against each other to such an extent that it is virtually impossible to decide whether the stories are fiction or nonfiction—but also impossible to ignore that issue. On the one hand, Borowski employs many of the standard devices of historical writing, as, for example, in details of chronology and num-

25. Thomas Keneally, *Schindler's List* (New York: Simon and Schuster, 1982), 10.
26. Tadeusz Borowski, *This Way for the Gas, Ladies and Gentlemen*, trans. Barbara Vedder (New York: Viking, 1977).

bers; such details have a prominence more usually reserved in fiction for the central elements of plot or character. On the other hand, the narrative is also so sustained and unified as to suggest that it must be fictional; an historical memoir (which Borowski's narrative superficially resembles) will ordinarily include extraneous or arbitrary events notwithstanding its unified view, since this is indeed how events unfold. And yet the nature of the events represented also seem to suggest that history, a lived experience, is asserting itself: what point would the imagination hope to realize by a conception of such objectified detail? The language and imagery of the stories, moreover, have an immediacy and spontaneity that artifice usually fails to achieve even in its most deliberate attempts to conceal its own presence.

The surrealistic effect of Borowski's writing, unlike the usual appearances of surrealism, which depend on the *exaggeration* of features of reality (as in such writers on the Nazi genocide as Jerzy Kosinski and Piotr Rawicz),[27] comes from the absence of the usual means for deciding whether the representation is "true" or not—at the same time that the decision itself is pressed on the reader. This effect could only be achieved (it would probably only be attempted) where the literary subject was so extraordinary—as in the events of the Nazi genocide—that it *could* not be exaggerated. In such circumstances, literary realism, which ordinarily still reveals itself as artifice, is virtually indistinguishable from historical discourse—with the effect, then, not of realism but of surrealism. It is as though, in respect to this subject, the pressure of history is so implacable that the imagination cannot exceed it or elaborate on it. Here, in other words, exaggeration *is* realism.

A last group of novels provides evidence of the blurred relation between fiction and nonfiction in imaginative writing about the Nazi genocide despite the fact that they do not appeal to the standard conventions of historical representation or make explicit claims of historical authenticity; the role of history is attested here *because* of its only tacit presence. For the authors in this group—these include Aharon Appelfeld, Edmond Jabès, Jakov Lind, and Cynthia Ozick—the role of the events of the genocide in the narrative structures of their work is presumed rather than expressed. The historical events are present in the impression made by their absence, suggested only by indirection and allusion. And yet that historical presence is crucial: unless the reader adds it to the author's text, the narrative itself remain unintelligible. In Appelfeld's *Badenheim 1939*, for example, life for the guests at Badenheim

27. Jerzy Kosinski, *The Painted Bird* (New York: Pocket Books, 1965); Piotr Rawicz, *Blood from the Sky*, trans. Peter Wiles (New York: Harcourt, Brace and World, 1964).

(only obliquely disclosed to be Jews at all) is gradually affected by certain restrictions.[28] These do not, however, essentially alter the atmosphere at the holiday resort, and the reader has then himself to understand the status of the guests and the nature of the events occurring outside the resort; it is also for the reader to anticipate the fate that awaits the unknowing vacationers. The power of the novel thus depends on the tension between a script written by the reader and a prior but only intermittent outline of plot and character by which the author evokes the other. Near the conclusion of the novel, when the guests of Badenheim board a train for an unknown destination, still impelled by a largely unstated causality, their main concern is over the cleanliness of the railroad coaches: the reader is expected to reflect on this blindness through his own knowledge, beyond the novel, of the destruction that awaits them. To be sure, contemporary readers would usually be aware of this connection, and it is also true that *some* presumptive knowledge is a condition for the reading of any text. But the knowledge assumed here on the part of the reader is neither commonplace nor tangential to the representation; it is central to the subject of the novel. Appelfeld's "fictional" text is literally immersed in history.

Presumptive knowledge of much the same order, in historical fact and in its relation of their literary structures, plays a significant role in other Appelfeld novels (e.g., in *Tzili* and *The Retreat,* and to a lesser extent, in *The Immortal Bartfuss*).[29] It figures largely, as has been detailed in chapter 5, for Jabès in *The Book of Questions,* and it does so as well for Lind in the novella *Soul of Wood*[30] and for Ozick in *The Messiah of Stockholm* (although not in other of her writings where the address is quite direct, for example, in the short story "The Shawl").[31] The role of historical reference in these works is not to provide information. History even as *absent* is here causally implicated in the fiction as both a motivating force and a continuing theme; the novels are "about" a subject that reveals itself through the responses to it by others—by the characters in the writing but mainly by the reader. This literary effect could be sustained, it seems, only if the subject itself were distinctive. Its details would have to be suf-

28. Aharon Appelfeld, *Badenheim 1939,* trans. Dalya Bilu (Boston: David Godine, 1980). See on this aspect of Appelfeld's writing Alan Mintz, *Hurban* (New York: Columbia University Press, 1984), 206.

29. Aharon Appelfeld, *Tzili,* trans. Dalya Bilu (New York: Dutton, 1983); *The Retreat,* trans. Dalya Bilu (New York: Dutton, 1984); *The Immortal Bartfuss,* trans. Jeffrey Green (New York: Weidenfeld and Nicholson, 1988).

30. Jakov Lind, *Soul of Wood and Other Stories,* trans. Ralph Manheim (New York: Grove, 1966).

31. Cynthia Ozick, *The Messiah of Stockholm* (New York: Knopf, 1987); "The Shawl," *New Yorker,* 26 May 1980, 33–34.

ficiently important that an unspecified "implied" reader would know them; it would, moreover, have to have sufficient weight historically to resist its own transformation into fiction and yet to serve as a basis for imaginative elaboration.

Poetry is the most difficult genre to reconcile with the assertion of an historical ideal in imaginative writing about the Nazi genocide, although this difficulty is to some extent an intrinsic feature of the genre. The concrete emphasis in poetic discourse that is, however, dislodged from any *particular* context ramifies any specific historical point of reference designated in poetry. The common difficulty of achieving critical agreement even on what the subject of a poem is presents further evidence of this; the difficulty does not disappear even when historical references are explicitly stated in the text itself (for example, in Yeats's "Easter 1916" or Whitman's "When Lilacs Last in the Dooryard Bloomed").

It is consistent with this disposition, then, that poetry which is most explicitly "about" the Nazi genocide—for example, Charles Reznikoff's "Holocaust"—introduces a documentary method of assertion and reference that brings the poetic text close to the prose of historical discourse; and that in writers such as Abraham Sutzkever (e.g., *Burnt Pearls*), William Heyen (*Erika* or *The Swastika Poems*), and Dan Pagis (*Points of Departure*),[32] who avoid documentary techniques, references to specific events in the Nazi genocide are nonetheless so explicitly detailed that historical assertion and poetic abstraction often clash. It may be excessive to claim that historical reference is *intrinsically* at odds with the poetic evocation of a universal ground of human experience—but the tension between those two impulses is unmistakable in much of the poetry mentioned, where particular moments of history are both intended to be but resist being part of the literary subject.

In the writing of Paul Celan, arguably the preeminent poet for whom the events of the Nazi genocide have been artistically decisive, the terms of this conflict appear with unusual clarity. On the one hand, it seems evident that even if in the reading of his poems all knowledge of Celan's biography were put to one side, his imaginative power and the coercive horror of his subject would be recognized. On the other hand, it is far from certain that if the poems were read under a "veil of ignorance" apart

---

32. Charles Reznikoff, *Holocaust* (Los Angeles: Black Sparrow, 1974); Abraham Sutzkever, *Burnt Pearls: Ghetto Poems*, trans. Seymour Mayne (Ontario: Mosaic Press, 1981); and see also, e.g., his *Fun Drei Velten* (Yiddish), (Buenos Aires: Society of Writers, 1953); William Heyen, *Erika, Poem of the Holocaust* (New York: Vanguard, 1984); Dan Pagis, *Points of Departure*, trans. Stephen Mitchell (Philadelphia: Jewish Publication Society, 1981).

from his biography readers would associate the poems with the subject of the Nazi genocide, or (more strongly) that they would require this association in order to experience the force of the poems. In "Aspen Tree,"[33] for example, Celan provides only two indefinite clues concerning the circumstances of the death of the mother of the person in whose voice the poem is expressed: the reader learns that she was shot and that this occurred in the Ukraine. That the cause of the mother's death is left vague and unstated may itself suggest the role of a large and impersonal force, but there is no more definite indication of what that force was. The brooding sense of loss and emptiness in the speaker's reflections, marked by the aspen tree as an emblem of place, is compelling—but nothing in that impression depends on a specific historical source or reference. (In the best known of his poems associated with the Nazi genocide, "Todesfuge," such references are more explicit—as in the proper names Margarete and Shulamith—but the issue raised here persists even then.)

To be sure, readers of Celan's poems often on their own apply information from his biography and from the context of the Nazi genocide. But in contrast to the group of novels mentioned earlier, for which such authorship by the reader is *required* if the work is to be intelligible, that necessity is less pressing and constant here. The possibility of poetic autonomy in this sense suggests a more general implication: that poetic reference to specific historical settings becomes increasingly attenuated as the text is more fully realized poetically. Is "Aspen Tree" *about* the Nazi genocide? Is it "about" the violent death of the speaker's mother? Is it "about" the enduring shock of loss? Even for texts in literary genres that are more discursive than poetry there is often disagreement in the identification of their subjects and "meanings"; such difficulties are compounded in respect to poetry because of its tendency to dehistoricize even its own quite explicit references. Portraiture is primarily a form of the visual rather than the literary arts, and one reason for this is that, in

33. Paul Celan, *Poems*, trans. Michael Hamburger (New York: Persea, 1980). The text of the poem:

> Aspen tree your leaves glance white into the dark.
> My mother's hair was never white.
>
> Dandelion, so green is the Ukraine.
> My yellow-haired mother did not come home.
>
> Rain cloud, above the well do you hover?
> My quiet mother weeps for everyone.
>
> Round star, you wind the golden loop.
> My mother's heart was ripped by lead.
>
> Oaken door, who lifted you off your hinges?
> My gentle mother cannot return.

contrast to the (specific) person who "sits" for a painter, the literary subject is less easily fixed in one—discursive—place. (To some extent, this resistance affects the reference of visual portraits as well: the "meaning" in 1988 of a Holbein portrait from 1530 has little to do with the person who was, and in a sense remains, its subject.)[34] It is as though the "frames" of poetry, even more than those of painting, sever the historical connections from which the works may set out.

Celan's poetry thus suggests a general paradox for imaginative writing about the Nazi genocide: the more specific and direct the historical address of such writing, the greater the constraints on its literary or poetic character. And conversely: the more consistently figurative or "imaginative" it is, the greater the distance between it and the claims of historical reference or authenticity. In poetry more than in other literary forms, the tension that separates these two impulses is unremitting. Even in his poetry most closely tied to themes of the Nazi genocide, Celan makes the effort to give up one of these in order to realize the other (a tension he himself describes in the account of poetry in his "Meridian" speech).[35] Other poets, such as Sutzkever, Nelly Sachs, and Abba Kovner, who attempt to sustain both impulses, disclose a resultant dissonance in their work—not because of their use of *poetic* figure, but because of the effort to move in two conflicting directions at once. In this sense, poetry reveals more clearly both the occasion and the impossibility of the project undertaken by all the genres of imaginative writing about the Nazi genocide—at once to incorporate and to forego history.

3. The Moral Space of Figurative Discourse

Even if the claim of an unusual role for historical strategies in imaginative writing about the Nazi genocide were accepted, this would not entail the second part of the thesis posed here: that documentary and historical writings about the genocide have been more adequate and more compelling—in sum, more *valuable*—than the imaginative writings about that subject. Indeed, it could be argued that by adopting the strategies of historiography, imaginative writing would combine the

34. On the question of reference in literature and painting, see Joseph Margolis, "Fiction and Existence," in Joseph Margolis (ed.), *The Worlds of Art and the World* (Amsterdam: Rodopi, 1984); Mark Roskill and David Carrier, *Truth and Falsehood in Visual Images* (Amherst, Mass.: University of Massachusetts Press, 1983). This issue is brought out with special force with respect to poetry in a poem by Primo Levi the *title* of which is "For Adolf Eichmann." Primo Levi, *Collected Poems*, trans. Ruth Feldman and Brian Swann (London: Faber & Faber, 1988).

35. "The Meridian," trans. Jerry Glen, *Chicago Review* 29 (1978), 29–41.

strengths of those two forms of discourse. But the second claim here argues the contrary: that the historical emphasis in imaginative writings about the Nazi genocide is symptomatic and confessional—at once reflecting the challenge for literary representation in the moral enormity of that event and conceding the inadequacy for such representation of the means available in figurative discourse. Imaginative writing about the Nazi genocide, in other words, attempts to enlarge on its usual means because, for *that* subject, its conventional resources fail. In this sense, imaginative writing "knows itself"—testifying to this by the impossible ideal it adopts of a form of writing that attempts at one time to be both literary and historical.

At this point, the line of argument in the present discussion becomes theoretical rather than practical, since the question is raised by what has been said so far of what, in literary or figurative discourse, could *account for* its failure—moral and then aesthetic—where a subject such as that of the Nazi genocide is involved. The language of this question is hypothetical: the claim of failure is still based here only on the evidence that imaginative writing about the genocide has insistently drawn on the genres and means of historical discourse. But to ask for an explanation of this emphasis is to raise questions about the nature of imaginative or figurative writing as such: what in that writing, when the subject is the Nazi genocide, would produce a shift to historical conventions? What is it that the one form of discourse lacks or inhibits that the other provides? The answers to these questions suggest that the unusual emphasis that has been noted is not accidental, and also that it is not a consequence only of the choice of the Nazi genocide as a literary subject. Something intrinsic or at least characteristic in the relation between literary and moral categories as that affects the two forms of discourse accounts for the invidious difference between them in this context.

The analysis of figurative discourse required by this account cannot avoid certain general questions of literary theory, but the point should not be lost that it is the exemplification of those questions in writings about the Nazi genocide—and before that, in the event itself—that is most immediately at issue. The evaluative thesis asserted is not meant to prescribe to critical judgment; if critical judgment contradicted the thesis—that is, if the imaginative writings about the Nazi genocide did in fact have a stronger critical basis than the historical writings, or if there were no grounds in critical practice for distinguishing between them—this would obviously count against the thesis. But the evidence points in the other direction, arguing—first from the historical emphasis in the imaginative writings and then from the critical assessment (and comparison) of the two sets of writings—for the privileged position of historical discourse. The need to determine what in the *nature* of figurative discourse explains or justifies this conclusion thus becomes pressing. If no such source can be found, the alleged contrast, if not simply mistaken, would be either accidental or a matter of circumstance. But the thesis here claims a stronger basis for the contrast, one set in the structure of imaginative writing itself. The evidence in this source involves three aspects of that writing; these are considered here under the headings of "literary space," "literary particularity," and "literary abstraction."

(i) *Literary space.* The characteristic use in imaginative writing of figures of speech (such as metaphor or metonymy) and tropes (for example, irony or tragedy) establishes a literary field or space between the writer and his writing and between that writing and what is written "about." Without such a space, the relation between language and what it represents would be unmediated; the event or referent *would be* the word. The term "trope" is itself significant here, since the meaning of "turn" or "turning" imputes to the literary subject a movement in a different direction from the one it would otherwise take. This definition does not imply the priority of literal discourse (that is, figurative language as a deviation from the literal norm); it claims rather that certain structural or functional properties in each of them turn into moral differences.

Defined in this way, the space established in figurative discourse implies that the relation between what is written and what is written "about" is contingent. The figurative turns of language occur in a field of alternative possibilities, and although writers do not exactly choose the figures which appear in their work from a list of alternatives that has been fixed previously, decisions of *some* sort are involved in these formulations—first in the turn to figurative language, and then in specifying the individual figures used (the latter choice, of course, excluding others).

Correspondingly, in order for figurative language to be effective, the reader must both realize that it *is* figurative and grasp what its specific figures are "of." Thus, to understand a metaphor is to recognize that it is meant metaphorically (including the fact that it is not meant literally) as well as to see the "tenor" or point of the individual metaphor. In becoming aware of the space between the metaphor and what it is of—and, by implication of the possibility of alternatives to the metaphor—the reader also acknowledges that it is the writer's decision or intention that takes the discourse in one direction rather than another. The reader thus retraces the "turns" of the writer (not necessarily approvingly: metaphors can be judged more or less adequate), with recognition of the writer's agency a part of the meaning itself. (Such recognition is an obvious requirement in attributions of style; one does not hear references to the "styles" of nature, for example, evidently because nature lacks this agency.)

As figurative discourse is "about" a subject that exists independently of the discourse, then, it purports to add to the subject something that it would otherwise lack. The effect of this supplement, however, does more than only elaborate this "single" subject. The assumption and then the disclosure of alternative ways of representing the subject itself becomes part of the representation. The persona or point of view which shapes the representation, moreover, is added to it as well. Thus, the figurative turn, whatever else it does in bringing the literary subject into view, also impinges on the content of that subject, adding itself and the decisions it presupposes. Why does the writer initiate this turn? How does what is added to it affect or alter the subject? Why does the reader collaborate with the writer in this turn? The moral features of literary space appear in the response to these questions.

(ii) *Literary particularity.* The space opened in figurative discourse between author and text and between the text and its referent begins to be filled in immediately—in the selection of one figure rather than another, and in the choices which constitute that figure. This process differs from the assertion of historical fact because of the framework of alternative possibilities within which the former occurs; the "particularity" of the point of view which expresses itself becomes a feature of the object represented. In some sense, all utterances are perspectival; but figurative discourse is distinctive inasmuch as the pattern of choices constituting it becomes part of its figuration. The reader does not notice or look *at* a metaphor but *by means of* it. The phenomenon of literary style, the combination of consistency and individuality in a writer's choices which make them unmistakably his—is the most substantial evidence for this representation of self as part of the figure. What the literary figure is a figure *of*—its meaning—thus shares in the perspective embodied in the figure itself.

(iii) *Literary abstraction.* In the same movement by which the clearing of figurative space provides a means for individuation, it also initiates a reaction against—or more precisely, beyond—that constraint. The turn of a literary figure occurs within a field of alternative possibilities, and the relation of the figure chosen to these possibilities has a generalizing effect. This effect is familiar from the role of more tangible framing devices: they focus attention on a subject by distancing it from its context, at once singling it out and bracketing its singularity. Figurative discourse "estranges" the subject of representation—and with this separation, a process of generalization begins which resembles in its form the movement toward universalization ascribed to poetry as Aristotle distinguishes it from history. In historical discourse, the references asserted preclude or at least defer generalization; by contrast, the alternative possibilities of poetry are constantly present (even after they are rejected). In figurative discourse, together with the distance between the figure chosen and its referent, there is set in motion a process of inference and generalization which becomes itself part of the text. This does not mean that "humankind" or "man in general" are simply to be substituted as a common subject for all figurative discourse—but this implication exerts pressure wherever a figurative space is established.

Although not always in the terms cited, these three "conditions" of figurative writing have often been acknowledged in formulations of the distinction between figurative and historical discourse.[36] They warrant a fuller exposition than is provided here, but even this brief formulation discloses a ground for the invidious distinction between imaginative writings with the Nazi genocide against the Jews as their subject and writings about that subject which are historical and nonfigurative. If, as the discussion in chapter 1 claimed, the act of genocide is directed against individuals who do not motivate that act *as* individuals, and if the evil represented by genocide also reflects a deliberate intent for evil in principle—in conceptualizing the group and in deciding to annihilate it—then, the intrinsic limitations of figurative discourse for the representation of genocide come into view. On the account given, imaginative representation would personalize even events that are impersonal and corporate; it would dehistoricize and generalize events that occur specifically and contingently. And the unavoidable dissonance here is evident. For a subject which historically combines the features of impersonality with a challenge to the conception of moral boundaries, the attempt to personalize it—or, for that matter, only to *add* to it—appears at once gratuitous and inconsistent, gratuitous because it individualizes where the subject by its nature is corporate; inconsistent because it sets limits when the subject itself has denied them. The effect of the addition is then

36. See, e.g., Kenneth Burke, *The Philosophy of Literary Form* (Berkeley: University of California Press, 1973); Northrop Frye, *Anatomy of Criticism* (Princeton, N.J.: Princeton University Press, 1957), *The Critical Path: An Essay on the Social Context of Literary Criticism* (Bloomington, Ind.: Indiana University Press, 1971); Frederic Jameson, *The Prison-House of Language* (Princeton, N.J.: Princeton University Press, 1972); Louis O. Mink, *Historical Understanding* (Ithaca, N.Y: Cornell University Press, 1987).

to misrepresent the subject and thus—where the aspects misrepresented are essential—to diminish it. In asserting the possibility of alternative figurative perspectives, furthermore, the writer asserts the process of representation and his own persona as elements of the representation— a further diminution of what, for a subject such as the Nazi genocide, is its essential core; beside it, an individual "perspective" is at most irrelevant. For certain subjects, it seems, their significance may be too broad or deep to be chanced by an individual point of view, morally more compelling—and actual—than the concept of possibility can sustain. Under this pressure, the presumption of illumination usually conceded to the act of writing (*any* writing) begins to lose its force.

These moral consequences appear concretely in the figurative process itself. As figuration imposes a particularized point of view, not only what is seen by way of the latter but its status *as* a point of view constitutes a theme. The discourse, in other words, is personalized; the writer obtrudes. And whatever the writer's motives, certain consequences of this obtrusion are unavoidable. The features of the literary subject, then, are heard, filtered through the writer's voice, with the personalization of perspective and the emphasis on the *means* of expression that this involves. When a literary subject is open to articulation of this sort—as in lyric poetry, where the subject is characteristically personal and emotive—then to shape it perspectivally by means of an authorial point of view may disclose features visible only by that means. But where impersonality and abstractness are essential features of the subject, as in the subject of the Nazi genocide, then a literary focus on individuation and agency "contradicts" the subject itself—a literary equivalent to logical inconsistency revealed through a disproportion in the moral correlatives mentioned earlier. Sentimentality or bathos, it has often been pointed out, are persistent failings in many of the novels and poems on the subject of the Nazi genocide. And understandable as the causes may be for the occurrence of such disproportions between feeling and fact where that subject is concerned, the failings are nonetheless accountable, both morally and literarily.

Even if such failings reflect mainly personal traits of particular authors, this would not be irrelevant. Egoism or vanity in individual character as they disclose themselves in the expressive means of writing will, for *some* subjects, constitute a literary and moral violation. The author's obtrusion, moreover, brings to a point the other effects of figuration that have been mentioned. Since by that obtrusion the subject is personalized, stylized—*figured*—the implication is unavoidable of a subject that could be represented in many different ways and that thus has no necessary and perhaps not even an actual basis. The figurative assertion of alternative possibilities, in other words, suggests a denial of limitation: *no* possibilities are excluded. And although for some literary subjects openness of this sort may be warranted or even desirable, for others it represents a falsification, morally *and* conceptually.

Another version of these same objections derives more immediately from "literary abstraction"—the process of generalization set in motion by the act of figuration. Where the specific historical character of a subject is crucial, the consequence of abstracting from that particularity—in the example at issue here, by representing the Nazi genocide as an instance of evil in general—is to distort the subject. The intrinsic connection of imaginative writing to generalization, in other words, raises a moral issue, since not every subject can be treated in this way. The playgoer who jumps onto the stage to rescue a threatened victim in a play has mistaken art for history: dramatic characters are *meant* to stand for something more and other than themselves, and this is a function of literary structure fixed in the terms of art itself. And just as the process of literary inference may be falsified by the playgoer who mistakes art's generalization in a single character, so the more extensive turn of history into art may be falsified as the generalized framework of art is imposed on the particular moments of history. To be sure, each individual or group in the nonliterary origins of a literary subject will in some sense be singular. But not every individual or group is assigned a role or fate historically *because* of that specification. This is, again, a distinctive mark of the process and then of the representation of genocide. Thus, the means of literary representation which can for some subjects generalize from specific cases without distortion are for other subjects open to exactly that charge.

To be sure, any representation of evil may understandably evoke general reflections on its nature. Certain figurative representations of individual evildoing, moreover, are aesthetically as well as morally compelling (so, again, Iago or Satan). But in these generalized representations, too, evil appears as the purpose and idea of an individual imagination or will; and rare as the evidence is for willed evil of this sort, it is still more difficult to find literary representations of evil for which a *collective* will is responsible. Literary agency is characteristically individual; thus, where what is crucial in the literary subject is the impersonality of its causes and reasons, to aestheticize or individualize those sources is to falsify or misrepresent the subject. For the reasons given, in respect to the relation between figurative discourse and its subject, the representation of a particular historical event in literary or figurative terms is intrinsically open to moral judgment; the impulse to overcome or at least to extend history in figurative discourse requires a warrant. And if this is a general condition to be met by the process of literary representation, imaginative writing about the events of the Nazi genocide faces the added difficulty of the "antirepresentational" features of those events themselves.

These antirepresentational features include a number of elements in the historical character of that literary subject. One important such element appears in the agency that shapes literary plot in narrative fiction and drama. The movement of narrative form is sustained by the motivation of the agents who appear within it—not only for what they do in the text, but for their "prehistory," what they have been or done at the point where the text begins. Thus, fictional narratives are judged at least minimally by criteria of plausibility and consistency—both of these criteria based on extraliterary evidence of human motives and conduct. Narrative representation thus presupposes individual agency prior to as well as within the representation. The importance of such agency is evident in the scarcity of texts from which it is absent. There are, for example, no literary representations "about" madness except where madness is set in a more basic framework of rationality and choice; in animal fables and allegories, the thematic basis is in the end human, and there are no "animal" novels or plays—because the freedom necessary for literary agency would be missing here.

This requirement of human agency cannot be met in writings about the Nazi genocide for the reasons that have been mentioned. The Jews were the victims in that process not because of anything they did individually, nor was it in their power, in terms of the act of genocide, to affect the future prescribed for them. To sublimate *this* basis into the individual agency required for narrative plot and character is to introduce a fundamental distortion: it is not the presumptive knowledge on which literary representation can base a narrative. Admittedly, in historical terms, as the victims of the genocide were faced by its imminence they could (and did) respond individually; it can be argued that at *that* point, they became agents who then, in historical fact and potentially in literary representation, could motivate narrative structures. In one sense, moreover, writing always starts in medias res: something will always have happened before a literary narrative begins. Thus, it could be held that the fact of the genocide may appear as a "given" in the development of literary plot—and the preceding section of this chapter refers to a number of writers who rely heavily on this assumption in order to avoid a direct representation of the causality involved in their own narratives.

The literary subject in this case, however, is closely tied to—depends on—the historical subject, and this relation holds also for what "happens" before the literary plot begins. Here, too, then, writing about the

Nazi genocide confronts the events of the genocide itself, in which individual agency, on one side at least, had no essential role. The Jews did not become victims as a consequence of their own decisions or choices. They were the objects—not the subjects—of genocide, and this means that in narrative fiction about the Nazi genocide, no literary basis is available for that one principal source of the discourse. In this respect, imaginative writing about the Nazi genocide is intrinsically arbitrary—since its starting point has no basis in even a marginally free definition of self by its main protagonists and only as much to do even with the Nazis as the choice of "principled" and impersonal evil can provide in the way of specific motivation. Admittedly, writers of fiction *and* of history have sometimes held that the role of victim is essential to the Jews in their history, or that the Jews were responsible either by collective action or by innate disposition for the decree of genocide against them. But even if such claims could avoid the charge of *literary* arbitrariness, the distortions they impose on the historical ground reappear in the literary representation. The requirements of consistency and coherence do not begin with literary representation; they hold there because they hold before that, at the point where history and literary representation meet.

To find agency in the role of the perpetrator in imaginative narratives of the Nazi genocide, moreover, is hardly a lesser problem than to find it in the role of the victim. To be sure, the motives historically of individual Nazis varied, and such differences might reappear literarily in their translation into imaginative characters. But if, as has been argued here, the Nazi genocide involves a knowing commitment to evil in principle beyond the psychological motives of its individual agents, the difficulties of literary representation will also be encountered there. Few literary characters choose evil for its own sake, and those few invariably have a mythological aura about them (again, as in Milton's Satan). The reasons for this are historical even more fundamentally than they are literary. What stories *could* be told of a person whose identity, whether in the representation or before it, was so constant as to suggest that no choice or decision had motivated them? And then, also historically, even the most infamous villains have tried to see themselves as acting on the basis of justified reason and purpose that by their own standards account for their actions. When the commitment to evil in principle is set in a network of bureaucratic and technological causality which further diffuses the role of individual agency, the options of literary representation are proportionately limited. One of the few and still among the most compelling representations of the Nazi as malefactor is that of Hannah Arendt's Eichmann—in what is an historical rather than a fictional work, and in which the claim is made for the "banal," not the radical or deliberate nature of his evil. Here, again, historical representation, which is not dependent on a role of subjective agency, is at once better able than figurative discourse—and more likely to try—to convey the features of the Nazi genocide.

Outlined in these theoretical terms, the failings ascribed to figurative discourse may seem a priori, oblivious to individual instances, actual or possible, of imaginative writing about the Nazi genocide. Furthermore, the differences in quality evident among various writings on the Nazi genocide indicate that the limitations that have been asserted here affect some of those writings less than others: here, too, the differences are quite real. But the evaluative thesis that has been posed does not deny the *possibility* of literary (and now moral) value in such works. It argues on grounds at once of practice and principle (in any event, not a priori) that the emphasis on historical authenticity among writings on the Nazi genocide has a basis in literary structure itself; thus, that for such writing, the risks—conceptual, moral, literary—increase in proportion to the distance the writing moves from that ideal. The logical implication of this view is that *no* imaginative representation of the Nazi genocide escapes these risks or the likelihood of failure, no matter how original or compelling it otherwise is. That there are valuable literary works on that subject does not mean that they are counterexamples; an alternative conclusion would view them as standing at one end of a continuum, with the shadow of moral liability cast over them as well; part of what they disclose is the contingency, even the arbitrariness of their achievement.

The general principle to which this conclusion is related extends well beyond the conclusion itself. When Hegel, early in the nineteenth century, heralded the "death" of art, he did this in the name of reason, as reason had allegedly caused and then marked art's passing. However that particular verdict is otherwise judged, it has the important consequence of identifying art as itself an historical phenomenon, dependent on contingencies not only at specific moments but in the whole of its history as well. The constraints on figurative discourse that have been identified make a less extensive but related claim: that for a particular literary subject, figurative discourse may not be the most adequate medium, indeed that it may not be adequate at all. Once this issue—the question of what *can* be represented imaginatively or literarily—is admitted, then the systematic framework of the discussion has at least a ground. This is itself a large step conceptually, since it precludes the more common view that offers a blanket endorsement to all subjects not only as literarily possible but as *equally* possible.

Especially in the light of these last comments, it can be argued that what turns out to be at issue here is, as Plato had asserted, the moral justification for literature or art as such, not for imaginative writings about a single subject, even one as morally charged as the Nazi genocide. Undoubtedly, this more general issue is affected by the thesis that has been posed, but the immediate implications of this relation bear on the consideration of writing about the Nazi genocide more than on the general issue. The implication recurs here, too, that the analysis of this morally extreme situation, far from leading to anomalous conclusions, discloses significant aspects of common experience and understanding. If genocide is distinctive among acts that are open to moral judgment— that is, with conditions of impersonality in the object and the will for evil in principle on the part of the agent—then, the claim has been made, figurative representation of that event will diminish the moral understanding of those events, not as it happens or for certain representations, but intrinsically. This same balance (more precisely, imbalance) may not affect every such instance of literary representation; still more evidently, it may not affect them all equally. On the other hand, the constraints on figurative discourse that have been alleged have at least one more inclusive implication: that in the relation between representation and its subject, the question of the moral status of literary form becomes unavoidable. As literary representation mediates between a subject and its reader, the process of representation becomes morally accountable in its consequences for each of them—and the imaginative writings of the Nazi genocide provide an unusual view of what is at stake in those relations.

4. Writing Against Silence

The discussion of the differences—conceptual, literary, moral—between imaginative and historical writing about the Nazi genocide has not addressed the more sweeping objection against *all* writing about the subject that motivates the "boundary question" referred to earlier. In most of its appearance this objection is conceptual rather than moral, asserting that the phenomenon of the Nazi genocide is beyond the grasp of human understanding, defying comprehension; the conclusion follows that *all* representation of those events, by the historian no less than the novelist, will fail. The indictment, then, does not question the intentions that underlie writing, nor is it based on limitations in the specific medium of literary representation. It is the opacity of the subject itself that is asserted, its inaccessibility either to reason or to the imagination. Even literary representations that acknowledge this constraint as part of their representation would not escape it; those that purport to overcome it would, in addition to exhibiting the limitation, be guilty of falsification. Imaginative writings with these failings, however, would not differ from texts in other kinds of writing, including that of history; on this account, the failure of representation is due not to the relation between a particular form of discourse and its subject but to the nature of the subject, which would be common to all such forms.

It will be recognized that the description of an event as incomprehensible or inexplicable is often itself a figure of speech; the aporia, an extreme instance of hyperbole, asserts just this—that words cannot convey or encompass a given subject.[37] Since the grasp of language normally extends wherever experience does, to claim of an event by this means that it defies language and understanding is meant to attest to its extraordinary nature, and this purpose has been evident in many references to the incomprehensibility of the Nazi genocide. But these claims themselves often appear as part of accounts that go on to speak in detail about aspects of the Nazi genocide. This is evidence, apparently, of the figurative purpose of such statements; at least *something* in their subject, we infer, is comprehensible and available for representation.

This does not mean, of course, that all assertions of the ineffability of the events of the Nazi genocide are figurative. Its context makes clear, for example, that George Steiner's statement that "the world of Auschwitz lies outside speech as it lies outside reason"[38] was intended literally (although Steiner subsequently modified this claim). But even such literal references have room for significant differences in meaning. So, for instance, when Raul Hilberg, the author of what remains the single most important study of the Nazi genocide, speaks of the "historical incomprehensibility" of that event, he takes this to mean that there were no sufficient reasons, in terms of *rational self-interest,* for the decisions and actions of the Nazis resulting in the Final Solution.[39] Since reasons of this sort are in his view required for historical understanding, the Nazi genocide against the Jews is in this sense inexplicable—although that does not mean that *other* forms of explanation (for example, psychological or economic) are not relevant.

A different but also literal meaning of the claim of incomprehensibility appears in religious or theological analysis; here the Nazi genocide is viewed in the context of the problem of the existence of evil in a world ordered by a just and omnipotent God—with the question formulated once again as "How was it possible?" In this context, the claim of incomprehensibility is interpreted to mean that the events of the gen-

37. See Arthur Quinn, *Figures of Speech* (Salt Lake City: Gibbs M. Smith, 1982), 36.
38. George Steiner, *Language and Silence* (New York: Atheneum, 1966), 123.
39. Raul Hilberg, "Concluding Discussion," in Lang, *Writing* (see chap. 2, n. 8), 274.

ocide are humanly unintelligible, although this conclusion would not be true—could not be true—within the larger framework of a divine will or understanding. (When the thesis of theodicy is extended to its logical conclusion, the phenomenon of the genocide becomes not only intelligible, but warranted—an inference that then raises its own problems for these authors.) On the more restricted issue of representation, however, the consequences of the literal claim of incomprehensibility are evident, pointing to the human inadequacy of the writer (and reader), not to an intrinsic opacity in the subject or any related inadequacy in the means of representation.[40] The events of the genocide are *humanly* incomprehensible (and thus ineffable), although this would not be true—could not be true—from the perspective of divine understanding.

The thesis that has been proposed concerning the limitations of imaginative writing about the Nazi genocide is not, however, tied in fact or principle to any more general claim of incomprehensibility or ineffability. The limitations described are associated with the forms of imaginative representation, and even then not equally among them. It may be, as certain theorists have proposed recently, that a characteristic distance and loss separates all literary representation from whatever that representation is "of," that language is always underdetermined. It is obvious, quite apart from this theory of language, that discourse is not *identical* with its subject. But general claims of incomprehensibility have no special bearing on any particular subject of discourse, and it is the distance between discourse and subject, addressed to the connection between ethical content and literary form in the subject of the Nazi genocide, that has been the focus of the discussion here. Admittedly, if, as in the Platonic view examined in chapter 2, evil as such is unintelligible and consequently incapable of representation, then all attempts to write about the Nazi genocide would be bound to fail. But there would then be nothing exceptional about that particular subject. In any event, the discussion in chapter 2 disputed the Platonic view—largely on the basis of evidence disclosed in the events of the Nazi genocide itself. Insofar as the view that evil as such is inexplicable is rejected, furthermore, the inadequacy of certain forms or instances of the representation of evil will be due to their specific features—in the subject or in the means or in the relation between them.

At least two questions crucial to the thesis proposed have so far been unmentioned. The first of these concerns the fact of imaginative writing

40. See, e.g., Eliezer Berkowitz, *Faith after the Holocaust* (New York: Ktav, 1973); Emil L. Fackenheim, *The Jewish Return into History* (New York: Schocken, 1978); Elizabeth Schussler Fiorenza and David Tracy (eds.), *The Holocaust as Interruption* (Edinburgh: T. & T. Clark, 1984).

about the Nazi genocide; that is, the widespread attention given to this writing by diverse audiences. Why, if the thesis asserted is warranted, should this active response to imaginative writings with the Nazi genocide as their subject not have been muted? (It is indisputable, moreover, that these writings have had wider currency than "historical" texts.) The second question addresses the logical basis of the thesis, specifically the distinction it assumes between "imaginative" and "historical" writing. It can reasonably be asked if historical discourse itself is not also imaginative. Does it not make use of the same figurative turns attributed to imaginative literature? Certainly there is strong evidence of the role of narrative structures and figurative discourse in historical writing—and this evidence only supplements the more basic fact that alternative historical versions invariably appear of the "same" event. Do not the objections that have been directed here at novels or the drama or poetry about the Nazi genocide hold with equal force against historical writing?

The first of these questions echoes a larger one that asks what it is in imaginative literature in general that draws readers to it. This is not the place to consider that question, however, except insofar as it bears immediately on the writing about the Nazi genocide. Admittedly, certain justifications have been given of a "Holocaust literature" which follow from a more general view of the significance of literature as such. But it is worth noting that these justifications, as they apply specifically to imaginative writings about the Nazi genocide, conclude precisely at the point where the objections that have been raised against such writings begin. So, for example, Lawrence Langer finds in the "art of atrocity" the value of creating "an imaginative reality possessing an autonomous dignity and form" that discloses perceptions about the "literal" world "which the mind ordinarily ignores or would like to avoid."[41] And Leslie Epstein finds in this writing an ability "to create a bond, a sense of connectedness between the reader and every aspect of the world that has been salvaged through imagination"; he remarks a "peculiar sense of responsibility" that the novelist, rather than the historian or theologian can instill.[42]

Neither of these statements implies that the novelist writing about the Nazi genocide uncovers new facts or information about its causes and means. Langer refers to the role of "perceptions"—what the writer calls attention to in his own response that others do not see (at least until

41. Lawrence Langer, *The Holocaust and the Literary Imagination* (New Haven: University Press, 1975), 30.
42. Epstein, "Writing about the Holocaust" (see n. 23), 264.

the writer shows the way); and Epstein emphasizes the possibility of a shared consciousness or identity, which historical discourse would supposedly impede. Both these views reflect more general theories of the capacity of literature to affect its readers, and as was suggested earlier in this chapter, those theories themselves are open to question. But a more immediate difficulty faces the proposals by Langer and Epstein, inasmuch as the literary features which they stress might be judged liabilities where the subject of the Nazi genocide is concerned—not, as they would have it, positive achievements. It might be acknowledged, for example, that imaginative literature in general provides access to aspects of experience that readers might otherwise avoid or find blocked off. So, for example, the representation of human motivation is sustained in imaginative writing to an extent not usually found in other writing, and the explanation for this appears in the requirements of literature itself. Because of the requirement of continuity in the lives of their characters, authors of imaginative literature follow the sequences of psychological cause and effect more closely than the historian does (or could) and do so whether historical evidence exists or not.

That this aspect of literary representation tends to draw readers, however, does not ensure that the grounds of the attraction are themselves always warranted—and indeed, a conclusion opposite to the one reached by Langer and Epstein might be inferred as it bears on the specific subject of the Nazi genocide. It is precisely the individual consciousness that is denied in the act or idea of genocide—and the imposition of a representation of agency on that subject, involving also the persona of the author, conduces to a distortion that is both conceptual and moral. It is not only that in much quasi-historical fiction about the Nazi genocide, conversations or other evidence of individual motivation and character are "made up" in order to create a narrative where, given the absence of historical evidence, there would be only a chronicle (so, for example, in Steiner's *Treblinka* and Keneally's *Schindler's List*)—but that the literary role of subjectivity as such is arguably misplaced here, as the basis of what the representation is "of." This is, it seems, the more general implication of Adorno's comment specifically directed against the literary representation of fascism: "The impossibility of portraying fascism springs from the fact that in it . . . subjective freedom no longer exists. Total unfreedom can be recognized, but not represented."[43] What is crucial here is not that among fictional recreations of the genocide *particular*

43. Theodor Adorno, *Minima Moralia*, trans. E. F. N. Jephcott (London: NLB, 1974), 144.

descriptions or statements can be shown to be unverifiable or false—although this is often the case and is disruptive when it occurs.[44] The more basic issues are literary and moral, not simply historical: that imaginative literature presupposes individuality and subjectivity in the representation of its characters and their actions, and that to represent certain literary subjects in those terms is a falsification. This does not mean that such representations are impossible; but it does mean that the moral strain within the literary subject, and between it and the historical subject, will disclose itself in the process of representation.

To be sure, the possibility always exists of literary and moral genius that may transcend these or any other supposedly intrinsic limitations. The history of literature provides notable examples of such accomplishment, and although even the most important writings on the Nazi genocide arguably fall short of this standard, they may nonetheless seem to overcome the limitations asserted here in the form of a general rule. To grant this possibility for figures like Celan, Borowski, or Appelfeld, however, need not undermine the main point of the thesis proposed. For there is no contradiction between conceding the possibility of literary significance and yet maintaining that no writer is immune to the moral and literary risks incurred when the subject of his writing is the Nazi genocide. The question remains to what extent writers are able to avoid these dangers, with the presumption that at best they will not escape entirely and that even insofar as they do the writings have to be read as a response to those dangers.

The second question mentioned at the beginning of this section concerns the privileged position that has been asserted here for historical writing relative to imaginative or figurative writing. This claim is based on the evidence that the potentiality of figurative discourse is limited where certain subjects or themes are concerned. But this assertion does not show that historical writing escapes the same objections. Without such evidence, which would have to demonstrate that historical writing is nonfigurative in at least some essential aspect of its composition, recent analyses of historical discourse which find in it a fundamental role for narrative—and thus literary—structure would hold.[45] The com-

44. Although criticism at this level also runs the risk of overliteralism; so, for example, Alvin Rosenfeld's objection to George Steiner's *The Portage of A. H. to San Cristobal:* "Why end it all . . . with Hitler's speech? Why give Hitler the last word?" (*Imagining Hitler* [Bloomington, Ind.: Indiana University Press, 1985], 98).

45. See Hayden White, *The Contents of the Form* (Baltimore, Md.: Johns Hopkins Press, 1987); Mink, "History and Fiction as Modes of Comprehension," in *Historical Understanding* (see n. 36).

bination of moral and literary failure that, according to the thesis presented here, affects imaginative writing about the Nazi genocide would thus, for the same reasons, also apply to historical discourse.

There is a difference, however, between acknowledging that historical representation makes use of narrative and figurative means and asserting the stronger thesis that historical discourse, like the genres of imaginative literature, is essentially dependent on those means. It is in rejecting the latter characterization of historical discourse that the contrast between imaginative and historical discourse emerges here—and it is the *fact* of the events of the Nazi genocide that serves (here, but also for the more general principle) as a basis for the contrast. It may be true that there are no "bare"—that is, without the means of representation—historical facts; and it may also be that there is no writing (historical or imaginative) that does not in principle engender what has been referred to here as figurative space. But neither of these possibilities denies the possibility of representation that stands in a direct relation to its object—in effect, if not in principle, immediate and unaltered. It is *this* possibility that stands at the crux of the distinction between historical and figurative discourse.

The evidence for this last claim might draw on a number of sources, but for the discussion here, only one is necessary: the *fact* of the Nazi genocide itself. Here, if anywhere, the difference between assertion and denial—on a different axis, between history and figuration—is clear, not only epistemically, but morally. To reject at this juncture the sharp distinction between historical and figurative discourse is, among its implications, to propose that reference to the Nazi genocide against the Jews is one of a number of possible figurative descriptions of a "fact" that does not exist outside such descriptions—or, more radically, to assert the possibility that the genocide did not occur, that it was not, is not a fact. Such implications hardly require elaboration; it seems clear that the existence of facts as such, the very possibility of knowledge, is at stake here. The enormity of denying the occurrence of the Nazi genocide is proportionate to the enormity of the occurrence itself; recognition of this proportion thus becomes itself part of the distinction between historical and figurative discourse proposed in this account.

This last claim does not mean that the occurrence of the Nazi genocide *cannot* be denied, and a number of writers, often grouped under the title of "revisionists," have done just this.[46] In one sense, this denial

46. The most widely known among these works include Arthur R. Butz, *The Hoax of the Twentieth Century* (Torrance, Calif.: Noontide Press, 1977); Robert Faurisson, *Mémoir en defense: Contre ceux qui m'accusent de falsifier l'histoire* (Paris: La Vieille Taupe, 1980)— this volume includes a supportive introduction by Noam Chomsky; Paul Rassinier, *Le*

is insignificant: it has not gained many or very credible supporters, least of all among historians. But in the context of the discussion here, the denial is important for reasons that extend beyond the premises of methodological skepticism that can be used to question *any* historical claim— the contentions, for example, that "facts" have social or ideological origins, or that alternative descriptions are almost always possible for a single group of data. So far as concerns these issues, a denial of the occurrence of the Nazi genocide is no different than the rejection of any other generally accepted historical claim. But that denial *is* different, with the difference related to the moral significance of the fact of the genocide (and then also of its denial). What alters the balance here is not that the empirical evidence is so much fuller or more compelling for the occurrence of the Nazi genocide than for any other historical event, but that the consequences of the affirmation or denial of the claim of its occurrence add *their* weight to the evidence itself. On these grounds, it is no exaggeration to hold that to deny the occurrence of the genocide is in effect to deny the existence of facts—and, to that extent, of history.

It was evidently this consideration that stood behind the statement published by a group of thirty-four French historians in response to the revisionist claim—the latter epitomized for them by the denial that the gas chambers in the death camps did, or even could have been responsible for, the killings associated with them. After providing a brief outline of the historical unfolding of the "Final Solution," the historians direct their conclusion against the revisionists:

Everyone is free to interpret a phenomenon like the Hitlerian genocide according to his philosophy. . . . Everyone is free to apply to it one or another means of explication; everyone is free, up to the limit, to imagine or to dream that these monstrous facts did not take place. They unfortunately did take place, and no one can deny their existence without outrage to the truth. The question should not be raised of how, *technically,* such mass murder could have been plausible. It was technically possible because it indeed took place. This is the obligatory starting point of any historical inquiry on the subject. . . . It is impossible to have a debate on the existence of the gas chambers.[47]

The statement points to the basis for joining the moral and epistemic features in the revisionist denial. If ever there was a "literal" fact—be-

Drame des juifs européens (Paris: Les Sept Couleurs, 1964); and Serge Thion, *Vérité historique ou vérité politique?* (Paris: La Vieille Taupe, 1980). See also the analyses of the revisionists by Nadine Fresco, "The Denial of the Dead: On the Faurisson Affair," *Dissent,* 1981, 467–83; and Pierre Vidal-Naquet, *Les Juifs, la mémoire et le présent* (Paris: Maspero, 1981).

47. *Le Monde,* 21 February 1979, 23 (B. L.'s translation).

yond the possibility of alternative formulations, among which reversal or denial must always be one—it is here, in the act and idea of the Nazi genocide; and if the moral implication of the role of facts needed proof, it is also to be found here, again in the phenomenon of the Nazi genocide. Denial here traduces not only one truth, but the possibility of truth as such—an "impossible" debate. It is ultimately *this* necessity, then, that grounds the distinction between historical and figurative discourse—and then also the claim derived from that distinction of the failings in imaginative representations of the Nazi genocide. However it may be conceived beyond that point, the fact of the Nazi genocide is a crux that separates historical discourse from the process of imaginative representation and its figurative space, perhaps not uniquely, but as surely as any fact might be required or able to.

The privileged position of historical discourse in this distinction does not extend to other forms of critical or theoretical discourse; for example, to writing in the social sciences or philosophy. Some accounts of these other forms hold that they too are nonfigurative, unmediated in their representations of facts. But even aside from the question of whether this claim can be demonstrated (it may itself be figurative), those forms of discourse disclose at least one characteristic that was judged also in the imaginative writings about the genocide to distort its subject. This feature is the process of universalization, which is more commonly associated with theoretical inquiry than with literary expression. The dominant explanatory ideal in the social sciences proposes a general understanding of the aspects of behavior studied—an understanding that can be translated from one context to another or at the very least be placed in a general schema of culture and human conduct. The concern with even the most specific evidence, then, is a concern with its generalizable features, which, systematically, are prior to the evidence itself.

This subordination of the particular to the universal which characterizes theoretical discourse is usually effected as though the subject "theorized" made no difference to the process—as though *any* subject could be addressed in this way. But this contention seems false in general, and specific examples in writings about the Nazi genocide demonstrate its failure at least where *that* subject is concerned. So, for example, in *The Informed Heart,* Bruno Bettelheim examines the patterns of responses among concentration-camp captives in terms of Freudian psychology.[48]

48. Bruno Bettelheim, *The Informed Heart: Autonomy in a Mass Age* (Glencoe, Ill.: Free Press, 1960). The method criticized leads elsewhere to an even more startling response to the evidence of the Holocaust: "Because of the nature of the psychoanalytic process, with its focus on libidinal and aggressive drives, psychoanalysts are in a unique position to guide the way in our attempt to master our enormous destructive potential, that is, the exacer-

Against that background, Bettelheim asserts, a close likeness appears between the identities that concentration-camp captives took on and the reversion to infantile behavior in a standard form of neurosis. Those who escaped this reversion, Bettelheim contends, were enabled to do so first by achieving an understanding of the pressures exerted on them, and then by opposing it on the basis of that understanding—by the "informed heart." The criticism to which this analysis seemed open is not that its instantiation of behavior in the concentration camps under a general theory could not lead to conclusions that might then be confirmed but that even if it did, the cogency of those conclusions would in effect be accidental. The imposition of a theory requires the translation into its own terms of the evidence—that evidence for which it has no categories of its own as well as that for which it has. In this sense, theory dictates rather than discovers what is then formulated in its own conclusions. When in criticizing Bettelheim Terrence Des Pres calls attention to the role in the camps of altruism and cooperation which Bettelheim does not mention, then, his objection is not that Bettelheim's account is insufficiently general but that the form or structure of the analysis itself is problematic, that theory, in this sense, suffers from an intrinsic "blindness."[49]

Again, writing on a different aspect of experience in the camps, Richard Rubenstein applies the motif of the "death of God" to the possibility of religious belief "after Auschwitz."[50] In thus linking the refutation of religious commitment to the occurrence of the Nazi genocide, Rubenstein subsumes the individuality of that event under a general abstraction. History is here dramatized and universalized; the Nazi genocide is made not individual but unique. Like all other such claims, the underlying rationale requires the denial of individuality in order (ostensibly) to emphasize it. So far as the occurrence of evil is a test of the existence of God, the Nazi genocide does not differ from an indefinite number of other historical occurrences of evil, most of them much slighter instances than the genocide. Again, Rubenstein's denial of this is the consequence of a method rather than of a failure to consider specific items of evidence.

These individual examples underscore the vulnerability of representations of the Nazi genocide to the distortion of generalization. Such

bated and unrelieved urge for violence." (Steven A. Luel and Paul Marcus [eds.], *Psychoanalytic Reflections on the Holocaust* [New York: Ktav, 1984, 5.)

49. Terrence Des Pres, *The Survivor: An Anatomy of Life in the Death Camps* (New York: Oxford University Press, 1976).

50. Richard Rubenstein, *After Auschwitz: Radical Theology and Contemporary Judaism* (Indianapolis, Ind.: Bobbs-Merrill, 1966).

theories as they preclude the possibility of disconfirmation, deny the
particularity even of the evidence of which they are purportedly representations. This feature of theoretical explanation does not pose difficulties when what is "theorized" is not singular to begin with; indeed, gen-
eralizability in this sense is a basic presupposition in the natural sciences.
But where particularity is an essential feature of a subject, the very concept of "explanation in general" comes into question—and it is also at
this point that practical judgment diverges from theoretical judgment.
Practical judgment—an inference leading to moral prescription and
act—differs from theoretical judgment precisely on the ideal of universalization. It is the particularity of a decision or event that is the focus of
practical judgment; the historically contingent features in the subject of
moral discourse—the fact that any judgment about it is tied to an historical context—mean that the attempt to universalize those features also
empties them of content. That theoretical or universal assertions can be
abstracted from features of the Nazi genocide is not inconsistent with
the conclusion that such assertions remain morally inadequate to that
subject; they are as remote as the physiological composition of a human
being is from his personality or moral character.

These last comments complete a full turn back to the issue of writing
itself as an occasion of moral judgment. Once writing is viewed as an act,
to be judged for what it "does" to its subject and to its readers, then the
enormity of the Nazi genocide in its historical or nonliterary character
necessarily affects—enlarges—the risks incurred in its literary representation. The judgment of literary representation depends, moreover, not
only on its treatment of its subject, but on the alternatives from among
which that one "act" was chosen and which might, in the critic's view,
have included another one that was preferable. The most radical alternative to any particular representation of the Nazi genocide is not a
different or contradictory one—but the possibility of not having written
at all; that is, the writer's decision for silence. And this then provides a
minimal but decisive standard by which all writing about the Nazi genocide can and ought to be judged, a standard that poses itself in the form
of a question: Would silence not have been preferable, more valuable,
than what was written? No writer could dispute the point of this question: in it, the stakes of writing are made proportionate to the weight of
its subject.

Admittedly, this standard in a more general form is applicable to *all*
writing. But for most literary subjects, a prima-facie presumption favors
what might be contributed by its representation; it is the moral consequence of an event such as the Nazi genocide that opens this prima-facie
presumption to question. The test of silence as an alternative, it should

be noted, does not measure writing simply by an absence or denial of value. Silence may also "speak"; because of what silence both does and does not say, it is turned to as a means for honoring or commemorating the dead. This ritual use makes silence a still more compelling standard of judgment for writings about the Nazi genocide; they are always to be judged as having displaced the value of silence.

When religious writers refer to the nature or will of God as incomprehensible or ineffable, this is mainly an assertion of conceptual inadequacy, attesting to the difficulty of representing God in human thought or language. The theological traditions have made unusual efforts to show how deep-seated these constraints are; for example, Maimonides turns to the language of "negative theology" (what God is *not*), and Thomas, to the language of analogy: we can speak only of what god is *like*. But the dissonance in the relation between the events of the Nazi genocide against the Jews and the writing about them is not conceptual, but moral. In terms only of historical complexity, the Nazi genocide does not differ quantitatively from other large-scale events involving many countries and masses of people. Its difference is in the phenomenon of genocide—a difference reflected in the dissonance which appears when the act of writing is judged in terms of what it does to its readers, and together with that, of what it does to its subject—that is, on both counts, morally. The risk of failure here is constant.

III

HISTORIES AND GENOCIDE

7

Genocide and Kant's Enlightenment

What is it to know man in particular? It is to know fools and scoundrels. . . .
The case is quite different with the study of man in general. Here he exhibits
greatness and his divine origin.
LESSING

The cosmopolitans boast of their love for all the world in order to enjoy the
privilege of loving no one.
ROUSSEAU

We [Christians] have burned you [Jews] as Holocausts.
VOLTAIRE

Human reason, even in the commonest mind, can easily be brought to a
high degree of correctness and completeness in moral matters.
KANT

The assumption runs silently but insistently through the history of philosophy that ideas have consequences and that those consequences
impinge on history as it is lived, not only as it is thought. So the writing
of ethics has been centered in the concepts of deliberation and choice, in
descriptions of the good or just life, and in proposals of what people
should do in order to realize that goal. Philosophers, in presenting these,
could hardly fail to hope that their readers would act and live differently
as a consequence of that reading than they otherwise would. Such inten-

165

tions could not ignore the fact that individuals or groups often fail to act on their own ideals, let alone on those proposed by someone else; but at least the hope of influencing other lives and other ways of viewing the world has been a constant premise of ethical thinkers and of philosophers more generally. This has been evident, not only in the tradition of such "practical" teachers of ethics as the Hebrew prophets or Socrates, but for systematic thinkers like Spinoza or Kant who were more purposefully detached from their surroundings. Even where we find an emphasis among these figures on knowledge for its own sake, that purpose is evocative: the truths discovered are understood to lead those who know them also to act on them.

Notwithstanding this assumption about the possible consequences of moral concepts and theoretical reflection, however, the question of what role ideas have actually *had* in effecting individual or social change and how this occurred has remained obscure; indeed the question itself has been generally ignored as either too small or too large: too small, if all that it asks is how an individual decides for or against ideas; too large, if it asks how ideas, as distinct from other causes, have influenced the course of world history. The difficulties in answering the latter question, an aspect of which will be the focus of discussion here, reflect the problem of tracing the causes of historical events in general. Even for economic or geopolitical factors, which are more readily quantifiable than ideas, explanations based on them have rarely been conclusive (consider, here, for example, the inconsistent accounts that have been proposed for the French Revolution).[1] The difficulty of determining the causal role of ideas, moreover, seems necessarily greater than that of other factors because of the problematic relation between individual minds and the process by which a social or political group makes *its* decisions—the "group mind." The latter, if it exists at all, cannot be assumed to be only a version of the former; yet individual minds and acts would undoubtedly have contributed to it, and the question of how this transaction occurs continues to resist the efforts of even those writers most deeply committed to its historical role.

Nonetheless, the pressure on historical writing to provide causal explanations is constant, mainly because without such accounts the

1. The differences range from the denial that the Revolution *was* revolutionary (Alfred Cobban, *The Myth of the French Revolution* [London: H. K. Lewis, 1955]) to the claim that it was an unexceptional part of a general process of social change (Jacques Gadechot, *France and the Atlantic Revolution of the Eighteenth Century*, trans. Herbert H. Rowen [New York: Free Press, 1965]), to the specific identification of (largely) economic cause and effect argued in Georges Lefebvre, *The French Revolution*, trans. Elizabeth Evanson (New York: Columbia University Press, 1962).

writing of history is restricted either to a bare assembly of chronicles or to narrative "storytelling" in which the line between fiction and nonfiction is blurred. That there has been an emphasis recently on just these conceptions of historiography[2] is undoubtedly due to the inadequacy of past efforts at causal explanation—but it is clear that these recent alternatives to the latter, whatever else they accomplish, rule out neither the possibility nor (more importantly) the need for explanation. The historical question of "Why?" remains unanswered—but it also refuses to go away.

Admittedly, attempts have come from various directions (for example, in Marxist or psychoanalytic historians) which would limit the problem of historical explanation by excluding from it any role for ideas, on the premise that ideas are themselves reflections or symptoms of more fundamental causes; on this assumption, reference to ideas as historical causes would also be precluded. The issues raised by this view extend beyond the focus of the present discussion, but assessed even superficially it is clear that the view involves a form of reductionism which offers no satisfactory explanation for the prima-facie evidence. Certainly, the assertion is common enough that ideas have consequences, and certainly decisions or judgments are often based on that assumption. Still more telling than this is the fact that historical events in which human agents figure would be unintelligible as deliberate or intentional unless certain conceptual forms could be identified in them. Obviously, such events do not occur only as ideas, but it is by way of ideas that they are almost invariably defined internally and even more obviously retrospectively; its conceptual form is to this extent a characteristic of the event or act—and this would be true even if no proof were available that a specific idea or set of ideas was in itself fully accountable for the outcome of any particular event or act.

This general claim does not imply that ideas should be privileged among historical causes. But it does mean that where ideas are intended or cited as causes within history, and even where they are not but where human agency has marked the events, there is a prima-facie basis for including ideas in the explanatory account of that event; to exclude them is, at least initially, to beg the question of why what happened did happen. As human agents invariably appeal to reasons to explain or even to describe what they do (for this purpose it does not matter that such statements are sometimes mistaken or deceptive), so historical events more generally, if human agency has been involved in them, have an idea-

2. See, e.g., Dominic LaCapra, *History and Criticism* (cited in chap. 6, n. 7); and White, *Tropics of Discourse* (see chap. 6, n. 7).

tional form that serves retrospectively as a representation of the elements comprising the event. In this sense, history is rational—not in *determining* thought or practice, but as a reflection or representation. Unless we acknowledge the forms of historical events as embodying ideas in this way, moreover, the possibility of understanding and, before that, of imagining those events will be seriously impeded. This stipulation, to be sure, does not solve the problem of how specific ideas are to be identified as causes or sources, but it at least recognizes that the question of what the historical role of ideas is does itself have historical justification.

To attempt to describe a framework of ideas which influenced the Nazi genocide against the Jews thus impinges on a number of general questions concerning the causal connections of genealogy of ideas; but these general questions will be subordinated here to a consideration of the historical consequences of one set of ideas in particular, those ideas which characterize the thought of the Enlightenment and which are epitomized for this discussion in the writings of Kant. The contention that there is to be found in Kant, or, more broadly, in the Enlightenment, certain conceptual or ideological origins of the Nazi genocide may appear initially either as tautological or as absurd. On the one hand, insofar as ideas are at all admitted as historical causes, the position of the Enlightenment at a crossroads of modern European social and intellectual history would *assure* it a role in the subsequent events of that history: to this extent, the tautology. On the other hand, to narrow this very general claim sufficiently to allege a direct connection or implication—to claim that specific motifs of the Enlightenment serve historically as an evocation of the events of the Nazi genocide—seems to strain the evidence to a breaking point. The span of 150 years which must be elided, the numerous factors (economic, geopolitical, psychological—in addition to other ideological elements) that have been otherwise established, the compelling moral and social ideals of the Enlightenment to which we are indebted for the very phrase the "rights of man": to find beyond these a contributory rule in the Enlightenment for an event as opaque in its rationale and as morally inhuman and notoriously "*un*-enlightened" as the Nazi war against the Jews seems more than any assembly of evidence that was not simply tendentious could support.

What will be outlined here, however, is a position that stands between these two alternatives, with the suggestion first, in the form of an analogy, that certain ideas prominent in the Enlightenment are recognizable in the conceptual framework embodied in the Nazi genocide; and, secondly, that if the relation between those two historical moments is not one of direct cause and effect (the one, that is, does not *entail* the other), the Enlightenment establishes a ground of historical possibility or causal evocation for the Nazi genocide. The concepts ascribed here to the Enlightenment thus appear as "manifest" in the principle of genocide that has been described in earlier chapters of this book. Clearly other ideas and even alternative descriptions of the ones cited here are also relevant in the same line of development (and some of these will be mentioned); quite different, *material* causes are also and perhaps still more directly involved. And even so, the problem of establishing an implicative or causal connection remains; that there may be an analogy between Enlightenment ideas and aspects of the ideological framework presupposed in the Nazi genocide does not in itself demonstrate an historical connection between the two.

These several qualifications can be admitted—together with the more obvious one that nowhere does the Enlightenment, Kant's or anyone else's, except in the most oblique way,[3] conceive the idea of genocide or its practice, against the Jews or anyone else. Such considerations may all be granted, and yet two opposing considerations weigh on the other side. The first of these, again, is the matter of prima-facie evidence: that it was in the same context of European thought for which the Enlightenment remained in the middle of the twentieth century an important focus of intellectual influence and social redirection—a continuing ideal—that the Nazi genocide against the Jews occurred. The second point is the more substantive and contentious thesis proposed here: that the ideational framework in which the act of the Nazi genocide was set involved—*required*—a number of concepts that had been central in Enlightenment thought. The contextual assertion suggests as a general possibility historical connections between the period of the Enlightenment and the ideas and practice involved in the Nazi genocide (that is, if ideas *ever* serve as historical causes); the implicative assertion purports to identify specific elements in this relation. It is obvious that ideas alone did not build the fences of the Nazi death camps or build their gas chambers. But it is no less obvious that those acts were not the work only of hands moving by themselves. Those acts also involved a variety of reasons and causes which were not hands at all; among these, ideas were one and an important source, and among these ideas were a number to which

3. This qualification is not simply an expression of academic caution. Consider, for example, Fichte's statement against extending civil rights to the Jews: "The only way to give them citizenship would be to cut off their heads on the same night in order to replace them with those containing no Jewish ideas." ("Beitrag zur Berichtung der Urteile des Publikums über die französischen Revolution" [1793].) And one can hardly miss the implied threat in Voltaire's entry on "Juifs" in the *Dictionnaire philosophique* which is the source for the epigraph at the beginning of this chapter. If Jews are not willing to give up *their* past, he insinuates, the Christian past in which the Jews were "burned as Holocausts" might be revived.

the Enlightenment gave their fullest and in certain respects their most deliberate expression.

1. Kant's Enlightenment

Kant may not be the most typical or representative thinker of the Enlightenment, but he is arguably the most significant one, both for his later influence in the history of ideas and for his systematic development of the fundamental themes of Enlightenment thought. He consciously presented himself, moreover, as an advocate of "enlightenment," both of the process and of the period; this combination of factors identifies him at the very least as an important spokesman for the intentions of Enlightenment thinking and also, it will be suggested here, for the subsequent lines of thought that emerged from it.

Kant's commitment both to enlightenment and the Enlightenment is formulated most explicitly in his essay of 1784, "What Is Enlightenment?"[4] That essay itself is brief and summary; it draws together a number of themes elaborated more fully in other works of Kant's critical philosophy, focusing in particular on the close relation between the theoretical principles of universality and rationality and the practical issues of moral decision and agency. The significance of this relation for Enlightenment thought and its influence on later, sometimes even antithetical formulations of the same relation, are the focus of the discussion here.

In the essay on Enlightenment, Kant refers to the term "enlightenment" as a process, not as a conclusion. "Do we now live in an enlightened age?" Kant asks. "The answer is No, but in an age of enlightenment" (8). The process, then, is current and incomplete; its principal feature, as Kant describes it, is the escape which enlightenment offers from intellectual "tutelage," an escape which depends on the employment of man's distinctive capacity of reason: "'Have the courage to use your own reason!'—that is the motto of the Enlightenment" (3).

Viewed against the long history of the rationalist tradition, this challenge on behalf of intellectual autonomy is hardly startling, but it is important nonetheless for what Kant means specifically to deny and to affirm by it. On the one hand, the assertion rejects claims of institutional privilege where knowledge, whether theoretical or moral, is concerned; this includes claims of authority by hierarchical structures such as the Church and, more generally, by appeals to tradition and history, what-

4. In Lewis White Beck (ed.), *Kant: On History* (Indianapolis, Ind.: Bobbs-Merrill, 1963), 3–10.

ever institutional forms they take. Reliance on such instances of external authority reflects "immaturity" in the individual which enlightenment is meant to overcome; in that earlier state, the individual's role as fully rational remains undemonstrated. In contrast to this, the alternative which is "now" open (Kant here refers to the ground laid by political as well as intellectual developments of the preceding decade) is intellectual independence in which the individual realizes the capacity to think on his own, without the mediation of institutions or the appeal to history that have been relied on previously. (The analogy recurs, for Kant and other Enlightenment writers, of the age of pre-Enlightenment as childhood and of the Enlightenment, then, as the passage to adulthood.) Kant does not assert in so many words that the reason which mankind is now in a position to actualize is a universal human capacity, but only because that claim can in his view be taken for granted. Enlightenment is open to anyone who relies on his own reason (that is what being enlightened *is*), with reason a natural faculty shared among human beings and in effect defining them *as* human. The latter fact does not assure universal agreement on all issues confronted by reason in the short run, but in the longer run not only the faculties of the mind but the conclusions reached by this means have universal force. Those conclusions will thus be identical for everyone; as in reason itself, variations or differences are insignificant.

Even in the compressed account of intellectual independence that Kant gives in the essay on Enlightenment, he calls attention to one form of judgment which may not achieve the autonomy of enlightenment in this strong sense, namely, the form which is subordinate to political authority. Kant distinguishes here between the "private" and the "public" uses of reason, affirming the possibility of enlightenment in the latter at the same time that he concedes restrictions on the former. "The public use of one's reason must always to be free, and it alone can bring about enlightenment among men. The private use of reason, on the other hand, may often be vary narrowly restricted without particularly hindering the progress of enlightenment" (51). To be sure, Kant does not here exactly endorse the constraints on the private use of reason—but neither does he characterize them as a necessary evil or indeed as an evil at all. Their justification seems in fact to be prudential: "It would be ruinous for an officer in service to debate about the suitability and utility of a command given to him by his superior; he must obey. But the right to make remarks on errors in the military and to lay them before the public for judgment cannot equitably be refused as a scholar" (5). The officer's private role would, on this account, be distinguished from and in certain cases given preference over his public role.

There is a question, to be sure, about the basis on which Kant draws the line between the public and the private uses of reason, although his own use of the distinction is consistent (so again: "The citizen cannot refuse to pay the taxes imposed on him"). Kant himself would later be rebuked by the King of Prussia, Frederick William II, for the views of religion expressed in *Religion within the Limits of Reason Alone* (1793), and it might be argued that his (Kant's) subsequent agreement to remain publicly silent on religious questions may have been inconsistent with the principle of his own private-public distinction.[5] But it is clear even so that the distinction itself reiterates a more basic conception of reason, whether theoretical or practical, which in Kant's view belongs entirely to the public domain and which is thus—especially in contrast to private reason—universal and independent of historical circumstances. The latter two features are themselves related: a prerequisite for judgment as universal is that it should not be bound by historical particularity or partiality. These features of judgment figure largely in Kant's epistemological, ethical, and even aesthetic writings. In all these areas, the autonomy to be realized by judgment implies the irrelevance of historical and cultural causality; if judgment is "enlightened," it necessarily leaves behind the historical context, which might otherwise be seen as an influence on it. This exclusion of history from the background of judgment is matched by the conclusiveness of judgment in its foreground: where disagreements in judgment occur, this will never be the end of the matter, since in principle there is only *one* judgment to be made, whatever obstacles must be overcome in practice in order to arrive at it.

The related characteristics of universality and independence of the historical context are prominent in Kant's conception of ethical judgment as practical reason—most notably in what is referred to as the principle of universalizability. That principle is concisely formulated in the first version (of three that Kant provides) of the Categorical Imperative: "Act only according to that maxim by which you can at the same time will that it should become a universal law."[6] A moral decision, in these terms, is to be based on the question of whether, for any other agent acting in the same situation, the principle governing the one action could also be willed for them. So—in an example that Kant provides—we test our inclination to make a promise which we know we cannot keep by examining the prospective act as universalized: is it possible that *everyone* should make promises that they know they cannot

5. On this issue in Kant's biography, see Hans Reiss (ed.), *Kant's Political Writings* (New York: Cambridge University Press, 1970), 2.

6. *Foundations of the Metaphysics of Morals*, trans. Lewis White Beck (Indianapolis, Ind.: Bobbs-Merrill, 1959), 39.

keep? If, as Kant concludes, the promise is impossible without "contradiction," then we cannot will it in the instance engaging us in the present.

It has often been pointed out by commentators on Kant that a significant difficulty in applying the Categorical Imperative turns on the question of how it can be determined that a particular act is or is not universalizable.[7] But Kant is quite explicit about one way in which that decision is *not* to be made, and this is by reference to the consequences of the act. That I should keep my promises because people will distrust me if I fail to, or because if I break my promises others will feel justified in acting similarly: such reasons appeal to prudential or "hypothetical" criteria which may be compelling on other grounds but do not, for Kant, provide a *moral* basis. The test of moral judgment is, in Kant's view, analogous to the test for logical contradiction: to make a promise while knowing that one will not keep it is self-contradictory inasmuch as it nullifies not only the particular "promise" expressed but the structure of promises as such. This assessment differs fundamentally from one which rejects a judgment because the *consequences* of the act in question would be harmful if "everyone" did it; the latter condition, again, is for Kant morally irrelevant.

Kant's turning away from the consequences of an act to its logic or form has itself important consequences for the procedure of universalization. For although there may be instances (as in the one cited) when the terms involved in a moral choice are unambiguous and can thus be captured by the test of universalization, many decisions evidently involve two *competing* obligations or goods, each of which, if it stood by itself, could arguably be universalized. In such cases, the problem then arises of how a choice can be made between the two conflicting "oughts" on the basis of the formal principle of the Categorical Imperative. Since Kant excludes consequences as morally irrelevant, the decision cannot be based on them (even, one supposes, if everything else is equal)—but it is not clear what other basis can be found that avoids such reference. Kant himself provides a notable example of this difficulty (the fact that he himself does not see it as a difficulty underscores the issue) in his essay "On a Supposed Right to Tell Lies from Benevolent Motives."[8] In the principal example he cites there, one person is asked by

7. See, e.g., T. C. Williams, *The Concept of the Categorical Imperative* (Oxford: Clarendon Press, 1968), 15–18; Keith Ward, *The Development of Kant's Views of Ethics* (New York: Humanities Press, 1972), 107–18.

8. "On a Supposed Right To Tell Lies from Benevolent Motives," in *Kant's Critique of Practical Reason and Other Works,* trans. Thomas K. Abbott (London: Longmans, Green and Co., 1948), 361–65.

another for the whereabouts of someone whom the second person
intends to kill. In this situation, too, Kant affirms, the test of universalization demonstrates that only the truth will do: to justify lying here is
to justify lying wherever it might be an option—and, furthermore, also
to make oneself responsible for whatever happens subsequently as a result of the lie. It might be thought (although the text itself ultimately
rules this out) that Kant is supposing here, not that there are *no* obligations to the victim of someone else's evil intentions, but that such
obligations are outweighed by the obligation to tell the truth. But on
this interpretation no less than on the likelier one, the principle of universalization yields an unequivocal verdict on what is to be done; the
initial construal of the situation as pulling the moral agent in two directions is thus seen to be mistaken. The action finally decided on is what
can be—what *is* to be—universalized; anything which might seem to
have been lost because of that judgment becomes, once the judgment is
formulated, irrelevant. There is no conflict between competing goods—
only adherence to the moral law, on the one hand, or the failure to, on
the other.

It might be objected to Kant's conclusion here that a different material
maxim from the one he adduces might obligate a moral agent to prevent
harm to a third person, whatever its source; or, alternatively, that where
human life is at stake, one has an obligation to violate maxims which
would otherwise be morally binding. Kant quite clearly, however, excludes these alternatives, and this rejection is only in part explained, in
the case of the threatened murder, by the fact that the "wrong" which is
likely to ensue is someone else's responsibility. For in addition to the
strong conception of moral individualism which underlies Kant's analysis here—only the "active" agent is finally responsible—Kant is also in
effect denying that the judgment which he (or any moral agent) makes
can be viewed as the lesser of two evils. Once a maxim is determined on
the basis of which a specific judgment is to be made, one can will and act
in accord only with it; the agent subsequently will not have chosen between two goods (in which case some other good would also have been
sacrificed), but between the good realized in the maxim which is asserted
and the wrong or contradiction entailed by the alternative to it. Once
practical reason has made its decision for one alternative, there is no reason left to any of the others—and this, it might be objected, hardly
matches the common experience within which many such decisions
are set.

Such systematic difficulties in the application of the Categorical Imperative are most immediately pertinent to the discussion here,
however, for the focus they provide on the central role of the principle

of universalizability and the further, "external," consequences to which that principle leads. These consequences are anticipated more pointedly in the "second formulation" of the Categorical Imperative, in which Kant shifts the focus of the test of universalizability from the moral will or judgment to the status of the moral agent. So, in this second formulation, Kant instructs the moral agent to "act so that you treat humanity, whether in your own person or in that of another, always as an end and never as a means merely."[9] The requirement of universalization is preserved here: *every* person is to be treated in the manner prescribed; thus, also, every act affecting that person must conform first to the requirement of universalization, whatever its particular content. In this way, Kant links the test of universalization to the traits that distinguish human beings as human beings (and so as ends in themselves); for it is on the basis of those traits—that is, of the "noumenal" or extrahistorical self—that man's claim to moral status, whether as agent, or more generally as subject, depends. On this basis, too, human beings are by definition alike in their essential nature. Any differences which foster apparent distinctions among human beings are thus at best morally irrelevant; at worst, insofar as they may obstruct the process of universalization, they are moral liabilities. The principle of universalization thus reappears in a slightly different form: man is to base his actions on a maxim insofar as it is universalizable because he is also *himself* "universalizable." So: "Every rational being must be able to regard himself as an end in himself with reference to all laws to which he may be subject. . . . For it is just the fitness of his maxims to a universal legislation that indicates that he is an end in himself."[10] Man's status as an end in himself is thus presupposed in the capacity for universalization, and the converse evidently holds here as well: any being without this capacity for universalization may be denied address as an "end in himself." Moral agents should be treated alike and as ends in themselves because, before that, they *are* alike—equal in worth because of what they are and as defining, by that same fact, what moral worth *is*.

The motivating principle of this argument, then, both in the moral agent and in the form of his acts, is the ideal of universalization—the contention, on the one hand, that universalizability is a condition of moral value, overriding any apparent differences in circumstance; on the other hand, that the formal principle of universalization is itself a value

9. *Foundations*, 47.
10. *Foundations*, 56. Or again: "Man finds in himself a faculty by which he distinguishes himself from all other things, even from himself insofar as he is affected by objects. This faculty is reason." (*Foundations*, 80.)

embodied in the moral agent. This conflation of what might be called formal and substantive categories is perhaps most evident in certain extreme examples that Kant provides and that disclose in their extremity that the principle of universalization is as fundamental a substantive element as it is a formal one in Kant's conceptual scheme. One of these concerns sexual relations. Here, in addition to a number of other moral qualifications that Kant enjoins, he calls attention to the violation, which is (allegedly) intrinsic, of the principle of universalizability: "Sexuality gives rise to the preference of one sex to the other . . . and [so] to the dishonoring of that sex through the satisfaction of desire."[11] Since sexuality (Kant here evidently speaks only of heterosexuality) is based on a difference in the other—a difference which is not morally supportable—whatever follows from that difference is "dishonoring." The satisfaction of sexual desire for any purpose other than procreation, Kant argues, will be instrumental—instrumental, again, because partial, and partial because the "judgment" on which the satisfaction is based is not universalizable.

A second and no less startling application of the principle of universalizability along the same lines appears in the Anthropology, where Kant criticizes the moral status of friendship: "Friendship is a restriction of favorable sentiments to a single subject and is very pleasant to him towards whom they are directed, but also a proof that generality and good will are lacking."[12] Friendship, too, then, because of the partiality which is evidently intrinsic to it (Kant does not demonstrate this feature but only, it seems, because it is obvious), is morally objectionable. Again, it is the principle of universalizability which motivates his conclusion and which, as applied to the particularism of friendship, leaves it, too, without a moral warrant.

These contentions may seem so much at odds with the common ascription of values as to raise questions not only about the specific examples cited but about the conceptual framework of Kant's view of practical reason as a whole. But what bears most immediately on the discussion here is the consistency with which these conclusions follow from the principle of universalization; with that as a premise of moral agency, there seems no way of avoiding the conclusions which Kant himself draws in the examples. To be sure, it has been often pointed out that the

11. *Lectures on Ethics,* trans. Louis Infeld (London: Methuen, 1963), 164.
12. *Anthropology from a Pragmatic Point of View,* trans. Mary J. Gregor (The Hague: Martinus Nijhoff, 1944), 31. In "Friendship" in the *Lectures on Ethics* (200–209), Kant presents a more positive view of friendship which nonetheless remains equivocal on the issue defined by the statement in the *Anthropology.* See also H. J. Paton's similarly equivocal defense of Kant's position in "Kant on Friendship," *Proceedings of the British Academy* 42 (1956), 46–66.

principle of universalization obviously could not apply to *every* decision or act (a person's decision to wear a blue shirt would presumably not have to meet the criterion of universalizability). But even putting such considerations to one side (and with them the difficulty of deciding, in Kant's own terms, when the principle of universalization is to be applied or not), the fact remains that insofar as the criterion is judged to be applicable, it leads consistently to conclusions of the sort cited. We recognize from the examples which Kant himself provides that wherever an act impinges on the autonomy of a moral agent, the doctrine of universalizability presupposes an equality, or stronger still, an identity among moral agents—and to the extent that that equality is qualified or hindered by anything related to the act itself, the act becomes morally suspect.

The exclusion of historical considerations from the process of ethical judgment is, moreover, a corollary of the pressure for universalization. The moral agent, acting himself or acted on by someone else, is held to be quite independent of any particular events or effects of historical influence. In this sense, universalization is not only horizontal, applying to all *contemporary* human agents, but vertical, holding for human agents irrespective of their particular pasts, and thus overriding any differences in cultural background or education that might distinguish them from each other. Kant does on occasion hint at the possibility of historically rooted qualifications in the principle of universalization. So, for example: "A man . . . who is brought up by gipsies [!] until the habit of evil conduct has become a necessity, is [morally] responsible to a lesser degree."[13] But by far the greater emphasis in his writings, for ethical and also for cognitive and aesthetic judgment, is on the universal applicability of such judgments quite apart from the context in which they are made or from the history of the moral agent to whom the judgment is directed. And this, too, it seems, is entailed by the principle of universalizability: so far as the application of the Categorical Imperative is concerned, individual or group differences are at best irrelevant; at worst such differences become hindrances or obstacles which then have to be overcome, and Kant, both in his ethics and his aesthetics, also offers suggestions about how this can be accomplished.

The one major point on which Kant seems ready to limit his conception of the role of universalization has already been alluded to, namely, in his view of the role of the state. For it might well seem that insofar as obligations are to be judged as universal, there could be no justification for attaching or subordinating them to a particular government or set of laws. For a variety of reasons, Kant does not draw this conclusion—but

13. *Lectures on Ethics*, 64.

those reasons themselves disclose and reassert his priorities as they have been described. So, in his essay on "Eternal Peace," Kant argues in behalf of a world federation of nations that would supervise lesser (including national) allegiances: "For states in their relation to each other, there cannot, according to reason, be any other way to get away from the lawless state which contains nothing but war than to give up (just like individual men) their wild and lawless freedom, to accept public and enforceable laws, and thus to form a constantly growing world state of all nations."[14] Even in this statement, admittedly, there is no sense that the nation is to be superseded, and Kant goes on to make this point more explicitly: "Unless all is to be lost, the positive idea of a world republic must be replaced by the negative substitute of a union of nations which maintains itself, prevents wars, and steadily expands." The nation is here a given, but the "given" is also, quite clearly, a grudging and limited concession, with the reason for the limitations more significant than what is limited. Thus, too, "patriotism and cosmopolitanism" are, in his view, compatible as ideals—with the Enlightenment emphasis, predictably, on the latter, and with both terms of the combination explicitly distinguished from the "folly" of nationalism. Kant thus acknowledges the tension, in the context of the Enlightenment more generally, between the impulse for the "universal rights of man" and the fact of nationalism, which historically was itself, in large measure, a consequence of that same universalist impulse.[15] There is in any event no question, in his recognition of the two sides of this tension, about the side to which Kant was himself principally committed. It is that theme and thesis of universalism, at once in the act of judgment and in the self acting and acted upon, which in its later structural turns would be incorporated in the structural framework of the phenomenon of genocide.

2. Conceptual Analogy and Common Principle

The introduction to the discussion of Kant in the preceding section acknowledged that a question might be raised about a view of the Enlightenment which took him as a representative or typical figure. But it also seems clear that the other likely representatives—Voltaire, Diderot, Hume, Lessing—are each open to similar objections, and it may well be that the Enlightenment is too diverse in its commitments and methods to afford a single exemplary spokesman at all. The difficulty thus raised is

14. "Perpetual Peace," in Reiss, *Kant's Political Writings*, 105.
15. See George Mosse, "Mass Politics and the Political Liturgy of Nationalism," in Eugene Kamenka (ed.), *Nationalism* (New York: St. Martins, 1976).

compounded, moreover, by the occurrence of attacks on Enlightenment views which are virtually coincident with those views and which are made sometimes (as with Fichte) by figures otherwise identified with the Enlightenment itself. (Norman Hampson goes so far as to suggest that "the reaction against the Enlightenment preceded most of the major works of the Enlightenment itself.")[16]

Even granting this complexity, however, the themes identified above in Kant's thought can be seen to recur, whether explicitly or as presupposition, in other Enlightenment formulations, and it is in fact impossible to identify or to describe the Enlightenment without reference to them. Among these themes, the impulse for universalization, with its implications for "practical"—i.e., moral and social—judgment and for the theory of human nature, is conceptually fundamental. To be sure, there is nothing distinctive philosophically in the Enlightenment conception of a universal or essential human nature by itself. What *is* distinctive there, and also exemplary of Enlightenment thought more generally, is the relation between the particular conception proposed and its exemplification in ethical and political practice. For in that relation, as the discussion of Kant has disclosed, universalization functions as both a substantive and a formal ground. On the one hand, persons or moral agents are defined in terms of certain common or universal characteristics; on the other hand, the test of any particular ethical judgment is whether it can in principle be universalized. The rights of the individual—what the individual may expect from others—thus depends on the recognition (from both sides: within the agent himself and in his judgment of the other individual) of a universal self.

This condition does not mean that selves are deserving of moral respect only when they act in prescribed ways (criminals, too, must be treated as moral agents; it is because of this that Kant takes the extreme view that retribution, not rehabilitation, is the only moral basis for punishment). But in order first to determine the self's status *as* a self, the requirement of commonality or universalization in the self must first be met, and the judgment of this depends at least as much on external or public scrutiny as it does on introspective judgment, which could hardly, after all, be disinterested. In this way, the conception of a universal essence (and of universal judgment) tends also toward a standard of universal conduct on the basis of judgment. (So Kant writes, "It is just this fitness of [a person's own] maxims for universal legislation that distinguishes him as an end in himself.")[17] The principle of universaliz-

---

16. Norman Hampson, *The Enlightenment* (New York: Penguin, 1982), 187.
17. *Foundations,* 56.

ability is thus not only a means applied by a moral agent; the capacity for moral universalization, which can only be assessed by measuring the acts based on it, constitutes the moral agent himself.

This requirement of universalization, as has been noted, is supported by an extreme version of individualism, according to which each self is fully and intrinsically constituted by the elements of its common nature. The social-contract theory, according to which governments are founded by the consent, explicit or tacit, of their citizens, epitomizes the political presuppositions of the Enlightenment. Again, not all Enlightenment thinkers subscribed to this theory (Hume, for example, was a severe critic, and Kant himself regarded the social contract not as historical but as a practical Idea of Reason).[18] But even where an alternative historical basis is proposed for the development of political structures, the state itself is still held to make only an instrumental and not an essential difference in the lives of its citizens, who thus remain, both initially and subsequently, independent of political and cultural history. Whatever else membership in a group or polity does for or to the individual, it does not constitute him as a person; his "natural" rights and the principles of conduct which mediate between those rights and his obligations are thus historical and independent of any particular context. It follows, then, that group identity—religious, social, political—is accidental and, where it exists, always defeasible; since it arose first in response to practical needs, it can then always be altered as need—or reason—dictates. The principle of universalization is in this sense vertical as well as horizontal: history makes no essential difference to character, and Hume, then, could answer his own question quite confidently: "Would you know the sentiments, motivations, and course of life of the Greeks and the Romans? Study well the temper and actions of the French and English."[19] There could not be significant differences.

These two themes, then—the impulse for universalization in the account of human nature and as a principle of both moral and theoretical "conduct," and the autonomous, nonhistorical (and thus also nonempirical) self—which are central for Kant's thought also identify him with central themes of the Enlightenment more generally, not only in its immediate historical context, but as it is subsequently appropriated in the nineteenth and twentieth centuries. To be sure, differences occur among

18. David Hume, "Of the Original Contract," in *David Hume's Political Essays,* ed. Charles Hendel (New York: Liberal Arts Press, 1953), 43–63. See also Reiss *Kant's Political Writings,* 29–30.

19. Admittedly, Hume elsewhere qualifies this ahistorical claim (cf., e.g., *Enquiry Concerning the Principles of Morals,* sect. 5, part 2).

Enlightenment figures in respect both to the grounds of these principles and to the implications drawn from them; there are predictable differences on those counts between materialists such as d'Holbach or Diderot and critics of materialism such as Kant himself. But the general themes are constant and efficacious, as they are translated into political and social practice and as they are addressed at the level of ideas. It is not difficult, moreover, to understand the importance that was attached to them. In the immediate social context, these themes were radical, because of the weight which historical precedent and social hierarchy had previously carried. Against the institutional strictures of the varieties of the *ancien régime* to which the Enlightenment opposed itself, the call to equality and fraternity was meant to—and did—have the force of liberation: one has only to refer here to the echoes in country after country of Europe of the slogans of the French Revolution. (We might, in a more limited example, recall the sober Kant, opposed in principle to all revolution, yet moved to extol *that* one and the ground laid for it in the writings of Rousseau, whose portrait looked out at Kant in his study).

Again, ideologically, the Enlightenment is a network of diverse, sometimes inconsistent concepts, and the same diversity persists in the lines of influence set in motion both within it and, still more evidently, in its aftermath. But even in this continuing diversity, the themes which have been identified—the formal principle of universalization which acquires the force also of a substantive content, and the ahistorical and asocial definition of the self, the two of them leading also to an antiempirical and thus ultimately subjective criterion of moral judgments—play a constant role. Subsequently, like other themes of the Enlightenment, these also turn in a number of different directions: provoking and fostering the Romantic reaction, contributing to the growth and professionalization of the social sciences in the nineteenth century, supporting a range of justifications for emergent nationalism—and then later, in the contention argued here, also providing a conceptual framework which would figure ideationally in the phenomenon of genocide.

In asserting the last of these points, the account here does not presuppose a corporate "mind" which had reasoned out and committed itself to certain doctrines and then also to their logical implications. Nor does it assume that even a *single* mind first formulated or intended a pattern of ideas and then drew the conclusion which had been claimed to ensure in the structural framework of genocide. As intentions are not known in any privileged way by the agent of an act (that is, an agent may be unaware of his own intentions and also may be mistaken about those he does name), so, too, the causality of ideas has an external form that does not presuppose conscious appropriation. The thesis, then, is that among the conceptual presuppositions which underlie the phenomenon of genocide, certain characteristic and central principles of the Enlightenment recur and thus appear as conditions of its later occurrence. The themes that have been identified in Kant's Enlightenment impinge on that later event first as the terms of a conceptual analogy and then (as the section following this argues) by a causal process of "affiliation" in which connections are established between certain common ideological themes.

Viewed schematically, the mutually reinforcing impulses of universalism and of judgment as reason oppose themselves to all claims for particularism, the more intensely as the latter claims base themselves on historical grounds. Judgment, whether theoretical or moral, holds conviction for the Enlightenment only in the present; thus, any claim on behalf of historical influence that might impede this judgment or that would support differences over which judgment, because of its universalist requirements, has no control becomes immediately suspect. There is no place here—because there is no justification by reason—for historical differences or for the historical self. The one accommodation that might be made where exceptions from the ideals of the universal self or reason are asserted is to treat the exceptions as inessential or accidental, as in matters of taste. Even these, moreover, are in principle remediable (taste itself can be educated); in any event, in comparison to the objects of other forms of judgment, the objects of taste are relatively less important. (Kant himself is, it may be pointed out, the main theoretical source for the isolation of aesthetic judgment in nineteenth- and twentieth-century thought from the other forms of judgment.) Any more fundamental assertions on behalf of particularism, whether in the self or in judgment, can, or, more precisely, ought to be denied; so far as they persist, they place themselves outside the norms of judgment. Exactly what response is warranted when such violations occur, and how we determine *when* they occur, would have to be based on formal criteria (such as the Categorical Imperative)—since there is nothing else to rely on. But those formal criteria, as has been suggested, do not provide the *substantive* basis which judgment requires in order to make the decision to exclude or include certain groups. The basis for such judgment is thus finally inaccessible—unknowable by external means even after the patterns of conduct are examined, and indeterminate internally, first because the criterion of judgment always is underdetermined, and then, beyond this, because the agent himself can never be known to be truly disinterested (i.e., universal) as a judge of his own intentions. In this sense, the articulation and then the assessment of moral agency, beginning with the assessment of one's own moral character, must be seen as problematic; an intrinsic opening is left for arbitrariness. The consequences of this opening reach their full force when an individual or group is alleged to cross the boundary by which the universal domain has been defined: the principles originally articulated within the sphere of the universalist ideal no longer apply. A radically different moral universe becomes possible, one that can nonetheless be held to be compatible with the first, since in each case its members as well as its principles have changed.

The consequences which follow from the convergence of these themes in the politics and civic life of the nineteenth century are to a certain extent predictable. Certainly those consequences are evident in the history of the "Emancipation" of the Jews during that time; less obviously, but more severely but still consistently, they persist in the subsequent background of the phenomenon of genocide. Accentuated by the development of nationalism, the pressure increases to base the rights of the citizen on the quality of a common and universal rationality that is defined and shared within the host group responsible for the definition. In turn, any attempt to maintain differences that are judged (whether externally or on the part of those who are different) as fundamental, in contrast to accidental ones, such as those of temperament (although in the extreme view which Nazism takes, these accidental features also become essential), can only be condemned as opposing the rational and moral ideals of commonality. On the one hand, then, in the Enlightenment ideals, emancipation and tolerance are offered to "man"—to all men—but the specification of those ideals, on the other hand, how they are to be applied, is left indeterminate by those principles and thus with no means of supporting (or defeating) any particular verdict. This absence itself adds to the pressure that those who receive the offer should be seen, and see themselves, as included within the primary group; it is even understandable, then, that the rights of citizenship should be extended only to those who succeed in this.

This account may seem to disclose only another, albeit complex, version of ethnocentrism, which has, after all, been a widespread feature of social history and which might be more readily analyzed by the psychological categories of prejudice than by a moral or metaphysical framework. But a significant difference in the Enlightenment appearance of this phenomenon distinguishes it from the more common forms of opposition between an established group and other alien or minority groups. In the aftermath of the French Revolution, sentiment grew rapidly in the countries of Europe to extend citizenship and thus the civic power of self-determination—of enlightenment—to the inhabitants of the individual nations. The allocation of civic rights on the basis of inherited status or class or of property holdings was thus in principle, if not always or quickly in practice, rejected. But emancipation and enlightenment based on the conception of a universal self meant that the self, too, was required to assume a new role, one integral to the life of the community; it was thus obliged to reject the particularist commitments—those, at least, which could not withstand the scrutiny of "reason"—that had otherwise confirmed the diverse identities of individuals or groups.

Religion as such was, of course, an obvious target of this Enlightenment criticism, although with important variations in nuance. So, for example, Enlightenment writers often found themselves walking an uneasy line in respect to the institutions of Christianity—committed, on the one hand, to criticism of the force of historical tradition and parochialism, wherever they might appear; on the other hand, restrained by other principles concerning the relation between religion and the state, and also at times by considerations of personal prudence. Thus, the anticlericalism of the Enlightenment, although never essentially in doubt, was sometimes muted where Christianity was concerned.[20] In respect to the Jews, on the other hand, there were no prudential reasons for concealing either the general criticism of religious commitment or practice or, beyond that, the more specific objections which, on Enlightenment grounds, might be directed against Judaism. It is likely in fact that some of the Enlightenment hostility toward Jews reflected an antagonism to Christianity that could be less readily expressed. But the conclusion is unavoidable, beyond these circumstances, that Enlightenment thought added its own reasons for disputing the acceptance of the Jews into the new post-Enlightenment social or political structure. The way in which these reasons at once reflect certain Enlightenment ideals and presage the ideological structure of genocide in the future is of immediate concern here. For the Enlightenment provided a "justification" for anti-Semitism that went well beyond the rejection of religion of Christianity as such, a justification based on the principle that motivated the Enlightenment reaction against the unenlightened past as a whole: that with the possibility of freedom and equality that was now open to them, all citizens of the new regime had an obligation to commit themselves to

20. There is an analogy here to the stance adopted by the Nazis in respect to the Catholic Church. Although the Nazi attitude to Christianity could have been in doubt to no one (and not only because of the origins of Christianity in Judaism), frontal attacks on the Church by the Nazis were rare; when they occurred, they were almost always directed against individuals on specific grounds, quite separate from more general questions about the status of religion. This policy evidently succeeded, at least as measured by the Church's refusal to confront the Nazis even when the lives of its own clergy were at stake (let alone for the lives of others). See, on this aspect of Nazi policy, Jacob Katz, *From Prejudice to Destruction: Anti-Semitism, 1700–1933* (Cambridge: Harvard University Press), 315–20.

those ideals by renouncing the differences that had characterized (whether as cause or effect) their previous tutelage. To choose to maintain differences of cult or custom—and thus, more fundamentally, of identity—in the face of an offer of commonality could itself serve as evidence that the offer had been misconceived.

There are few figures of the Enlightenment in fact who in their common defense of toleration do not qualify that principle where the Jews are concerned. This fact alone would be significant for assessing the Enlightenment in relation to its ideals; it becomes still more significant in the light of evidence that this attitude toward the Jews was not accidental or simply the recrudescence of earlier prejudices, but was engendered by doctrines of the Enlightenment itself. In Kant's view, for example, Judaism does not even achieve the status of a true religion, since its practice is entirely external, a "cult" of rituals and observances which are not rationally motivated, but "heteronomous"—the result of external commands.[21] In this sense, the religious practices of Judaism are entirely removed from the moral realm, which could not have an heteronomous basis. For Voltaire, even if one puts aside the conventional slurs that he willingly took over from the past (for example, in his references to the Jews as "the most contemptible of all nations . . . robbers, seditious"), one sees the themes of universality and ahistoricism at work. The Jews, in his view of them, were so bound by—or worse, committed to—an obscurantist tradition that there was little prospect that they either would or could leave it behind them. They were *themselves* intolerant: this was demonstrated by the persistence with which they maintained their separateness. And whatever else a principle of tolerance might entail, it should not, for Voltaire, be extended to those who did not accept it themselves. (The fact that nothing seems to have *followed* from this alleged intolerance on the part of the Jews, for example, in terms of social disruption, evidently made no difference to Voltaire.) The range of discourse here extends, moreover, from the abstract level of principle to much more commonplace moments of social exchange. So the benign Hume would write to the chairman of the India Company, in what was obviously meant to be a cordial letter of support (28 August 1767): "Allow me to recommend to your Patronage, M. [Isaac de] Pinto, whom I venture to call my Friend, tho' a Jew."[22]

It should be noted that judgments such as the ones cited were not di-

---

26. See Kant, *Religion within the Limits of Reason Alone*, trans. Theodore M. Greene and Hoyt H. Hudson (New York: Harper and Row, 1960), 116–18; see also on this point Nathan Rotenstreich, *The Recurring Pattern: Studies in Anti-Judaism in Modern Thought* (London: Weidenfeld and Nicolson, 1963), chap. 2.

22. Cited by Richard H. Popkin, in "Hume and Isaac de Pinto," in William B. Todd (ed.), *Hume and the Enlightenment* (Austin: University of Texas Press, 1974).

rected among Enlightenment figures only against the Jews, and that for some of those figures (most notably, Lessing), the Jews were even excepted from what otherwise recurs as a general mood of prejudice against differences and particularism:[23] against the American Indians and also against the European settlers of the New World; against the Gypsies; against "foreigners," even, in certain instances, when the foreigners were citizens of other countries of Europe itself. It might be argued that such prejudices can be more favorably understood as a response to new possibilities opened by the principles of equality and universality: people of origins or backgrounds which previously had not even been acknowledged were at least being considered in terms of those principles. But historical apologetics of this sort are finally less compelling than the fact of the continuing criticism of difference itself and the ideological structure underlying it; here the practice of exclusion coexisted with and seems even to have been evoked by the principle of tolerance.

In a social or conceptual structure which stresses equality of rights as a function of the equality of persons, individual differences and a fortiori group differences become suspect and the rights that would "normally" be ascribed to them, problematic. What starts out then as a commitment to tolerance turns out to be, not acceptance of diversity in its own terms, but a tolerance of difference within the margins fixed by a stipulated conception of reason. For anyone outside those margins, questions of degree—how far they are outside—hardly matter: what is crucial is that the person or the group has been excluded. This does not automatically determine what the *consequences* of such decisions will be, and indeed there is much discussion, during and after the Enlightenment, about the "degrees" of rights to be accorded the Jews. So, for example, Fichte and Friedrich Ruhs argued that elementary "human rights" should be extended to them, but not civil rights: the original Declaration of the Rights of Man, which was endorsed in Paris on 27 August 1789, did not include the Jews (or for that matter, the Protestants) under its purview.

23. See on this point, e.g., Tzvetan Todorov, *The Conquest of America,* trans. Richard Howard (New York: Harper and Row, 1984), 247–54. A measure of how deep-seated these attitudes and the "rational" principles underlying them are can be seen in a statement by John Locke in his *Letter Concerning Toleration:* "Nobody is born a member of any church; otherwise the religion of parents would descend unto children, by the same right of inheritance as their temporal estates, and everyone would hold his faith by the same tenure he does his lands; than which nothing can be imagined more absurd." The issue here is not Locke's view of what religion *should* be, but his a priori rejection of a position which is by no means uncommon and which is precisely the conception of religious identity held in Judaism.

For both of those groups, subsequent legislation was required.[24] What is crucial here, however, is less the particular recommendations that were made than the fact that the principles themselves provide no means for deciding such issues. The principles pertain to the rights and obligations of those who come fully within the domain of citizenship (and to that extent, of humanity). To place anyone outside that domain is to open the way to arbitrariness, not only in the first judgment of who has or has not the right to a civic identity, but also in the subsequent judgment of how those who do not have that right are to be treated.[25] (Even Kant's argument for a proportionality between crime and punishment stems from a thesis independent of—and possibly inconsistent with—that of the Categorical Imperative.) Formal concepts such as the Categorical Imperative or the rational will provide no substantive help in specifying how the results of their own applications are to be judged outside the domain for which they are formulated.

In a teleological ethics such as Aristotle's, certain practical recommendations can be ruled out on the basis of the end desired; if temperance is identified as a virtue, for example, it is evident that certain types of conduct are more likely to lead to that goal than others, and this determination is itself open to public discussion and judgment. The emphasis on a goal or outcome, moreover, allows for variety in the means, since there may well be alternative ways of reaching a single end. Where the means is also conceived as an end, however, where the ethics is "deontological," then the occurrence of variety or pluralism, either as a feature of judgment or in the objects of judgment, itself becomes suspect. And although certain differences may in the event be judged not to be ethically or politically significant, the burden of proof rests always on the differences themselves and those in whom they are found. The initial presumption is against them both, with no formal means provided for overcoming that presumption or for deciding what consequences follow from it.

The conceptions thus outlined mark out an analogy between the elements embodied in the "principle" of genocide as that has been described above in chapter 1 and the structural form exemplified in the

---

24. Arthur Hertzberg, *The French Enlightenment and the Jews* (New York: Columbia University Press, 1968), 339. See also Katz, *From Prejudice to Destruction*, 77.

25. Talmon argues that "totalitarian democracy"—of both the left and, as in Nazism, the right—adopted a "too perfectionist attitude" toward the values of eighteenth-century liberal individualism (which otherwise would in his view have evolved into a version of John Stuart Mill's conception of liberty). The contention here has been that this "too perfectionist attitude" is built into the position itself. (See Jacob Talmon, *The Origins of Totalitarian Democracy* [New York: Praeger, 1960], 249.)

conceptions of the universal self and of the ahistorical, universalizing judgment which have been proposed here as basic themes of Enlightenment thought. In the conceptual framework presupposed in the phenomenon of genocide, a crucial distinction is asserted between members of a group to whom certain rights are ascribed by virtue of that membership and individuals who are not members of that group, whose humanity is thus brought into question and whose "rights" then become contestable. Furthermore, if the rights at issue (and correlatively the definition of the group) are fundamental—for example, as such a definition might distinguish between humans and subhumans—exclusion from the first group means that virtually no controls remain for the determination of the status (or rights) of those who are excluded. This does not by itself ensure that the consequences of such exclusion will be severe, but it does mean that there are no limits *in principle* to what those consequences may bring. The fact of difference becomes in effect a prima-facie justification for whatever response is made.

The discussion of genocide in chapter 1 suggested that the Nazis, even when they assumed power in 1933, had not, either conceptually or practically, fixed on the goal of genocide—but that this purpose evolved in a number of stages, each of which was first fixed by them and then successively breached. Formally, the single most decisive stage in this progression was the abrogation of citizenship for the Jews of Germany, in the Nuremberg Laws of 1935—a step by which the Nazis began the quite specific exemplification of the conceptual framework that has been outlined here. For once the Jews were formally excluded from the body politic—on the grounds that *by their nature* they did not qualify for the rights of citizenship—there were no limits in principle to what steps might be initiated against them, even if in point of fact it required five or six years before the most extreme of those steps, that of genocide, was taken.

The stages progressively reached in this period, then, followed as opportunity presented itself and in the absence of resistance from other sources either within or outside Germany; once the process began, certainly in the absence of opposition, there was no reason for it to stop at any particular point. And if genocide could be set in motion and even justified in this way in respect to the Jews of Germany, who were first formally disenfranchised in order to assure the "legality" of further measures directed against them, the justification would be only stronger for genocide directed against Jews who had not been German citizens in the first place and who were also alleged to be a threat against those citizens. There were no constraints of moral or of political principle to prevent this; the various international conventions of war governing the treat-

ment of civilians or of prisoners of war, which had relied for their force
on a combination of tacit understanding and the power of public and
international opinion, were simply overridden, on the grounds that
where the Jews were concerned the principles did not apply and that in
any event public opinion would be indifferent. (With respect to the latter point, of course, the Nazis were quite correct at least in reference to
the time when the crucial decisions were being made.) It may be too
much to claim that the more than two million Russian prisoners of war
(and Polish, British, and American prisoners of war in much smaller
numbers) who were killed by the Nazis were killed because the genocide
against the Jews nullified the conventions that might otherwise have
protected them; but certainly it was the justification invoked for genocide that would also "justify" the violation of the conventions that
might have protected the other prisoners of war. As nothing was forbidden or precluded for the Nazis in their genocide against the Jews, the
right to transgress limitlessly was readily extended to other and, in some
sense, to all laws.

3. The Affiliation of Ideas

The analogy of ideas outlined in the preceding section between certain
Enlightenment themes and the conceptual framework of the phenomenon of genocide does not yet prove a causal connection between
the two, and the difficulty of establishing such a connection is evidently
greater than that of establishing the analogy (there will, after all, be *some*
likeness between any two events). The relation proposed, then, is stronger than analogy or likeness, although more oblique than that of direct
physical causality. It will be referred to as "affiliation"—in which certain
features of one ideational structure reappear as features of a second and
later one, serving in both structures a similar motivating role and con-
necting them also at specific historical junctures. In the accounts of the
two ideological frameworks juxtaposed here, the impulse for universalization or totalization is pivotal—first, for conceiving the individual
self in terms of a formally general definition, thus precluding concrete
and historical differences; and then, for basing the definition of that universal self on formal criteria which cannot, however, be applied formally.
So long as the terms "human" or "rational" are defined ahistorically,
without reference to the historical ground on which both those concepts
and their referents are based, an opening is left for a definition and for
the moral implications to be drawn from it, which is at best arbitrary in
its practical applications and at worst, as in the Nazi definition, a pretext
used to conceal other purposes. The opening to such arbitrariness is

manifest in the Nazi conception of racial determinism and in their application of it—for example, in the Nazi persecution, on the same ground of racial inferiority that was applied to the Jews, of the "Aryan" Gypsies—and, on the other side, in the transformation by fiat of the Japanese into "honorary" Aryans. (A still odder example was the Nazi decision that the Karaites were not "really" Jews—a verdict that saved the members of that small community.) The criteria applied in these cases depended on a practical standard for which the conceptual framework itself provided no basis one way or the other; *any* conclusions asserted would then be consistent, even if they might have been less flagrant than they were in fact.

The notion of a universalist definition of the self contains the basis of this inconsistency within itself, since it implies that the concept of humanity is not exclusionary, but at the same time makes clear that the concept is inapplicable without a criterion of exclusion (without such a criterion, there would be nothing that was not a self). The definition thus presents itself as a formal principle; when it comes to be applied and thus used to distinguish between one group or person and another, however, it turns into a substantive and then arbitrary standard. The progression here is thus neither accidental nor a misconstrual of the principle. Where the ideal of universality is proposed as an abstract and formal standard, there can be no place in it for the consideration that people live and act within groups or as individuals, not (or not only) abstractly or generally, but historically and particularly. Moreover, where social decision and ethical valuation within a fixed moral universe of discourse depend finally on the individual intention of the agent, with its inaccessibility to verification, no tests or checks of those decisions are possible other than that of conformity; anyone who violates what is otherwise a social consensus places himself outside the community and is thus liable to its challenge.

The danger thus posed is more fundamental than that of the "tyranny of the majority" (in Mill's phrase), inasmuch as groups or individuals may be excluded on the basis of principle in such a way as to deny them the status even of a minority. Since the criterion of discrimination is itself exempt from historical or empirical scrutiny, the properties ascribed in applying the criterion are similarly inaccessible and beyond argument. Under the guise of reason, then, the principle as applied may do exactly as it chooses to, on decisions concerning not only particular rights but in respect to the ascription of rights as such. And the arbitrariness which this invites is exemplified, not only in the conclusion reached by the Nazi pseudo-science of race which has been cited, but also in the apparently haphazard turns that marked the path leading to the Final Solution. It might well seem, for example, that there is an unfathomable disparity between the fact that in September 1941, more than eight years after they came to power, the Nazis would be arriving at the conclusion that thenceforth German Jews should be forbidden to ride in public transport during rush hours and the fact that five months later the Wannsee conference would formally set in motion the extermination of the Jews. In terms of the contentless principle which underlies the reasoning leading to those conclusions, however, the incongruity in the proximity of these two steps is only apparent.

The claim made here for a relation of affiliation between the themes cited from the Enlightenment and the structural presuppositions of the phenomenon of genocide amounts to more than the negative thesis that there is no inconsistency between them, although it should be recognized that this minimal contention would itself be significant. (So Andre Glucksmann writes: "It is not fair to accuse the master thinkers of having organized the concentration camps, rather of not having *dis*organized them in advance.")[26] For some moral or theoretical commitments, certain potential "transformations" are so unlikely as to be for practical purposes impossible. Admittedly, this constraint applies more often to the social consequences of economic or material conditions than to the role of ideas: to wage a war, for example, presupposes certain resources without which a decision to initiate the war would be unlikely (or beyond that, simply irrational). But the relationship between ideas and their consequences may be similarly proportioned, and this evidently applies both to their individual and their "corporate" appearances, even if it is most explicit at the level of the individual. It may be too much to claim, for example, that given John Dewey's theoretical ideals of experimentation and pluralism, he *could* not have aligned himself politically with fascism, but surely such a commitment would have been for him only a step short of impossible. One might, as a check on this claim, compare this potential relation in respect to Dewey with the analogous possibility in respect to Heidegger. This difference in probability amounts, at the level of ideas, to a test of consistency.

But, again, it is not only the absence of inconsistency that characterizes the relation of the two structural frameworks that have been outlined. A more positive connection figures in that relation, and the principal exemplification of this is the lure of universalism, as the Nazis imposed their own totalizing definition of the self, and their supposed right to assert that definition, on a group which insisted on its own divergent particularity. The fact that the Nazis were nationalists, appealing

26. Andre Glucksmann, *The Master Thinkers*, trans. Brian Pearce (New York: Harper and Row, 1980), 96.

also to the *völkisch* Teutonic ideals, is not at odds, as might seem to be the case, with the emphasis ascribed here to the principle of universalization. It was not only that the Nazis repeatedly emphasized that they were thinking always of their own place vis-à-vis everyone else but that the principle of universalization was applied wherever they had power; they had, in effect, incorporated that principle into nationalism. In doing this, the Nazis were in effect urging the replacement of history by a version of reason, imposing this, where the Jews were concerned, on a group for which, in the Nazis' view, history was intrinsically related to identity. At the point at which this opposition became explicit, there was no room for compromise—not for the Jews, since there was nothing they could do about the identity ascribed to them, and not for the Nazis, since it was their definition that was being applied.

The crucial issue here for the history of ideas is not whether the Nazis *could* have given the ideas they appropriated and applied a different form, or whether they could have rejected them entirely (both of which were evidently possible), but whether the conclusions they reached were somehow native or implicit in the ideas and whether they were so conceived (as ideas) by the Nazis themselves. The argument presented has asserted that both of these were the case: that in respect to the phenomenon of genocide the Nazis chose to act on the concept and, before that, to "have" the idea itself, enlarging in these choices on a basis already extant. Ideas, whether of individuals or groups, come to life in quite varied ways. At one extreme, the process may begin with the appropriation of an idea directly from an earlier context; at the other extreme, a reactionary idea may be provoked in opposition to the original. Between these extremes, a mediate possibility occurs in which implications latent in earlier ideas are imagined and affirmed—made manifest. Such explication may take place contemporaneously with the act in which the idea is embodied, but it serves even then as a means of "having" the idea. Seen from this perspective, the affiliation of ideas need not be conscious, any more than intentions have to be explicitly or fully conceived before they are acted on. The latter condition, as was suggested in chapter 1, is a feature of the intentionality of genocide, as the idea of genocide may in certain respects have been coincident with or even posterior to the act itself. But in those circumstances also, ideas retain their identity as ideas and their potential role as reasons—with the responsibility entailed by this on the part of those who have and act on them. It is too much to claim that the Nazis, consciously and as a group, arrived at a death sentence for the Jews on Europe by deducing it from premises which had announced first, long before, an abstract definition of the self and then that the Jews were excluded from that definition—

the two of these then pointing to a conclusion in the "principle" of genocide. But an alternative view of the process, as making manifest in the later moment what had been only latent in the earlier ideas, can represent the historical connection between them without any such rationalist assumption; the process is that of bringing to the surface what had been present before as an internal and broad condition.

It is evident that a claim for even the limited form of causality by affiliation that has been proposed here between structural elements of the Enlightenment and the phenomenon of genocide faces a number of serious objections—most immediately, that the Nazis held themselves and have generally been considered by others to stand in sharp opposition to Enlightenment ideals. The cogency of this objection is evident from the standard formulations of those ideals. So, for example, Peter Gay characterizes the Enlightenment thinkers as calling for "a social and political order that would be secular, reasonable, humane, pacific, open and free."[27] It is difficult to conceive of the Third Reich, even in its own terms let alone in those of others, as exemplifying these goals. The Nazis themselves, moreover, explicitly attacked the principles of the Enlightenment and the humanistic tradition in which it stood. The Nazi theorist and apologist Ernst Kriek would write that "the idea of humanism . . . is a philosophical principle of the eighteenth century caused by the conditions of the time. It is in no sense binding upon us as we live under different conditions, in different times."[28] Heidegger's "Letter on Humanism" is more diffuse than Kriek's statement, but the implication is clear there as in other of Heidegger's writings (including but by no means restricted to his notorious Inaugural Address in 1933 as Rector at the University of Freiburg) that the themes of Enlightenment humanism, and especially the principle of "tolerance," are indeed under attack.[29] Furthermore, when Nazi ideology is categorized among the currents of ideas in the nineteenth and twentieth centuries, it is commonly seen as a reaction *against* the Enlightenment—emphasizing intuition and feeling in contrast to reason, nostalgia for the past against "modernism," collective identity over individual autonomy or responsibility.[30]

27. Peter Gay, *The Enlightenment* (New York: Knopf, 1969), vol. 1, 397.

28. Cited in Max Weinreich, *Hitler's Professors* (New York: YIVO, 1946), 6.

29. Martin Heidegger, "Letter on Humanism," in David Krell (ed.), *Martin Heidegger: Basic Writings* (New York: Harper and Row, 1977), 189–242; cf. also "'The Self-Assertion of the German University': Heidegger's Rectoral Address," trans. Karsten Harries, *Review of Metaphysics* 38 (1985), 470–80, and "On the Essence of Truth," in Krell, *Martin Heidegger*, 113–42.

30. See Emanuel Levinas, *Difficile Liberté* (Paris: Albin Michel, 1976), 357–64; George Mosse, *The Crisis* (see chap. 1, n. 7), 13; Leszek Kolakowski, "Genocide and Ideology," in

All of these conceptual features, moreover, say nothing yet about the actual policies of the Nazis, which, if anything, appear still more distant from the impulses of the Enlightenment. Whatever reasons or justifications they gave to others, it is evident that the Nazis did not believe themselves bound by the new assembly of moral and social conventions which had emerged in the post-Enlightenment milieu of Europe and which, however weak in their formulation and in the public consensus about them, provided at least a superficial bond among nations (and had been professed by German regimes prior to the Nazis). Even if the Enlightenment had spoken less emphatically than it did about the principles of tolerance, equality, and reason, the claim for a connection between such principles and the acts of the Nazis would appear problematic.

Such objections are in one sense undeniable—but they argue past rather than against the thesis posed here, which is based on the internal structure of ideas, not on what is said about them. Once again, the prima-facie evidence is a reminder of the need for such analysis: unless the Nazi genocide against the Jews is viewed as aberration or madness, a break in history itself—and there are both historical and logical arguments against this—the one possible alternative is to locate that event in relation to its historical antecedents. The prima-facie evidence, furthermore, is enlarged in the relation of affiliation that has been proposed between conceptual cause and effect. As has been suggested above, the imprint of an idea may be evident in its aftermath or "effect" in a form less one-sided than either direct incorporation (obviously not the relation to be found here) or contradiction. In a third alternative, ideas persist by clearing a conceptual space which their implications or affiliations then occupy. On the latter account, a projection from the original occurs which, although not directly incorporating the original, extends certain of its features which retain their original form to another quite different context. Extremity in that later context may have been muted in its earlier appearance; it is true as well that what is latent does not always *have to* find expression. But where the expression is indisputable, the tests of consistency and relevance point the way back to its source.

It is this last type of connection that has been proposed between the Enlightenment principles cited and the conceptual structure presupposed in the phenomenon of the Nazi genocide. The abstract, ahistorical self posited by the Enlightenment as an ideal of humanity entails in its converse appearance the implication that historical difference (and all

Lyman H. Legters (ed.), *Western Society after the Holocaust* (Boulder, Colo.: Westview Press, 1983), 19–20.

the more, an historical definition of identity) will be suspect; the principle of universal reason or judgment implies that the grounds on which such distinctions are based may be—should be—challenged: not only can everyone be judged by the one criterion, but the consequences of being included or excluded by it are, in terms of the principle of universalizability, without limits. The "difference" of the Jews was judged by the Nazis to be fundamental—and with this decision, there was nothing to inhibit the decision subsequently made about what followed from that judgment: there was no "reason" *not* to destroy the difference. To be sure, the Nazis were themselves "particularist" in their nationalism and in the distinctions they emphasized between themselves and other nations and races. But more important than the Nazis' insistence on establishing their own place is the fact that their assertions of particularism were characteristically formulated in the terms of universalist principles. Louis Dumont has called attention to the contrast for the Nazis between the values of *Allgemeinheit* ("universality") and *Gesamtheit* ("entirety," "totality") to which *their* version of individualism is tied and the narrow and egotistic individualism by which other races (and especially the Jews) are, according to the Nazi account, constrained.[31]

The account of this conceptual affiliation does not mean that anyone committed to the original principles would foresee, or, if he foresaw them, would concur in the conclusions that were thus subsequently to be drawn. Put more strongly, there is no implication here that the future represented in the Nazi genocide could not have moved in a different direction than the one it took. Affiliation does not amount to inevitability; what is latent does not *have* to become manifest. The more problematic question is whether the relation between the principles initially distinguished and their aftermath is plausible in terms of historical transmission, on the one hand, and, on the other hand, in terms of the general freedom of ideas to move from one context to another. Given the initial principles that have been identified and the historical absence of countervailing pressures, the connection that has been described provides a conceptual framework for the transformation of the initial principles into the presuppositions of genocide.

This claim does not imply that no other ideas are involved in the conceptual framework of genocide in general or in the Nazi genocide against the Jews in particular; it is obvious, in fact, that other ideas (perhaps related to the Enlightenment principles noted, perhaps not) might have,

31. Louis Dumont, *Essays on Individualism* (Chicago: University of Chicago Press, 1986), 163, 167.

or had, significant roles in both these connections. So, for example, S. H. Bergmann suggests that "when we ask ourselves, which philosophy it was that paved the way to Nazism, we will have to say that it was that philosophy of the 19th century which—under the mistaken and mistaking influences of the methods of natural science—taught men to see humanity as a zoological species and tried to eliminate the abyss between man and beast."[32] The biological motif thus cited appears, for Nazi ideology, in the conception of racial inheritance (which extends to personality or character as well as to physical features); in the system of eugenics (and thereby in euthanasia), which was based on the theory of race; in the version of Social Darwinism maintained by the Nazis; and even in the biological metaphors of disease appealed to as justification for the genocide against the Jews. There is, however, no conflict between the relevance alleged for this cluster of ideas and the principles emphasized previously; if the universalist conceptions of self and judgment are taken as central, these other ideas disclose themselves as compatible with them.

Again, however, a relation stronger than compatibility or consistency holds between these ideas and the Enlightenment themes that have been cited. It seems clear, for example, that the direction taken by nineteenth-century biological theory, concluding in theories of evolution, racial differentiation, and genetic transmission, was indebted to the Enlightenment ideal of history as progressive—an ideal itself linked to the conception of a developing and potentially universal reason. At some point, admittedly, such broadly drawn connections become so inclusive as to be trivial. But when the concepts of the ahistorical self and universal judgment are joined to the materialism of such Enlightenment figures as La Mettrie and d'Holbach (and even, it should be added, the marquis de Sade), the affinity alleged between the moral ideals of the Enlightenment and the biological theories of the nineteenth century becomes increasingly plausible and with this, too, their subsequent convergence in the concept of genocide.

That there is no litmus-paper test of relevance for assessing the process of affiliation does not mean that certain supposed connections may not be judged implausible or problematic. An important instance of this can be seen in the common references by both Nazi theoreticians (like Alfred Rosenberg and Alfred Bäumler) and independent commentators to Nietzsche as an ideological influence on Nazism.[33] This connection is

32. S. H. Bergmann, "Can Transgression Have an Agent?" *Yad Vashem Studies* 5 (1963), 14.

33. See, e.g., Alfred Bäumler, "Nietzsche und der Nationalsozialismus," in *Studien zur deutschen Gesitesgeschichte* (Berlin: Junker and Dannhaupt, 1937).

most frequently alleged for the translation of Nietzsche's conception of the *Übermensch* into the doctrine of the Aryan "master race," and there is no denying points of resemblance between the two, insofar as they both represent certain individuals as naturally superior to others in power and then in merit. But the disanalogies between the two positions, even in respect to this one claim, are crucial, especially as concerns the racial theory which is so essential a part of the Nazi view. The status of the *Übermensch* for Nietzsche is quite explicitly not racial or inheritable. So far as genetic theory is concerned, in fact, Nietzsche was a Lamarckian, and it is in any event the individual, not the group or species, on which his claims for the *Übermensch* are founded.[34] When this difference is joined to Nietzsche's own and repeated attacks on anti-Semitism—a phenomenon already sufficiently common in his time for him to cite it as further evidence for his view of the basic German "stupidity"—the misreading required to identify him as a source of authority for Nazi ideology is evident.

Admittedly, it is Nietzsche, not Schiller or Goethe (or Kant), who was taken up in this way, and that fact, however understood, is surely not accidental. "One can't falsify just anything," Derrida writes about the subsequent history of the "Nietzsche text."[35] Nor is the argument more compelling for ideas than it is for technology that creators are exempt from responsibility for the uses to which their inventions are put, whatever their own original intentions were. But difficult as the judgment of relevance or irrelevance may be in this connection, the judgment itself is inescapable, and *some* of the distinctions with which it concludes are more than only plausible. The fact that a chair can be used as a weapon does not prove that the "idea" of a chair is the source or "cause" of an attack in which it is used: latency is not the equivalent of logical *possibility*. In this respect, the chair differs from a bomb, the primary function of which is to destroy (or to threaten to do so). To be sure, misappropriation has causal consequences no less certainly than does affiliation, and, again, there is no certain line between the two. But for Nietzsche's historical aftermath, what is at issue is an instance of misappropriation, not

34. See on this point Walter Kaufmann, *Nietzsche: Philosopher, Psychologist, Antichrist* (Princeton, N.J.: Princeton University Press, 1967), 294–5.
35. Jacques Derrida, *The Ear of the Other*, trans. Peggy Kamuf (New York: Schocken, 1985), 24. The distinction asserted by Derrida does not take a position, more positively, on what the nature of the connection *is*, apparently deferring it because of the "still-open contours of an era . . . I do not believe that we as yet know how to think what Nazism is" (*EAR*, 31). We do not in any event find in Nietzsche even an approximation of Goethe in *Wilhelm Meister:* "We do not tolerate any Jew among us; for how could we grant him a share in the highest culture, the origin and tradition of which he denies."

198 HISTORIES AND GENOCIDE

of deduction and not even, in the term proposed here, of affiliation. Far from being entailed by the premises underlying Nietzsche's position, the conclusions drawn are inconsistent with them. To reconstruct in the imagination the events leading up to the Nazi genocide against the Jews without the name or presence of Nietzsche is to be compelled to change almost nothing else in that pattern. This contrasts sharply with the results of the same experiment as it might be applied to a number of other ideas and thinkers whose absence would entail significant revisions in the process of Enlightenment affiliation—even, perhaps in its eventual outcome.

One further methodological issue needs to be mentioned in relation to this process. From the claim of a qualified causal connection between certain ideas, it follows that had a *different* idea been substituted for the "cause," the outcome, everything else being equal, would also have been different. A test for this claim, then, is in identifying an alternative hypothesis—the different cause that would have produced different consequences. Again, factors other than ideas—economic, psychological, geopolitical causes—undoubtedly also affected the occurrence of the Nazi genocide.[36] But insofar as a specific idea or group of ideas figure as causal factors there, it should be possible to propose others that would arguably have led to different consequences.

Since the affiliation of ideas that has been described focuses on the roles of universalization in judgment and the ahistorical concept of a universal self, an alternative schema would entail changes in these factors. One such alternative, then, would associate historical or social identity intrinsically with human nature—in contrast to an ahistorical "essence"—stipulating that its related conception of human rights would depend, not on the conformity of all persons to a single ahistorical ideal, but on an indefinite number of possible ideals. What appears here is not a *broadened* version of tolerance, but a revision of that value vertically, on the ground that at least certain social differences are not accidental (to be tolerated in the sense of being overlooked) but determinant aspects of individual identity. Civil rights accorded the individual in the latter case would be granted not in return for a conformity exacted by the definition of a universal self, but in the interest of individual or group self-realization which might well disclose significant variations or differences in that process.

To be sure, even on this alternative version of the principle of tolera-

36. Richard Rubenstein proposes a version of the latter in *The Age of Triage* (Boston: Beacon Press, 1983).

tion, discrimination or oppression might occur—when a majority group imposed itself on a minority or when groups relatively equal in power came into conflict with each other; but such occurrences would then be aberrant, not impelled by the principle itself. The ideal underlying this alternative version, with its basis in an historical and socially contingent self, would be anti-utopian, opposed to notions of human perfectibility and a universalist standard of human nature and society on which such notions are based. That the Enlightenment version of these doctrines is only one among many in the history of social thought should not obscure the persistence of an opposed tradition in which the pluralist view dominates. Perhaps the single most important formulation of this appears in the Aristotelian conception of polity which identifies an historical ground at the basis of political or social structures, with the implication which follows from this of a plurality both of grounds and structures. The strong distinction asserted by Aristotle between theoretical and practical reason according to which it is precisely a feature of the latter *not* to meet the standard of universalization required by the former provides a methodological basis for the defense of ethical and political pluralism.

Admittedly, universalist elements also appear in Aristotle's *Politics* and in other of his writings (as in the *Nichomachean Ethics*). But the issue here is not so much the question of consistency in Aristotle's writings as their disclosure of an alternative to the Enlightenment design of universalization. Both in Aristotle, and more significantly for the present discussion, in a number of contemporary writers on ethics and social theory whose work incorporates this alternative basis, the possibility of a pluralist view is clearly posed.[37] This does not in itself demonstrate the advantages of that or any other alternative, but it adds weight to the contention that as the themes of the Enlightenment did not lead inevitably to the "affiliation" which has here been identified with them, the possibility existed of alternative themes or ideas—then as also now.

37. As, for example, in MacIntyre, *After Virtue* (see chap. 2, n. 17), esp. chaps. 4–6; Bernard Williams, *Ethics and the Limits of Philosophy* (Cambridge: Harvard University Press, 1985); Stuart Hampshire, *Morality and Conflict* (Cambridge: Harvard University Press, 1983), 143–54. Thomas Nagel, in *The View from Nowhere* (New York: Oxford University Press, 1986), takes a pragmatist rather than an Aristotelian position, but the view ("from nowhere") which he criticizes closely resembles the one against which these other writers are also reacting. The affinity should be noted, moreover, between these proposals and other recent attempts, mainly in the social sciences, to identify the typological features of political or social structures conducive to the occurrence of genocide. See, for example, Wallimann and Dobkowski, *Genocide* (see chap. 1, n. 1), part I.

4. Universalist Reason and Particularist History

In addition to the specific difficulties that have been acknowledged in respect to the account given so far, the broader objection might be raised that speaking in the name of history, the account itself remains ahistorical. For even on the assumptions that historical events have an ideational form and that the ideational form as it has been outlined figures in the structures both of the Enlightenment background and the phenomenon of the Nazi genocide, these do not address the question of why that form should, in its actual history, have had the particular agents and objects that it did. Why, with the principles ascribed here to the Enlightenment spread broadly across Europe, should the eruption of genocide have occurred in Germany? And why, whether in connection with this question or independently, did that eruption, among the diverse groups who might have been singled out, take the Jews as its object? The conjunction of those two groups is decisive in the occurrence of the Nazi genocide, and this issue is thus unavoidable; that the answers to it seem bound to remain problematic hardly diminishes its urgency.

It has already been acknowledged here that to require necessary and sufficient conditons in historical explanation is to pose an impossible demand. At the very least, the contention that history is underdetermined, on the scale of mass movements no less than at the level of the individual, has history on its side, if only in the failure of all past efforts to demonstrate why specific historical events *must* have turned out as they did. In this sense, it would be as excessive to argue that the occurrence of the Nazi genocide *had* to have the Nazis as its source as it would be to assert that the Nazis individually had no option in acting as they did. Either of these claims would preclude any ascription of moral responsibility, and this is only one, although a central one, among other objections to their plausibility. That genocide is an idea as well as an act—more precisely, that it is an idea *in* the act—further underscores this point. If we ask why someone, whether an individual or a group, "has" a certain idea or then acts on it, it is usually possible to point to certain sources as implicated consciously or unconsciously in that process. But such references remain at most only probable, with the degree of probability related inversely to the novelty of the ideas and to the break they represent between the past and the present. The most radical or "original" historical developments are by definition the least predictable—a condition no less applicable to ethical or political ideas or acts than to scientific or artistic innovations.

This does not mean that the Nazi genocide could just as readily have had other agents—that it would have been equally possible for the English or the French or the Americans to have initiated it (or equally possible that it should not have occurred at all). Writings about the history of the Third Reich have made amply clear the number of factors which distinguish German history in the nineteenth and early twentieth centuries from the histories of these other countries; these include a variety of material constraints and institutional presuppositions at the foundation of the phenomenon of Nazism and its genocidal war. The economic and political exigencies which affected the Weimar Republic, the causes within the social and institutional framework of Germany that had earlier contributed to World War I, the definitions of civil and social class in Bismarck's Germany which preceded *that:* these only begin to touch on the distinguishing features later implicated in the policies and actions of the Third Reich.[38] But it is also evident that the causal chains constructed around these elements remain underdetermined so far as concerns the requirements of explanation for Hitler's Germany: the supposed causes are not by themselves sufficient to the effect. Many similar if not identical factors are evident in countries other than Germany; even if this consideration were put aside, moreover, there is insufficient evidence in German history itself to support the conclusion that an effect (here, the Nazi genocide against the Jews) had followed necessarily from the causes cited.

It might be argued, admittedly, that the feature of underdetermination characterizes all historical explanation, much in the way that it applies even in the more restricted and straightforward form of biographical narratives which detail the histories of individual lives. There, too, each effect recalls an additional or prior cause, and the chain of explanation is both unending and insufficient at any moment to "deduce" any particular biographical event. But if this is characteristic of historiography in general, it has a special point in respect to the Nazi genocide against the Jews. This is due in part to the displacement of the factors of self-interest which usually figure largely in attempts at historical explanation. As has been argued in chapters 1 and 2, the question "*Why* did the Nazis do what they did?" constantly runs up against the fact that in certain notable ways the Nazi genocide against the Jews was in direct conflict with the "interests" of the Nazis. If it did not do so initially, the Nazi war against the Jews eventually diminished the chances for German victory in the larger war in which the Germans were engaged—and at a relatively early point this was evident to almost

38. See, e.g., Gordon A. Craig, *Germany 1866–1945* (New York: Oxford University Press, 1978); David Calleo, *The German Problem Reconsidered* (Cambridge: Cambridge University Press, 1978).

everyone aware of the juxtaposition of the two. There is no doubt something to the claim, now increasingly being pressed by a number of German historians, that various decisions made independently of each other converged to provide an impetus to the Nazi policy of genocide.[39] But to admit this as a factor is not to demonstrate that there was no encompassing intention in that policy or that that policy was not affirmed as a policy and even when weighed against the interests of Germany victory—or indeed survival—in the war as a whole.[40]

When the latter considerations are added to those already cited—that it is impossible to demonstrate any necessity that impelled the Nazi genocide and, on the other hand, that the combination of act and idea was not accidental or a matter of circumstances—the remaining possibilities of explanation are sharply narrowed. They return in fact to the features of genocide that have been previously cited: that in the Nazis' war of extermination, a basic principle was held to be at stake by them, and that they both chose that principle and chose also to act on it quite apart from the consequences of these decisions for other of their goals. It is obvious that material circumstances contributed to Nazi policies before and during the twelve years of their rule, and undoubtedly these circumstances affected Germany distinctively and in any event more directly and severely than they did other countries in the same period. But even this basis was not determinant of what ensued—a fact which leaves only one alternative in the pattern of explanation, namely, that the Nazi genocide against the Jews was intentional and the result of a decision: the Nazis did what they did because they both wanted and chose to. In historical terms, this conclusion will seem simplistic or moralistic, even ahistorical. But it arguably emerges from the history of the Nazi genocide itself, and it emerges only as the alternatives to it disclose themselves as still more problematic, on both historical and moral grounds.

39. See, e.g., Martin Broszat, "Hitler and the Genesis of the Final Solution," *Yad Vashem Studies* 13 (1979), 61–98; and "Plaidoyer für eine Historisierung des Nationalsozialismus," *Merkur* 39 (1985), 373–85; Mommsen, "Die Realisierung des Utopischen" (see chap. 1, n. 8), 381–420. See also Arno J. Mayer, *Why Did the Heavens not Darken?: The "Final Solution" in History* (New York: Pantheon, 1988).

40. Consider, for example, the statement by Himmler himself in a letter to Ganzenmüller, Secretary of State of the German Transport (23 January 1943): "I well know what dire straits the railroads are in and what demands are always being made on them. Nonetheless I am forced to appeal to you: help me and supply me the trains." Cited in Arad, *Belzec* (see chap. 1, n. 14), 133. That the stakes involved in the issue were fully articulated is unmistakable in the position Göring took (and in large measure lost) in arguing against Heydrich: "It is more important for us to win the war than to implement racial policy." (Werner Prag and Wolfgang Jacobmeyer (eds.), *Das Dienstagebuch des deutschen Generalsgouverneurs in Polen 1939–1945* (Stuttgart: Deutsche Verlags-Anstalt, 1974), 336.

The second "particularist" question referred to above moves, with strong irony, along parallel lines to the first. Obviously, the Jews did not choose or decide on their fate as victims in the Nazi genocide. But it also seems clear that the role forced on them in that genocide was not accidental or unrelated to the historical choices by which they had shaped and confirmed their own identity. This conclusion becomes increasingly compelling when it is judged against the only possible alternative to it—namely, that the decision underlying the Nazi genocide against the Jews was a random decision, one that might have been turned equally plausibly against any other of the number of distinguishable groups of which the Germans would have been aware. The latter view, as has already been mentioned, is not without its proponents, either as applied to the history of anti-Semitism generally or to the Nazi genocide in particular. Sartre's *The Anti-Semite and the Jew,* written in the context of the events of World War II, epitomizes this "scapegoat" view of those events, according to which the agents of anti-Semitism, moved mainly by a generalized desire to blame and punish in order to escape their own freedom and responsibility, were indifferent to the particular object onto which that desire was projected.[41] On this account, the choice of the Jews was arbitrary; neither anti-Semitism in general nor the extremity it reached in the Nazi genocide could have even a contextual, let alone a determinant, basis.

It will be evident that Sartre's account takes a distinctively ahistorical view of an event with an unusually dense historical background (it is sufficiently ahistorical to lead Sartre to ignore even evidence that might support his claim—for example, the fact that the Nazis also intended genocide against the Gypsies). As Sartre draws on the conception of personal "bad faith" which he had earlier elaborated in *Being and Nothingness,* anti-Semitism on his account reflects not even the history of the agent, let alone that of the victim. In this sense, Sartre's thesis goes further than only the contention that the Nazis chose to do what they did; Sartre admits no reason for any choice *within* the choice, and indeed the act of deciding, as a whole, appears to him intrinsically unrelated to reason. There is only the will to find an object for blame, to escape the responsibility of personal freedom—and then the act itself.

Admittedly, to dispute this or similar explanations does not imply that they are not relevant. The syndrome of the scapegoat recurs at many historical junctures, and the long history of anti-Semitism has surely included that impulse among others. (The history of scapegoating begins, one supposes, with the first choice, in the biblical account, of the

41. Sartre, *Anti-Semite* (see chap. 5, n. 4).

scapegoat itself.) But to claim this as a *sufficient* reason or cause for anti-Semitism is to reduce broad complexities of history and reason to a single psychological or conative category—a restriction which is implausible in principle and fact. Most importantly, it denies an historical role or identity to anyone other than the individual or group immediately responsible for the act—and where the Nazi genocide against the Jews is concerned, this seems a clear misrepresentation of that act and the decisions underlying it.[42]

The fact remains that in the face of the various prescriptions imposed on them externally (sometimes also in the acceptance of those prescriptions from within), Jews after the Enlightenment hardly less than before it retained an identity set in their own terms—a definition that was bound to test severely any prescription for universalism. If Jewish identity had been a function only of religion or creed, this might have been confronted externally (as it was in the history of Christian anti-Semitism) by means of forcible conversion or expulsion. (It is significant that notwithstanding the other important differences between Nazi and Christian anti-Semitism, the Nazis initially adopted one of the latter's traditional policies, namely, expulsion.) If, on the other hand, the particularism of the Jews had been exclusively ethnic or cultural, this too might have been undone: in its post-Enlightenment appearance, the religious alternative of conversion was replaced by its secular counterpart, assimilation. But the Nazis themselves devised a category of particularism, namely, race, which established the identity of the Jews as a biological "fact." And with this basis none of the traditional repsonses would suffice. Assimilation as it might mediate ethnic differences became instead a danger, since the process would further the transmission of biological characteristics. Assimilation which had occurred in the past was for the Nazis a continuing problem, both on practical grounds and "in principle." The Nuremberg Laws of 1935, according to which three Jewish grandparents were required—there were also less stringent, cultural requirements—to establish full Jewish identity, were themselves a revision of the earlier (1933), more stringent *Arierparagraph*, according to which one Jewish grandparent was sufficient to warrant exclusion from the category of "Aryans." (The arbitrariness of such definitions did

42. Max Horkheimer and Theodor Adorno, in *Dialectics of Enlightenment,* trans. J. Cumming (New York: Herder and Herder, 1972), present an extreme version of this thesis. Not only could "the fascist leaders just as easily replace the anti-Semitic plank in their platform by some other" (207), but the victims themselves could "take the place of the murderers . . . should they be invested with the title of the norm" (171). It is unclear how Horkheimer and Adorno can find such a view consistent with their own attack on Enlightenment "abstraction" and ahistoricism.

not, however, block the application of the general "principle.") Where the biological phenomenon of race was at issue, moreover, expulsion—in addition to its "impracticality"—would offer no more likely an alternative than assimilation: the alleged racial menace of the Jews would, on the analogy with disease, be a threat wherever and as long as they lived.

It can be argued that it was this specifically racial definition of particularism by the Nazis, not the opposition to particularism on behalf of universalism, that led them to conceive of the Final Solution. But, as has already been suggested, these views are not independent of each other in the development of the Nazi genocide. The drive for universalization was accompanied, first latently and then explicitly, by the requirement of exclusion and the rejection of particularism—both of these objectified for the Nazis in the identity of Jews vis-à-vis Germany. Nothing in this related set of intentions, moreover, would stand in principle against the most extreme repression of the particularism to be excluded; genocide was, at the very least, consistent with the same ground on which exclusion was based.

It is another one of the harsh but undeniable ironies of the history of the Nazi genocide that the conception of race in Nazi anti-Semitism has certain analogous features to the conception by the Jews of their own identity. Even before confronting the modernist and secularist distinction between religion and culture, the Jews had viewed themselves neither only as a religious fellowship defined by doctrinal commitments nor only as a cultural or ethnic group. The predominant representations of Jewish identity had asserted a conjunction between those two elements. The conjunction was not exceptional in the classical or the medieval Christian world, but it was noticed even in those times as asserted by the Jews, and it became more pressing an issue with the increasingly important post-Enlightenment distinction between religious and civic identity: the Jews would even then maintain their particularist commitments which seemed to challenge the universalist ideal. This challenge presented a large target; the Jews were all too clearly a test of what the impulse of universalization, detached from history and radically extended, would tolerate. That extension did not make the genocide against the Jews inevitable, but it did mean that the fact that the Jews became the objects of the Nazi attacks and ultimately of their genocide was more than an historical accident, that the "choice" which the Nazis made of them was deliberate in the same sense—and in the same act—as was the intent then joined to it to annihilate them as a group.

Within Judaism itself a strong universalist impulse is evident, initially in the monotheistic covenant in its historical origins, and then, directed toward the future, with the messianic vision of a future in which all people and peoples will unite. But this universalist view has been located consistently in a particularistic medium, with the implication that if the universalist ideal is to be realized, that will occur because of what transpires within history itself, as individuals and particular groups are engaged there. The irony thus becomes more intense that the Jews were killed in the name of a universalism that could tolerate many other things but not the one claim which is the basis on which all other historical claims depend, including even the claims on behalf of universal justice and universal reason. That is, the aspiration of individuals or groups to live their own lives—that is, to live.

8

Zionism in the Aftermath

Why ask about *Zionism* after the Nazi genocide? Isn't it *Judaism* that has to find a place for that event in the life of a religion and culture—in its claims, for example, of a just God, and, more generally, in the will now, still to persist in the assembly of traditional beliefs and commitments, of which Zionism, however important, has been only one? Well, yes, of course—but that does not deny that it was Zionism that became historically intertwined with the actions of Nazi Germany as no other communal or social feature of Judaism did and to an extent that will continue in the future as in the near past to affect the definition of Jewish identity. The connection here is stark, bitterly ironical, part of it so close to the center of recent Jewish history that with it the double vision of irony almost breaks apart. Can one do more than acknowledge, and then, as at the scene of a terrible accident, look away from the fact that the Nazi genocide did more to further the progress of Zionism than any other single event in modern history? Certainly the evidence is strong and nonpartisan that without the Nazi genocide the State of Israel, the most constant goal of Zionism, would possibly not have come into existence at all, or that if it had might well have soon disappeared. Indeed, even *after* the facts of the genocide were known—when the nations of the world, including also those who had fought the Nazis, stood condemned for negligence, culpable as bystanders willing to observe the murder of millions of people rather than to extend to them immigration permits or to modify strategies for fighting the war—even then, the decision in November 1947 by which the

207

General Assembly of the United Nations voted for the partition of Palestine and so for establishing a Jewish state was far from a foregone conclusion, with a number of political surprises contributing to the difference. And so it is a virtual certainty that *without* the genocide, without the hundreds of thousands of "displaced persons" left after the war as a presence in Europe, without the influx to Palestine of many of those refugees, without the twinges of conscience for past omission that nations allowed themselves at the prospect of a remedy that would cost themselves little—without these, it is as likely as anything can be among complex historical causes and effects that the decision by the world community to authorize a Jewish state in Palestine would not have been forthcoming, at least at that time. One need not linger here, then, on the maddening claim of an individual Eichmann that he had considered *himself* a Zionist to recognize the improbable congruity of history that brought Zionism and the Nazi genocide together. After two thousand years of dispersion, of being forced to live in countries that were not "theirs," the Jews were led back to Zion, if not wholly, decisively, by the same act of genocide that killed more than a third of their number and would, if it had had its way, have killed them all.[1]

If this were the whole of the connection between Zionism and the Nazi genocide, that link might be viewed as an isolated historical moment, perhaps, like a natural catastrophe, as a breach in an otherwise regular and predictable order. But that one connection and the consequences to which it led turn out in fact to have been part of an issue of longer standing, reflecting a continuing tension in Jewish history between the will of Zionism, for which one particular land had been a focus of memory and aspiration, and the energies of a Diaspora strong in its belief that it had realized a viable synthesis of Jewish and secular existence outside of Zion. How to mediate between the conflicting pulls in this tension has been a major preoccupation of Jewish thought and culture, one prefigured even in that early biblical "promise" of a land, a promise which was to lose its future-directed basis only twice (and then temporarily) in the long course of Jewish history—that is, when the Jews, after the Exodus, actually entered and inhabited the land and then again in the period of the Second Temple. Attempts to resolve this tension have historically been various but constant; they range from the flat denial of Zionism—in nineteenth-century Reform conception of Juda-

1. See David Horowitz, "The Holocaust as Background for the Decision of the United Nations to Establish a Jewish State," and Yehuda Bauer, "The Holocaust and the Struggle of the Yishuv as Factors in the Establishment of the State of Israel," in *Holocaust and Rebirth* (Jerusalem: Yad Vashem, 1974).

ism as a "protestant" religion with no institutionalized spiritual, let alone territorial or political center—to the conclusion drawn by the Zionists that the tension was nothing less than a contradiction, that with the establishment of a Jewish state, life in the Diaspora would be unintelligible, and that *without* the land and their habitation of it the continued existence of the Jews as Jews would be impossible.

It was the latter contention that claimed to find a source of evidence in the Nazi genocide. For Zionists, as for others who were moved by quite different motives and ideological lines, the question of how the genocide could have happened was inevitable. And even more than these other questioners, Zionists found themselves tempted by the harsh conclusion that, in some measure at least, the initial situation of the victims of the genocide and then their response to the genocide as it unfolded had themselves been factors in its occurrence. The argument here at first seemed plausible, almost benign: that as the Jews for some reason had been singled out as the object of genocide, so, too, for some reason (perhaps related to that initial situation), the process of their systematic extermination had been *possible*. The simplest rendering of these events, moreover—simple because it required for evidence only the indisputable fact that the genocide had occurred—pointed to the incapacity of the Jews to prevent it (since, surely, if they *had* been able to, they *would* have). And an explanation for this incapacity, too, was then ready at hand: that it was due to the identity the Jews had taken on as an alien—dependent and debilitated—people in Europe, a pattern of identity that had thus provided at least a means and perhaps even the occasion for the intentions of anti-Semitism. The conclusion accordingly emerged in so many words that the Nazi extermination of the Jews was confirmation—criminal, unspeakable, but nonetheless actual—of the Zionist analysis of life in the Diaspora. Certainly for the political Zionists, especially for the socialists among them but hardly less for those committed to other political or moral ideologies, the evidence was unmistakable. That the Jews in their marginal and deracinated existence had taken on identities—occupations, roles, self-images—which made them unfit to act spontaneously or independently, which turned them into caricatures of the bourgeoisie (who were already, after all, caricatures of full human beings) lacking either the practical efficacy of the working class or the political weight of the ruling classes; that European Jews were first compelled and then became accustomed to live by rules established by others in a condition of continuing dependency; that there was not elsewhere a Jewish state that could represent them to the community of nations: all of this, item by item, constituted, on the one hand, the Zionist rationale for its own ideals and then, on the other hand, a quite specific account of what made possible the near-realization of Nazi intentions.[2]

And, of course, the next step in the argument, moving then from the past to the present and future, also was obvious. Because just as evidence from the period of the Nazi genocide could be taken to confirm the Zionist diagnosis of Jewish history in the Diaspora, that evidence spoke, also, not only of what might in the past have averted destruction and loss, but of the future, what would or should yet be. What had been confirmed was, in short, a directive for future Jewish existence: that a national state was required—necessary if not inevitable—and that Jews, perhaps as laborers who would then escape the debilities of bourgeois existence, but at least as citizens in a nation chosen and constituted and defended by themselves, could expect to live fully safely, at home, only within it.

Now it is clear that there are gaps in the several stages of this argument and not only because of the abbreviated account given it here. Some of those gaps are serious enough to challenge the sequence as a whole; almost all of them have implications that go beyond the argument itself. The terms of one such implication are so highly charged, in fact, that it is easy to overlook the fact that the implication is only a variation on the general theme. For again, harsh and unnerving as the claim is, it is recognizable as a corollary of the most basic thesis of Zionism: that the European Jews were in good measure responsible for their own destruction, since if they *had* understood and acted on the alternative that Zionism made available to them—politically, economically, spiritually—they would not have been victimized by Hitler at all. They would not have been living in Europe: or if they were, they would not have been singled out for destruction; or if they were, the record of their resistance in the ghettos and death camps would have been much stronger than it was. The history of the Nazi genocide, in other words, would have been quite different—and probably not a history of *genocide* at all.[3]

This is not the context in which to consider the question of how the

2. Raul Hilberg, in the original edition of *The Destruction of the European Jews* (Chicago: Quadrangle, 1961) extends this argument with his notion of the "anticipatory compliance" which led the Jews (allegedly) to do to themselves what was threatened from the outside, to include Zionism itself; the latter also appears for him as a form of sublimation, a refusal by the Jews to face directly the conditions of their present (see pp. 14–17, 666–69). These terms recur in the revised edition of the book (see chap. 2, n. 9, above), pp. 23–24, although with some shift in emphasis; the role of Israel is now also referred to as an instance of the "mechanism of flight" (p. 1193).

3. Hannah Arendt gives an extreme (and much-criticized) version of this thesis (in *Eichmann*—see chap. 1, n. 18), chap. 7.

Jewish response to the Nazi genocide—the latter first as a threat and
later as an actuality—affected the course of that series of events. But two
facts which cannot be ignored have emerged in the numerous discussions of that question. The first of these is that there *were* significant acts
of overt resistance by the Jews, individually and collectively, and that
they were greater in number and more complex in their detail than was
acknowledged in the early verdict on Jewish behavior and especially in
the awful simile which had a part in that verdict, of the Jews going to
their deaths "like sheep being led to the slaughter" (awful even if accurate, but especially if false).[4] The contention that there was resistance
would warrant consideration even on a narrow definition of resistance as
requiring direct physical action; the claim would be stronger still, if, as
the studies of resistance have suggested, the narrow definition deserves
to be broadened to include indirect and even symbolic resistance. That
the Nazis succeeded in killing two-thirds of the Jews of Europe and Russia has usually been regarded as proof by itself that the acts of Jewish
resistance were few and at any rate ineffectual—but it should be obvious
that any such conclusion is meaningless unless it is accompanied by an
assessment of the conditions under which such resistance would have
had to take place.

The second relevant fact is comparative: that the response of the Jews
was not, on the whole, different from the response of the many other
victims of the Nazi machinery of destruction, certainly not as these
other victims found themselves within the concentration camps and
death camps, but outside the camps as well. The members of these other
groups who were funneled into the death camps seem to have responded
to the process that first gathered them and then acted to destroy them in
the same way that the Jews did—first with the hope of deferral; then,
occasionally, with overt resistance; but, most often, compliantly and
nearly always with a sense of incredulity at the fate which confronted
them. The murder of more than two million Russian prisoners of war
(who had, after all, been fit enough to be soldiers), and of a million and a
half Yugoslav civilians, the massacre in the French town of Oradur-

<hr />

4. See, e.g., Lucien Steinberg, *The Jews Against Hitler*, trans. Marion Hunger (London:
Gordon & Cremonisi, 1978); Isaiah Trunk, *Jewish Responses to Nazi Persecution* (New York:
Stein and Day, 1982); and A. Zwi Bar-On, "The Jews in the Soviet Partisan Movement,"
in *Yad Vashem Studies* 4 (1960), 167–89. There is an obvious difference between a judg-
ment which in retrospect uses this phrase and a statement made at the time by Jewish
partisans, designed to enlist support for the resistance—as in the Proclamation by the
United Partisan Organization calling for a revolt in Vilna, 1 September 1943, published in
Arad et al., *Documents* (see chap. 3, n. 7), 433.

sur-glane; and the annihilation of the Czech village of Lidice—these acts of different orders of magnitude and others like them accompanied the Nazi genocide against the Jews; and here too, the record of overt resistance makes only a slight impression in comparison to the magnitude of the events. Unlike the Jews, moreover, the victims in most of these groups were often on home ground, in the midst of compatriots and familiar surroundings. Whatever it was that had supposedly "unfitted" the Jews could hardly account for the reaction of these other groups, and it is reasonable to assume, then, that a quite different explanation is required for understanding this often common response to the Nazi apparatus of extermination.

Thus, the charge which alleges that somehow the history of the Jews in the Diaspora had peculiarly disabled them to react to the Nazi threat loses much of its invidious character. Indeed, all that seems left of that charge, aside from the implication that large numbers of people were not (and perhaps *could* not be) prepared to react to the imminence of mass extermination, is that the Jews in Europe were *present*—available as objects for a genocidal apparatus. And this diminution of the initial thesis in the end also makes a difference well beyond the interpretation of Jewish history alone, for it nullifies the claim that the Jews were to an extent Hitler's creators, that they made *him* "possible"—which is the logical conclusion of the contention that the Jews had collaborated in their own destruction and thus in realizing that central purpose of Hitler's design.

To be sure, the question of why the Jews were singled out by the Nazis in the first place is not answered by the statement that the Jews were present—"available." That question has in fact been largely left blank in accounts of Jewish history, even in the standard histories of anti-Semitism; it is also muted in accounts that link those histories with the history of Zionism, presumably because any explanation the latter might provide would be tied to the (allegedly) debilitated character of the Jew in exile: not only would that character have affected the Jewish reaction to the threat of genocide—it would, in an earlier appearance, have contributed to the origins of that threat.[5] Even less ideologically charged efforts to address the same question, moreover, are so complicated by

5. It is a harsh lesson in the ways of ideology to see the convergence of certain formulations of Zionist theory on the claims of anti-Semitism itself. This convergence extends even to the use of common metaphors and in particular the charge against the Jews of the Diaspora of "parasitism" (alleged by A. D. Gordon and Y. H. Brenner) or of being "diseased" (Max Nordau). (On the usage of these terms in anti-Semitic writers, see Bein, "The Jewish Parasite" cited in chap. 1, n. 13), 3–40. Brenner could write that "in every place they do not accept us—and perhaps they are justified," and Jacob Klatzkin would speak of the "rightfulness of anti-Semitism."

the history of social and religious anti-Semitism which extends back to the Church Fathers, by the nineteenth-century development of nationalism, by the economic history of post–World War I Europe, that they too have been and will no doubt remain partial or inadequate. The acknowledgement of such difficulties does not, however, bear decisively on the relation between the Zionist analysis of Jewish life in the Diaspora and the Jewish response to the Nazi genocide. For however the question of why the history of anti-Semitism took the form that it did is resolved, what remains now of the Zionist contention that the response of the Jews to the Nazis confirms the premises of the Zionist ideal is not much more than the claim that if the Jews had not believed that they could live in Europe (whether by assimilation or as Jews), they would not have become victims of the genocide—and this near-tautology gives little support to the inference from the same premises that Jewish existence is possible only in a Jewish state. Certainly at least two other conclusions are more obvious and no less pertinent: that willed barbarism empowered by modern technology and a willing bureaucracy has the capacity for great evil, and that human beings—by the conventions they have evolved and perhaps by nature as well—are or at least were ill-prepared to anticipate or to defend themselves against that barbarism.

These two conclusions do not themselves answer the question of why the Jews became the primary object of the Nazi genocide, but it is important to recognize that a response to *that* question which is different from—indeed, antithetical to—that offered by the Zionists has been proposed; this is the contention that it was certain distinctive achievements of Jews in exile that motivated the origins and events of the Nazi genocide. This perspective, too, has been appropriated by ideologies and also subsumed under more general explanations of anti-Semitism—for example, in the claim that the Jews were attacked by the Nazis because they had challenged a reluctantly Christian culture to be truly Christian, or in the claim that the ethical ideals of Jewish existence were a continuing threat to nationalism, on the one hand, or, contradictorily, to internationalism, on the other.[6] With such claims, too, it is difficult to sort out the different threads of psychological and material causality.

Such explanations do not have to be judged, however, to win acknowledgment of one of their presuppositions that might also stand quite independently: namely, that Jewish existence in the Diaspora and especially in those countries of Europe where the Nazi genocide was centered, far from being effete or depleted, had in fact been active and

6. See, e.g., George Steiner, "The Long Life of Metaphor: An Approach to 'the Shoah'" *Encounter* 48 (February 1987), 55–61, reprinted in Lang, *Writing*.

productive—creative—both in its own communal life and in its contributions to the cultures in which that life was set. In the aftermath of the
Nazi genocide, it is difficult to imagine what would now constitute European Jewish existence if the Jews killed in the genocide had been able
to live out their lives, had reared a later generation, had maintained the
development of Jewish and secular life in the centers of Vilna, Warsaw,
Vienna, and Berlin. The immediate horror of the death camps has made
it difficult to conjure the lives that might have been in lieu of the deaths
that were—but this, too, obviously constitutes the actual and continuing loss. Whatever else is true of Jewish history in the Diaspora, it is
beyond dispute that that history was productive in terms of elaborating
the texture of Jewish culture and (most notably since the Emancipation
but before then as well) of contributing to the secular culture as well;
there is no reason to believe that these would have changed if the Nazi
attack on the Jews had not occurred. Also *this* testimony, then, stands
against the one-sided diagnosis by Zionism of a people incapacitated by
the conditions of their dispersion.[7]

In other words, far from confirming or even clarifying the conclusions of Zionism, the Nazi genocide leaves the question of the relation
between Zionism and Judaism *less* settled than it had been before. If,
moreover, as the evidence indicates, the Jewish response in the face of
genocide had little that was distinctive about it, nothing, in any event, to
demonstrate that life in the Diaspora had been culturally or morally incapacitating, then what remains of the claim that the Jews were somehow
inculpated in the act that was directed against them is the tautology that
if the Jews had not been in Europe in 1933 or even in 1939, they would
not have been within Hitler's reach. And this is no more an argument for
political Zionism than it is an argument that the Jews—and also, one
supposes, everyone else who was to become a victim of the Nazis—
should have been foresighted enough to join the earlier waves of emigra-

7. *Shliluth Ha-galuth*—"Negation" or "Denigration of the Diaspora"—has been a sufficiently common concept in Zionist writings to become an institutionalized phrase. Aside
from the willingness of this view to deny the achievements both for Jewish and secular
culture of the Diaspora, it ignores the fact that imagination and energy from this source
also initiated and sustained the Zionist movement itself. Ahad Ha'am, in his 1909 essay
which uses the phrase *Shliluth Ha-galuth* as its title, offers there a prescient criticism of that
attitude. (Cf. Arthur Hertzberg (ed.), *The Zionist Idea* (cited in chap. 4, n. 3), 270–81.)
Eliezer Schweid argues that the "Shliluth Ha-galuth" is intrinsic to Zionism, although it
may take more or less severe forms (in *his* case, severe: see "Shtay Gishoth L'Rayon
'Shliluth Ha-golah'," in *ha-tsionuth* (Tel Aviv: Kibbutz Hameuchad, 1984). See also, for a
criticism of Ahad Ha'am for not carrying his advocacy of a role for the Diaspora even further, Jacob Neusner, *Stranger at Home* (Chicago: University of Chicago Press, 1981), chap.
12.

tion that set out from Europe for other lands, for the United States or South America no less than for Palestine. Even the plausible, although by no means self-evident, contention that the existence of the State of Israel makes attacks on Jews outside of it less likely does not in itself resolve the question of what, *as individuals,* the attitude of Jews to Zionism should have been before the genocide (except that they ought in general to have been more prudent), or how they should act now, in its aftermath.[8]

I say that these arguments do not determine an answer to the question but this does not mean that they do not *affect* it. For surely there are implications from the fact of the genocide for the relation between the Jew and Zionism. And although these implications are unequivocal in certain respects, in others no less central, they only underscore the traditionally problematic character of that relation. What has become increasingly evident, for example, is that far from settling the role of Zionism in Jewish life and culture, the existence of the State of Israel— itself, as argued here, related to the occurrence of the Nazi genocide— has substantially complicated that issue. The founding of Israel meant that for the first time in two thousand years, a version of the Zionist ideal was within reach of most Jews: life in a Jewish state was possible. This might have been supposed to resolve at least *that* tension in the tradition, providing ready access to a dimension of Jewish life that claimed both biblical and cultural authority. But what emerged in fact was less a resolution than a reiteration of the original issue, and in a more highly problematic form. Those Jews who have been free to move to Israel have by a large majority refused to do so; where they have not been free to make the choice—mainly, in Russia—the evidence about what decision they would make if they *were* free is at best equivocal; Israel itself now confronts the phenomenon of emigration by numbers of its own citizens. Whatever the statehood of Israel has demonstrated, it has evidently not yet provided a convincing answer to the question of the relation between Judaism and Zionism, of what place in that relation the land or state of Israel should have. The differences in commitment between Jews who choose not to live in a Jewish state and those who do

8. I speak here of a "plausible" contention, but its opposite is also plausible—that the existence of Israel makes attacks on Jews in the Diaspora more, not less likely, by adding fuel to the charge of dual or divided loyalty. The latter had been an element in anti-Semitism before 1948, but the attraction of anti-Semitism to nationalism could well be increased by the challenge of a competing nationalism. (Cf. on this point Jacob Katz, *From Prejudice to Destruction* [see chap. 7, n. 20], chap. 26.) It is another of the ironies in the history of Zionism that the same spirit of nationalism which contributed to the currents of anti-Semitism also provided a model for the Zionist reaction against it.

would seem to be, if anything, less clear now than had been the case before its founding, since now the alternatives are, for most Jews, genuine
options.[9]

To be sure, it might be objected that because Jews outside Israel (and
some inside it) do not *recognize* the answer represented by a Jewish state
for the problem of Jewish identity does not mean that the answer is not
there to be found. As European Jewry falsely imagined, often even after
1933, that they too could continue to lead "normal" lives both as Jews
and as citizens, so—the objection would go—the same kind of illusion
might be responsible now for the attitudes of Jews living in Europe or in
the United States. History alone, of course, will finally decide the matter,
but what is more important for the present—since, after all, every Jew is
forced to judge the claim now, in the present—is the way in which this
argument reduces the Zionist thesis to a counsel of prudence which is
not altogether convincing even in its own terms. As repugnant as it may
be to consider the vulnerability of Israel to external force, to the exigencies of survival, those possibilities are real ones (I refer here to Israel in
the present, not as it might be with the return of all Jews to Israel; together with everything else that the latter would accomplish, it would
also add still another point of vulnerability). To the extent that the
Zionist ideal is essentially political, and to the extent that that political
ideal rests on the premise that a Jewish nation-state, better than any alternative (or even alone among alternatives), assures the security of its
citizens from alien and specifically anti-Semitic threats, current political
realities again suggest that the claims of Zionism are questionable.
There is, in other words, no conclusive evidence, and substantial counterevidence, for the assumption that Israel is more likely to assure the
safety of its Jewish citizens than is the United States or the countries of
Western Europe; surely this is one factor (among others) in the refusal of
Jews elsewhere to immigrate to Israel when they have the opportunity to
do so ("refusal" is in most cases too strong a term; more often than not,
the option is not seriously considered).

Whether the sense of relative political security outside Israel is false or
not, moreover, that sense underlines a practical flaw in the line of argument for Zionism as essentially or even largely political in character. For
unless the political argument is based on the largely a priori grounds

9. One way of putting this issue is in the contention that with the founding of Israel,
there could no longer be any "first person" Zionists, only "third person" ones; whoever
was inclined to say "I am a Zionist" could not meaningfully say it living outside Israel—and
in Israel it would be redundant. Ben Gurion would state the point more simply: "There are
no more Zionists." See M. I. Urofsky, *We are One: American Jewry and Israel* (New York:
Doubleday, 1978), 288–9.

often appealed to by nationalism—to the effect that Jews could not *possibly* be assured of freedom or security or "selfhood" except in a Jewish state (like Italians in an Italian state or Algerians in an Algerian state)—then insofar as there is evidence either for the independence and security of Jews in other countries *or* for the insecurity of Jews living in the Jewish state, the case of Zionism is to that extent weakened. And there is at least some evidence on both these counts. It may be that western liberal democracies as they are now constituted are ill prepared to defend the minority groups living among them, or that they may themselves nurture threats to minority existence; but the weight of evidence, if not fully against these possibilities, is at least equivocal—as it is also (on other grounds) against the view that the apparent threats to Israeli security are in the end not serious. Insofar as Zionism after the Nazi genocide would base its justification on the prudential grounds of self-defense, that justification is far from self-evident.

The latter conclusion, to be sure, does not by itself argue against Zionism as including political considerations; but since I have been suggesting that even the course of the Nazi genocide did not add weight to the argument for political Zionism as an exclusive or primary conception of Zionism, the possibility seems remote that other historical events will be more effective. Insofar as Zionism is impelled by a *political* rationale in providing an analysis of the Nazi destruction of the Jews, that analysis seems an instance of special pleading, based on evidence that is partial and even tendentious and that raises as many questions as it answers. There is little to distinguish this view in principle from Zionism expounded at another extreme—that of the politics of spirit, where the return to Zion is based on messianic hopes and the promise of the reconstruction of the Temple. In both these views, individual faith and commitment provide the basis—and however compelling either of these is in its own terms, their proponents seem willing to ignore history, including the history of Zionism itself and a third alternative which that history also discloses.

For political Zionism, on the one hand, and for messianic Zionism, on the other, Zionism revolves around a single center, in Israel the state or in the New Jerusalem. The Diaspora is by contrast provisional and defective—and it is by challenging that conception of the Diaspora that a third alternative discloses itself. This alternative is not itself novel, although, like the others, it is altered by the facts of the Nazi genocide. The history of this view extends backward at least to the beginning of the twentieth century, and it has had a number of significant proponents since those origins, although its conception of Zionism as binary—with

HISTORIES AND GENOCIDE

Israel and the Diaspora mutually fostering and extending each other—has consistently been relegated to a position of marginality. Admittedly, the ideal of "cultural Zionism" that has come to be associated primarily with the name of Ahad Ha'am flourished first at a time when the political existence of a state of Israel was at best an improbability: *that* was the reason, it might be objected, why Ahad Ha'am was willing to settle for a notion of "bipolarity," according to which Zion as a center would at once support and draw from the resources of the Diaspora, and in which the Diaspora was in effect recognized as a probably permanent element of Jewish existence.[10] But it is clear that there was more behind Ahad Ha'am's view than only a willingness to make a virtue out of necessity; there was the conviction that a Judaism, even a *Zionism,* that maintained two sources, one in Israel (i.e., the Jewish land), the other in the Diaspora, might well possess an effectiveness and energy—and still, also, a consistency with the tradition—that was at least viable and possibly even more so than would be the case if either one of those sources did not exist. It was clear for Ahad Ha'am that *the* center would be in Zion. It is also clear that this conception of a "spiritual center" quite independent of (and in some ways opposed to) a political structure could not be easily translated into practice (even in Ahad Ha'am's own terms). But what is crucial in this conception and itself part of his emphasis on a "spiritual center" is the recognition that a geographical or political "ingathering" by itself would not settle the problems of Jewish identity or, for that matter, those of Zionism.

There are many problems with the conception of bipolarity, including the question of whether it is a conception of Zionism at all.[11] But these difficulties, too, may seem less intractable than the ones, both practical and in principle, which attend the alternative monistic theories of Zionism. The events of the last half century—Zionism during and in the aftermath of genocide—add to the force of this contrast and deepen the shadow of suspicion that the genocide throws on these more standard views. To begin by challenging this conception of bipolarity because of its concession of a role to Jewish existence outside Israel—which is the usual starting point for attacks on this position—is already to skew the discussion, since it presupposes that in principle as well as in practice the Jews of the Diaspora have an unequal (in fact,

10. See, e.g., "The Jewish State and the Jewish Problem," in Hans Kohn (ed.), *Nationalism and the Jewish Ethic: Basic Writings and Ahad Ha'am* (New York: Schocken, 1962), 66–89; and "Ha–Tzionuth Ha–Medinith," in *The Writings of Ahad Ha'am,* 135–40.

11. So, for example, Yehuda Bauer's contention that "for the sake of the existence of Israel as a prosperous entity, a viable American Jewish Diaspora is desirable." (In Moshe Davis (ed.), *Zionism in Transition* [New York: Arno Press, 1980], 259.)

insurmountable) part of the burden of proof. Any theory which simply assumes that problems in determining the character of Jewish existence outside Israel do not also pertain (directly or indirectly) inside Israel, however, comes close to begging the question. It is *this* question, after all, that any conception of Zionism has to address—of whether, and to what extent, Jewish existence *does* become unproblematic for Jews who have "gone up" to Israel. The assumption often made to this effect seems openly mistaken, both because certain questions concerning Jewish existence are entirely separable from the issue of "place" and because even among the problems that do relate to it, many are shared between Jews living in Israel and those living elsewhere.

For certain of the shared problems, in fact, the principle of bipolarity is, if not a requirement, at least a useful step toward providing an answer. Even viewed strictly in political terms, in fact, the existence of Jewish communities outside Israel, far from challenging its existence or detracting from it, is in fact beneficial—to the extent that it is at least arguable that the advantages overbalance even the alternative which would have those other communities move collectively to Israel. The substantial dependence of Israel on Jewish communities of the Diaspora is only one aspect of this relation, although on that ground, too, it might be argued that it is desirable that Jews outside Israel should maintain their existence there, even—from the point of view of political Zionism—if this means that they would have to sacrifice themselves in doing so.[12] I refer here not only to the financial and political support given to Israel by the Jewish communities of the Diaspora, but to the importance for Israel of their social and cultural contributions as well: the significant indebtedness of Israeli institutions—academic, technological, artistic, even religious—to Jewish, non-Israeli sources around the world is indicative of this relation. And although it may be objected that the contributions made to Israel by these sources reflect current historical circumstance rather than a long-term or intrinsic relation and that this historical circumstance, even as it now exists, would be outweighed in importance by the movement of the communities of the Diaspora to Israel if that occurred, the unlikelihood of any such move is not the only or the strongest argument against the view that Zionism or Jewish identity more generally would be most consistently served by a general return of the Jews to Israel.

12. Even this conception of a "shared identity" can be easily skewed. For example, Eliezer Schweid writes that "so long as the entire Jewish people is not living in its homeland, all sections of the people share equally in the advantages of the homeland and the defects of the Diaspora." (Davis, *Zionism*, 245.) If there is, as I have been suggesting, more than this to share from both sides, what Schweid proposes would hardly be an "equal" division.

The contention that Israel, the state or the land, *needs* the Diaspora, that the role of the Jewish communities outside Israel is integrally related to the role of Israel itself, is in any event based on more than either the cultural or material circumstances which, at least for the moment, point to the same conclusion. If the bond between the Jews and Zion itself is not only political, if the "promise" of the land requires witness to the promise as well as to the land, then for at least part of that sense it does not matter where Jews live: as the promise enjoins a spirit of communal obligation and religious purposiveness in ways for which "spatial" or political identity play no special role, Jews might realize that promise wherever they are. For these aspects of his commitment, moreover, the Jew living in Israel may be as distant from what is entailed even in the Zionist ideal as the Jew living in Ethiopia or in the Argentine, for, again, the physical—or political—properties of a place or polity do not exhaust the terms of that promise. Beyond this, furthermore, there is always the special danger for Israeli Jews of mistaking the land itself as fully constituting the promise they think to have realized. (The political, quasi-religious movement for a "Greater Israel" that now has so strong a grip on Israeli thought, although undoubtedly a *version* of Zionist doctrine, is certainly not implied by or even consistent with all of its versions.)

Admittedly, the danger also exists (at the other extreme) of inverting the particularity of Zionism into a generalized abstraction or a heuristic device. What is said here is *not* meant to propose a role for Zionism as a metaphor for incompleteness or historical finitude—the sense that Zionism might provide a focus for Jewish existence only as it remains unrealized. This conception, which parallels and is related to traditional messianism, figured psychologically in the view of Zionism held by many Jews in the Diaspora before the founding of the State of Israel and, to some extent, has figured since then as well. (For Jews who see the authentic return to Zion as requiring the advent of the Messiah and the rebuilding of the Temple, this metaphoric role continues to serve even if they live now in Israel.) The existence and accessibility of Israel diminishes the role of this factor in the Zionist ideal, and that diminution has had an unbalancing effect on traditional conceptions of Zionism and the status of the Diaspora. (Here again an unlikely connection appears between Zionism and the Nazi genocide—for it seems probable that the continued attention paid in the Diaspora to the "Holocaust" is undoubtedly due to some part to the fact that it is "bipolar," an event shared equally by Jews inside and outside Israel; this fact also explains why commemoration of the Nazi genocide has to some extent displaced the role that Zionism itself previously had in the Diaspora culture.)

To be sure, this shift in balance also suggests the deeper possibility that the Zionist ideal and the Diaspora had previously coexisted fruitfully *because* the Zionist ideal was privileged by both; a change of the sort described here might then hinder rather than advance the chances of bipolarity. It might be held, in other words, that the privileging in Zionist thought hitherto of Zion over the Diaspora was necessary to support what was in fact a reciprocal relation between the two, and that a revision of the former might dislocate that relation. If assessment of the Diaspora has generally been, as Ahad Ha'am described it, "subjectively negative, but objectively positive," then the task for Zionism now, based on the principle of bipolarity, would be to overcome the subjectively negative view of the Diaspora—a view hitherto common, as Ahad Ha'am recognized, both in the Diaspora and in Israel—without altering its role as objectively positive. There seems no intrinsic reason that this cannot be done—but that is far from providing assurance of its possibility; the test, evidently, is yet to be made.

To be sure, this proposal does not define the *means* for a bipolar rather than a monistic relation between the Diaspora and Israel. A fuller account of how communities of the Diaspora could exist collaboratively and reciprocally with Israel is needed, something more than the claim that such a relation is possible and desirable, or even, historically, that it has in fact obtained (although the latter is surely significant). This issue is too large to be addressed here, and indeed it is so closely tied to predictions about the future situation of Jews inside and outside Israel that any prescription, however detailed, will undoubtedly be insufficient and probably mistaken. But the outline of such a relation is intimated in the references made above to the cultural Zionism of Ahad Ha'am, which is, as he suggested, consistent with other protoconceptions of Zionism antedating the largely political versions of the late nineteenth century. There has been no doubt raised in these accounts, for all their differences in *specific* interpretations, about the fact of a special relation within Judaism between the people and the land of Israel: in this sense Zionism, with a center in Zion, is intrinsic. And although Jewish identity is largely nondoctrinal, the privileging of the land of Israel would be counted, if not among the most basic tenets (for example, it is not included in the Maimonidean creed), as not far from such tenets in importance. How exactly to understand that relation—even to say that it should be understood *literally* is not much help—has been a persistent question whose complexity is itself underscored by the oversimplifications of political Zionism. What can be inferred in common from the principal accounts of it historically include a reverence for communal origins and for a bond which is located specifically in space and time but yet is not exclusively conventional or political. These premises point to a factor that would distinguish the issue of Jewish identity from that of doctrinal creeds, on the one hand, and from that of nationalism or other primarily political systems, on the other. Such terms are minimal and unsatisfactory, but even so they confirm the elements of subjectivity and particularization that Zionism has characteristically prescribed.

There is, to be sure, an opposing impulse in the Jewish tradition to this claim on behalf of particularization, an impulse away from the very idea of a specific location (even metaphorically) for religious and cultural commitment. This opposing impulse is not only directed against parochial abuses—for example, in the tirades of the Prophets against those who emphasize the letter of the law at the expense of general principles of social justice—but also has a positive character of its own, as universalizing and thus as externalizing the practice of Judaism. The Reform tradition has undoubtedly exaggerated this aspect of what it misleadingly represents as "prophetic Judaism" (as though the Prophets were simply antinomians, upholding a spirit of the law against its consistently repressive letter); but there is also no doubt that what may be thus exaggerated is nonetheless real in itself. It is from a conjunction between this side of the tradition and the other particularistic side that a positive role for the Diaspora may be evoked, not only as inevitable, but also as warranted.

There is, it seems, a substantial difference between a conception of Judaism as looking inward, and thus focusing its attachment exclusively on Israel the land and the religious and cultural institutions engendered by that entity, and a conception in which this one view is joined by another which faces outward, addressing the world, and thus translating what impinges from the outside into the texture of Jewish tradition. The historical particularity of that tradition is undeniable, and Zionism, however understood, is linked to this particularity; neither the prescriptions of Jewish religious law nor the identity of the people can, without distortion, be made into metaphors or abstracted from their content. An important element of this particularity, moreover, is constituted by the land and (to a lesser degree) by the ideal of an autonomous existence in that land. But the specificity of Judaism is not only a matter of practice or doing. For whatever the emphasis in Judaism on practice or the law as independent of "reasons" or even of ideals, this hardly means that there are not general principles at stake in that practice. It would surely be too much to claim that *only* Jewish existence outside the land of Israel represents or gives voice to the universalist and externalizing impulse of Judaism, assuring it a concrete presence in the world at large; or that without this appearance the universalist impulse and perhaps, by implication, even the ideal of transcendence, would simply be lost. But there can be little question that historically the Diaspora has in fact contributed to these ideals, and that, so long as it exists, it may well continue to do so. It is in this sense that the Jewish community within the State of Israel finds an allied presence in the Jewish communities outside those boundaries—both of them are involved in a common design which then supports each community individually. It is probably an exaggeration to assert that Judaism (and so, directly or indirectly, Zionism) *requires* a Diaspora, but even the more moderate claim of consistency or compatibility or mutuality between the two sides has important consequences.[13]

To be sure, there is one land of Israel and many lands and communities of the Diaspora, no one of which counts for Jewish identity in the way that Israel does by itself. But imagine for a moment the sudden disappearance of those other communities (not by cataclysm, but perhaps even by the translation of those communities to Israel itself). Would this disappearance not alter, beyond the patterns of political geography, the very conception of Jewish commitment and practice? As much as this development might be viewed as fulfilling one part of traditional aspirations, surely it would also compel revision in other respects of the theoretical and moral structure of Jewish identity. The consequences of this "thought-experiment" ought to be taken seriously. Just as the new existence of the State of Israel, by the possibilities it opened up, compelled Jews in the Diaspora to reconceive what Zionism would thenceforth mean for them, so this other possibility may compel recognition, from within the State of Israel as well as outside it, of the legitimacy of the Diaspora. Both may be viewed now as integral to Zionism and thus as motivating it. The metaphoric analogues of the relation of an outside to an inside, of the spokes of a wheel to its hub are too condensed to represent the complexity of the two terms of the relation between the Diaspora and Israel, but they usefully suggest the *kind* of relation that the notion of bipolarity entails. If both elements are necessary, talk about which is more or less so will itself matter less and less.

Such comments do not imply any doubt about the importance of the State of Israel for Zionism and Judaism, especially as features are included in that relation which are not only political but moral and religious and cultural. If it were for no more than the revival of the Hebrew language, the expressive thread that runs through Jewish history not simply instrumentally but substantively, the debt of Jewish

---

13. One of these appeared in the not quite unequivocal but much debated declaration ratified at the Twenty-ninth Zionist Congress in 1978 that "the continuity of Jewish life in the Diaspora is a reality and Zionism seeks to strengthen Jewish life and self-realization."

communities outside Israel would be unmistakable; that revival has had important consequences for Jewish religious and classical education in the Diaspora as well as for Jewish popular culture. If one adds to this, other evident aspects of Jewish learning and consciousness which the existence of Israel has elaborated or initiated (for example, the practical recovery of the study of Jewish history), the past and continuing importance of Israel for the Diaspora would be clear, however one judges the political elements of Zionism.

And yet it also remains to say that even if these developments could not or would not have taken place without a State of Israel and even if Jews outside Israel had not also contributed to them (neither of which is strictly true), this would still not be a sufficient basis for claiming for Israel independence of the Diaspora, much less to propose such independence as the single end toward which the existence and efforts of the Diaspora itself ought to be turned. The very diversity of idioms in which Diaspora Jewry speaks and reformulates its common concepts and practices is in itself a contribution to Jewish identity, but more important than this, however fraught with dangers and potential failures, is the position of the Diaspora between Judaism (and Israel) and the world—and what, from that position, it has in the past transmitted in both directions. The Diaspora is in these terms not a mere metaphor for universalism but an active means directed toward that goal; it is thus directed also toward the goal of Zionism itself, insofar as that goal, too, is one part of the more general ideal of Jewish identity.

The objection may be made to the conception of a bipolar Zionism as it has been outlined here that, looking in two directions at once, it hardly seems like Zionism at all. It appears, in effect, only to ratify what is from most sides admitted as a problematic status quo (so, for example, the satirical definition of Zionism as the commitment of someone to send someone else to Israel). But surely the objection is question-begging, since it privileges one conception of Zionism to the exclusion of others when it is precisely the question of what Zionism can now be that is at issue—of whether Zionism *does* entail the traditionally dominant view of itself as asymmetrical, pointed exclusively in the direction of Israel.

The objection is more difficult to respond to in that it invites prescriptions for change when whatever may yet ensue is unlikely to happen just because it has been prescribed. If by "status quo" the objection refers to the coexistence of Israel and a Diaspora, then indeed that relation is at once a fact and, on the terms proposed here, a prospect. So long as the Diaspora is seen (by itself as well as by others) as intrinsically defective, then its purpose will be defined in terms of the character and, before that, of the existence of Israel; Israel itself will be inclined to take those features—focused on itself—as its own premises. Where bipolarity is urged, in contrast, the definition of a different and common goal is assumed—one in which the reciprocal relation between the two sources then becomes no less important a feature of Zionism than what each of the poles provides independently. But surely this is consistent with the tradition in which even Zionism is not, or not only, an end in itself but an ideal among a number of others which, like them, serves also as a means within a more general structure of identity and commitment. Only through such an understanding does the contention that the existence of Israel strengthens the communities of the Diaspora in their will to persist in the Diaspora become the truth it has historically been, rather than the contradiction it would become in the monistic views of Zionism.[14]

All of this assumes in Diaspora Jewry both a sense of purpose and the requisite means to maintain their share of the dual effort, and it would be foolish to ignore the possibility that these may fail, that assimilation may so impair the will of the Diaspora as to produce a situation in which for practical purposes Jews *had* returned to Zion—since there would be none left outside it. (Ben-Gurion used the trenchant metaphor the "kiss of death" to describe the lure of this attraction.) It is difficult to know how to assess such a prediction, because both the evidence for it and the evidence that points in the opposite direction—the ambiguous fact of the *survival* of the Diaspora for over two millennia (including almost two centuries of "Emancipation"), in a large variety of social and cultural contexts—do not come from settings exactly like that of the present. It is almost as if the position one takes on this question is not prior to but part of a larger decision of where to cast one's lot. It is not surprising, then, that those who argue for the viability of the Diaspora tend to live there, and those who are skeptical about it do not (although these biographical facts should properly be quite independent of the predictions). The latter point is important as a counterbalance to the ostensively (but misleadingly) scientific predictions of the demise of the Diaspora by assimilation—not because there is no evidence, but because we cannot be certain of how to interpret the evidence; *and* because it calls attention to another issue in the discussion: the fact, namely, that the future of Judaism, whether in the Diaspora or in Israel, is related not only to the positions taken by Jews but also to the position of religious and cultural values and ideas in the contemporary world more generally. The differences between Judaism and other religions hardly exempt the former

14. For a discussion of contemporary positions on the status of Diaspora—most of them opposed to the view proposed here—see Arnold Eisen, *Galut: Modern Jewish Reflection on Homelessness and Homecoming* (Bloomington, Ind.: Indiana University Press, 1986), chap. 7.

from the effects of historical—political, social, cultural—changes that affect the letter. And to the extent that religion as such faces increasing pressure from a threatening hegemony of technology and secularism, these effects are bound to be felt—have already been felt—in Judaism and Zionism, not only in the Diaspora but in Israel as well (and also in the fundamentalist reaction against that pressure). With this challenge, more than ever, one might conclude, Judaism requires the efforts—including also the variety—of its two sources.

These are, then, reasons that the Zionist ideal can—and ought to be—an element in Jewish existence both inside and outside the State of Israel. Those reasons stand, of course, in conjunction now with the existence of Israel as a predominantly Jewish state that is also home for three and a half million Jews. On the account given here, it is evident that a threat to this existence would unavoidably also be one to Jews outside Israel, not because of a potential "domino" effect (although that is possible) and not only because of a shared identity (this would be true of Jews wherever they lived), but because the definition of the community as a whole has this as one of its two principal sources. Thus, more positively, Israel ought to remain an important focus of concern and attentiveness for Jews elsewhere *because* the relation between them is reciprocal. On the other hand, Israel, too, would have an involvement in Diaspora Jewry that is more than only prudential: its own identity, its commitments as well as its resources, are linked to that of the other. Thus, too—from the first direction—recent discussions of the "right" of Jews outside Israel to a voice in the policies or, more generally, the character of Israeli society often misconstrue the issue. It is obvious that non-Israeli Jews are not citizens of Israel, that they do not serve in Israel's army or vote in its elections, etc. But that they have a right to concern themselves with what happens in (as well as "to") Israel seems also evident—or as much as any statement about such rights can be. Certainly the argument that Jews of the Diaspora ought to be involved with Israel but should express this only by being advocates for the political party that happens at the moment to govern Israel has little to support it except for the fact that certain Israeli groups would prefer it. Views such as Shlomo Avineri's assignment of a "normative" role exclusively to Israel in its relation with the Diaspora[15] assert just such a disjunction, according to which the Diaspora has only obligations and no rights, in contrast to Israel, which has all the rights and no obligations in respect to the Diaspora. There is no reason for believing that this imbalance is more viable—or more just—

15. Shlomo Avineri, *The Making of Modern Zionism* (New York: Basic Books, 1981)

for a conception of Jewish identity than it has been when applied to political governance more generally.

Such reference to Zionism in the present (and for the future) moves far from the initial point of this discussion as it proposed to view Zionism after the Nazi genocide. But for reasons also set out initially, the account here was meant to consider what the aftermath of that event entailed for Zionism, wherever that might lead. To be sure, it may seem from what has been said that the Nazi genocide changed very little *objectively* in the character of Zionism. But this in itself turns out to be significant because of the enormity of the event; like the discovery of a structure that stood unmoved in the midst of an earthquake, that fact itself needs to be understood. The way in which the Nazi genocide impinges historically on the history of Zionism *without* making it a purely historical or political phenomenon thus provides a strong determination of what Zionism ought and may yet be. The crime of the Nazi genocide warrants constant retelling; to follow the course of Zionism in the twentieth century is significant among the ways of retelling that event, and this is true both despite and because of the bitter contact joined at certain points between the two. Anyone who finds in this contact the easy moral that some good may come even out of great evil discredits his own judgment—but neither can it be doubted now that the Nazi genocide *had* consequences for the practical course of the history of Zionism and for the conception of what Zionism had often been alleged to be. Certainly the conclusion emerges clearly here that to situate Zionism in political terms alone is to conceive the State of Israel exclusively as either a memorial to the past or a refuge against the future—and neither of these will suffice to sustain a people or a religion or a culture and probably not even a country. There is, however, an alternative.

9

Speaking, Writing, Teaching: Institutions of Memory

1. Institutions as Memory

It is forty-five years since the Nazi genocide against the Jews came to an end. The millions of deaths, the single moments and their accrual of suffering, the constant expectation of anguish, would have no additions. And immediately that past, situated and turned, began to move from memory into history. Understandably, the history was in its first years mainly a history of silence. The obvious items for counting became available: names, numbers, dates. But evidence is a medium of abstraction, and the recent past did not easily give way to this; there were, in any event, no measurable units of pain, of loss, of futures broken by which the immediacy of what had taken place could be translated into reflection. Thus, for those who had faced the attempt at annihilation and by a combination of chance and will had survived; for those who had intended and perpetrated genocide, then to see it end in their own defeat; for those who as bystanders watched, sometimes detached, sometimes with warmer intentions but even so with incapacitating doubt—all these found themselves at a moment when there was little to be said, when nothing that might give a shape to the future seemed likely or even possible beside the actuality that had occurred.

So it is not surprising that the first years after the end of the war were ones largely of silence, in which those who had been directly affected but survived took the opportunity to leave behind a clamor constituted of so many different sounds that together they would have seemed less like sounds than like noise. Some of that first silence was willed: the survivors stopping for breath and looking, incredulously, at the promise of a future; the spectators, taken by shame at the end of a tragedy in which they suddenly discovered themselves as actors; the agents of genocide hoping to forget or, more often, to be forgotten. But much of it was a reflex, an exclamation without sound: history, for once, was at a loss for words.

But that silent exclamation, the most immediate and definite response, passed quickly. Even under the burden of massacre, life seems bound to discourse—to rehearsal, to recollection and reflection, and then, too, beyond its own impulses, to answering questions asked by a new generation searching for its own voice: all these representations of the self entered their claims. And so the survivors found words, at first softly, often in new and alien languages, but always, even in their pauses, with an extraordinary compulsion: there was something they knew that was unknown to anyone else. What they had seen was unbelievable to the sight; it thus reached for public acknowledgment, as though only that could bring a measure of understanding to the terrible and isolated reality inside them. Also the bystanders, tardily, began to try to do what they could, asking—often invidiously, rarely innocently—how what had happened had been caused to or allowed to. The scholars reached for their pens. And so the chronicles, the expositions, the narratives, began—and together with these labors of mind and imagination, also the theses and hypotheses, accusations and denials, the work of judgment. Culture now would turn individual memory into the systematic forms of expression: the axioms of historical explanation, the compilations of statistical data, the devices of fiction and poetry, the aspirations of theological summary. And then it would move further to turn these single lines, isolated still by their sources in individual consciousness, into institutions with a larger and corporate reach: laws and trials, museums, libraries, centers of research, courses of study, conferences, monuments of bronze and stone. The individual memory, the individual imagination, the individual conscience—sometimes moved directly, sometimes vicariously—organized themselves.

The spread of this development is understandable personally, sociologically, reflectively; given the magnitude of the events which constituted the occasion, it was inescapable. There could in any case be no doubt about the social warrant for institutionalizing the events of the Nazi genocide: even for historical occurrences less highly charged, for the celebration of a single death and the life on which that pronounces, the process of institutionalization is assumed. And yet, even with this validation, a second aspect of the same development increased in intensity as the institutions commemorating the events of the Nazi genocide began to emerge—what have been spoken of as the "deformations of the Holocaust." For as with any reformulation or abstraction moved by events opaque in their density or menace, the way was open in this institutionalization for a variety of falsifications: in the self-justification pursued constantly by theories and ideologies, by individual and cultural sentimentality which sought by a turn to the past to elude the severities of the present, by the temptation that disruption encourages for settling old scores, by the competition among injured voices for recognition. As these were added to normal lapses of tactlessness and carelessness, the outcome was predictable; and although it is necessary to recognize that the deformations of the Holocaust have not been as extreme as they might have been, still the evidence is plain of violation and exploitation: in the political rhetoric which directs charges of genocide or Nazism against acts that, terrible as they are, are clearly not *that;* in the designs of fiction and film which would exhibit this subject too by the configurations of melodrama or romance; in "shows" of art or music, mounted as social celebration; in the many varieties of Holocaust "business" from which writers and speakers on the Nazi genocide have been unable or unwilling to dissociate themselves; in the extremity of denial—almost too blatant even to be a violation—which would now claim that the events of the Nazi genocide, quite simply, never occurred. The likelihood that such deformations will accompany *any* process of institutionalization only underscores a more basic issue: could it not be objected that for certain subjects or topics this price is too high? Why should we not insist that at times institutionalization ought to be rejected altogether? And would not this insistence apply most immediately to events or subjects of such moral weight that even their slightest deformation would be culpable?

It has been suggested earlier in these pages that the threat of deformation in the aftermath of the Nazi genocide applies not only to the most obvious institutions; it extends also to the individual writer or teacher, if only through his dependence on the "institutions" of language and literature. Certain aspects of those institutions have been discussed, and it should then be clear that the dangers of their deformation extend further than language or literature in their own terms; they impinge on the institutional or social constraints which surround the writer himself. Thus, the writer who thinks personally to avoid the pressures of institutional deformation soon learns better, since he too depends for the elaboration of his work on editors and publishers and their publics, on the establishments of education, on library collections, and on foundations. Thus, he finds himself responding to purposes which may be quite at odds with his own; even when this is not the case, those other agencies are present as uninvited but constant guests.

The possibility that falsification stemming from these sources will be a feature of *all* institutionalization is not a warrant for concluding that it ought then simply to be accepted as a price to be paid. The issue of such acceptance, in any event, would arise only after a prior one had arisen, one which asked what purpose, in the translation of the events of the Nazi genocide against the Jews into the new forms of history, the process of institutionalization would serve. The fact of institutionalization is indisputable, evident in the libraries and museums, in the courses of study and conferences, in public ritual and civic monuments. The writing of history itself, it seems, is the most immediate institutional form that individual memory takes when the process of objectification begins, and we may then, reading backward through these various expressions, understand them as cumulative evidence of the turn from memory to history.

The reasons for that turn, speculative as such consideration will be, are clear in certain features. It serves, on the one hand, as a means of reiteration, of the repetition of subjective memory; it serves also, on the other hand, as a means of objectification—a form of collective address which provides an external view of individual and subjective expression and thus joins those expressions together. It is arguable that neither collective nor individual expression would even be possible apart from the process of institutionalization; in this sense too collective memory is prior to individual memory. The institutionalization of the Nazi genocide against the Jews is thus not symbolic of a collective internal awareness so much as its cause. The suggestion was made in the opening chapter of this book that this awareness, in its representation of the phenomenon of genocide, extends also to institutions that on the surface seem to have little to do directly with that phenomenon. The United Nations Convention on Genocide is an explicit example of institutionalization in the aftermath of the Nazi genocide; but other more obliquely relevant examples, which also would not have taken the form they did without the events of the Nazi genocide, have emerged from the same process. This pertains not only to Jewish history and to German history but elsewhere as well. Here as in its other appearances, memory is inseparable from social practice; it constitutes an important part of the "mind" which social practice requires and engenders if it is to move at all.

Certain accounts and analyses of the Nazi genocide appeared almost instantaneously, at the same time as the events themselves. But it was only a decade later that these events began to comprise a theme in scholarly writing and teaching, at the same time as the events themselves. It was still later than this, especially after the Six Day War of 1967, that "the Holocaust" took on the generally recognized public form that is now has. Among the reasons for this "lag" (the term suggests an inevitability to breaking the silence, although there is no reason to assume that history will always find a voice), at least one seems inescapable: that it was only then (that is, recently) and not, looking toward the future, for very long, that those who had endured the Nazi genocide saw a vanishing opportunity to give accounts of what on their ways as "survivors" they had seen and known, indeed of what "survival" could even mean for those who had passed through the act of genocide and for the culture in which it had occurred. It is undoubtedly this precarious sense of anticipation, adding recognition of the future to the burden of the past, that accounts for the recent flaring of consciousness and the more concerted summoning of institutional memory to the events of the Nazi genocide. It is understandable that at this point, too, as the individual consciousness concedes its limits, individual memory should turn most deliberately into history. Thus, the desire of history and of the other institutions of memory is to reach beyond the individual moment and place, to evoke the future in the name of the past when the distinction between the past and the present is about to disappear—that is, when there are about to be no more survivors. Institutionalization that comes after this brings with it a sense of improbability, even of arbitrariness, since it then has the task, in addition to its own, also of inventing subjective memory; institutions or monuments, if they are not initiated within memory of the events they commemorate, are thus unlikely to occur at all.

Among the presuppositions that underlie these comments, the most central is the assumption that memory, even for the individual but still more surely collectively, is deliberate, a matter of choice. It need not be held that everything included in or excluded from memory is effected voluntarily to recognize that a large part of its power comes from the consciousness of its own capacity. The selectivity of memory, even when it may seem accidental, is purposive not only in the sense which requires that some things should be *forgotten* (also, after all, part of the design of memory)—but inasmuch as social and linguistic meanings themselves reflect the shapes of memory. In contrast to the imagination, memory and the features of personal identity that depend on it are distinguished precisely by this intentional feature. Explicitly commemorative monuments—gravestones, steles, statues, buildings—are the most palpable emblems of the shapes of memory, but they are only more open in this disclosure than other of memory's "decisions." Especially in such monuments is the convergence of the several sources of commemorative meaning evident: a chronicle—that is, designation of the event or persons commemorated; an interpretation—of what is commemorated (and thus a statement of the values from which it set out); and then a combination of resolve and imperative—directed at once to the past and the future, and meant with that conjunction to define a role for memory in terms of its consequences. The anticipation of these consequences (which include also a sense of what would occur *without* them) points toward the future more insistently than toward the past; it is there that monuments realize their purpose or not—and it is also in this function of pointing that the institutionalization of memory attests dramatically to a crucial feature of institutionalization more generally. For in the terms by which monuments have here been defined, institutions themselves also appear as monuments, as themselves testaments of social or collective memory, and in certain respects the most powerful bearers of such memory. Not all institutions are willing to acknowledge this historical character (some, for their own purposes, deny it altogether); few of them, moreover, are explicitly intended as commemorative; the more usual guise is as a *resolution* of the past, a response to specific problems. Yet history discloses itself through them as surely as the layers of an archaeological excavation disclose the impression of a lost civilization. Thus, to refer to the process of "institutionalizing the Holocaust" is not—should not be—pejorative. The prospect offers stronger assurance for the coherence of past and future than anything that individual efforts of memory could realize by themselves, although it also places the burden of history on social consciousness, which by itself would be inclined to be free of it.

Whether in the metal or stone monuments fashioned in the image of the victims of the Nazi genocide or in the more abstract figures of the social institutions also shaped by that event, it is important, then, to recognize a common source and purpose. Part of that purpose, moreover, is the denial or rejection of its alternative, which for both of those forms would be oblivion or silence. It is no doubt true that in the presence of some events silence is an honest and discerning response—perhaps the *most* honest and discerning one. But silence, too, can be institutionalized—given a warranty of permanence through repression or displacement. That this should constitute the response of history and memory to the events of the Nazi genocide would, however, be a larger deformation than anything that the institutions of discourse, individual or collective and with all their potential for misrepresentation, have engendered or could yet. To criticize the deformations of the Holocaust—

the exploitation, the sentimentalizing, the distortion of fact—without measuring them against the enormity to which even those deformations themselves are an alternative would itself lead to misrepresentation in both; the same enormity that makes the deformations morally culpable also makes them bearable. And it is in the institutions of the Nazi genocide, in them *all,* that we find those two sides; the truth is that we cannot escape either.

2. Teaching the Holocaust

Most university or college teachers would deny that the courses they teach have anything to do with ethics, let alone that they as teachers could be found guilty of indoctrinating students with their own values. But they, too, despite this reticence, do of course openly commit themselves on ethical issues in ways that become part of the impressionable record which their students take away with them. How could it be otherwise, since each time a teacher answers (or avoids) a question, he also makes a statement about his own role, about the ideals of education, about how students—that is, people in the role of students—deserve to be treated?

In the range of commitments tacitly presented in this way, the ideal of tolerance and the related value of pluralism rank high. The phrase that repeats itself as a motto of higher education—the "disinterested search for knowledge"—is itself emblematic of these qualities, proposing to anyone who approaches that every position or action deserves a hearing; that differences in perspective are not only likely but welcome; that where evidence or argument run out, then conflicting judgments and tastes, whatever their consequences, must live together; that moral or practical reason begins only after theoretical (that is, disinterested) knowledge ends—that the two are quite separate. John Stuart Mill's essay *On Liberty,* which stands both as a symbol and as a source for much contemporary political and moral thought, puts the argument for tolerance, not only as a civic virtue, but as an intellectual and ethical ideal: falsehood is *valuable* for illuminating truth. It is, then, as though truth ought for its own sake to moderate its claims, to leave nourishment for its antagonist. Nothing is to be fully ruled out, nothing need be left without some claim.

Even a superficial view of political and social history since the eighteenth century shows that the struggle which had to be undertaken against parochialism and the established hierarchy of values in order to win a place for the values of tolerance and pluralism was hard-fought—

and this history often leads us to overlook the fact that the values of tolerance and pluralism themselves exact a price. The occasion that made this overwhelmingly clear to me was also the first time that I introduced the topic of the Nazi genocide against the Jews in a university class; it has been repeated a number of times since, in the same setting. There was for me, on these occasions, no surer proof of the difference between teaching ethics and teaching *about* ethics, between the role of the philosopher and the role of the professor of philosophy.

The first of these occasions was the discussion in a small seminar for undergraduate students of two books, Hannah Arendt's *Eichmann in Jerusalem* and Simon Wiesenthal's *The Sunflower*. Arendt looks back in her study of the "banality of evil," through a description of Eichmann's trial in 1961, to an account of the events that led up to it; Wiesenthal, in *The Sunflower*, asked a number of writers—philosophers, theologians, jurists—to pass judgment on his response (and to offer their own) to a dying SS man who asked Wiesenthal, at the time a concentration-camp inmate, to "forgive" him for an atrocity against Jews in which the SS man had participated in a town on the Russian front. I had introduced the two books, together with other readings from history, philosophy, and literature, as a series of reflections on the nature of evil. Those sources would, I thought, offer diverse views of ethical (and unethical) action, together with an outline of the concepts which these entailed. Anticipating the discussion of these issues with a group of students which was itself diverse, I felt secure at least of a common starting point: that for the texts considered and the roles in them of evil and wrongdoing, we—students and instructor, together with the authors—would share a common recognition at least of the *appearance* of evil, the phenomenon which we would then be attempting to understand.

But this assumption turned out to clash surely and directly with the reality of the seminar itself, and never more so than in the discussion of the two books which had the Nazi genocide against the Jews as their subject. The strongest reaction by the students in the seminar to Arendt's book focused on the trial of Eichmann itself: Was not that trial illegal? Were not the Israelis at fault, as wrong morally perhaps as Eichmann in abducting him, bringing him to trial, and then executing him? The persistent reaction to Wiesenthal's book was a denial of the question it asked: The SS man had acted as a soldier; his education and training had shaped his behavior, and there should thus be no issue *either* of forgiving him or of not doing so. As there could be no claim for responsibility, there could also be none of guilt. In moral disputes between nations or cultures, there is no means of resolution. The SS man had done what at the time he believed he ought to—and that was the whole of the matter so far as *moral* judgment could be summoned, especially from a distance in time and space.

This was not, it need be said, a careless or indifferent group of students who responded in this way. They were intelligent and "good" students who read conscientiously; presumably they had decided to enroll in the seminar because of an interest or even a concern for its topic, which had been summarily listed as "The Concept of Evil." But then, when the phenomenon of evil actually *appeared*, the students were—to my own first sharp reaction—simply blind to that appearance, substituting for what was plainly there before their eyes a set of oblique replacements. And the dilemma—the *moral* dilemma—forced by the students on the instructor was, in that same moment, oppressive. On the one hand, their response itself was honest enough: they had read the books; they knew from that and from other reading the general outline of facts concerning what had happened during the Nazi genocide; the questions they raised were, as questions, reasoned and sincere. They thus in a sense had earned their doubts; and this, on the principle of tolerance to which my own training and commitment had been attuned, meant that the issues they raised should receive serious and measured discussion, levelheaded, level-toned. On the other hand stood the facts themselves, speaking—if ever facts did—for themselves: one-sided, partial, not at all tolerant. To be sure, Arendt herself called attention to the issue of legitimacy in Eichmann's trial—but for her, too, finally, it was Eichmann and *his* actions, not the trial, that were on trial. Wiesenthal indeed asked his readers to judge his response to the SS man's request (Wiesenthal had turned away in silence, denying forgiveness). But never, in inviting judgment, does Wiesenthal doubt the character of the occasion of the SS man's request. "Look at them!! Can't you see what they're writing *about*??": this side of me wanted to yell out, to shake the well-meaning, decent, intelligent group of young men and women before me whom I supposed as a group to be as unlikely as any that might be found to justify those actions, let alone to will them themselves.

In fact, I did shout—but not much. Mainly, I sweated, with the heat that comes not from honest labor but from being forced to move in two opposite directions at one time. Tolerance? Openmindedness? Of course. Yet these did not come close to answering the occasion, which was so evidently one-sided. Pleading? Cursing? Well, no doubt. But these would hardly be intelligible when juxtaposed to the expectations nourished in the students by their educational pasts—the tolerant suspension of disbelief, the characteristic academic gathering of views. I

forced myself—quickly at the time, more slowly, later—to try to understand why a reader of those two books would first or even later single out
the conclusions that the students had drawn. How, in considering
Arendt's description of Eichmann and his history, would a reader with
no disposition to favor him or anything else about the Nazis, with no
inclination (I was willing to suppose) even to the varieties of polite anti-
Semitism, be led *first* to consider the legality of Eichmann's trial? How,
responding to Wiesenthal's request for advice in judging the SS man,
could readers object that there was no judgment to be made?

To be sure, the students themselves offered various reasons for reaching these conclusions, and spoke also, variously, of the degree of their
commitments. But, still, the similarities in their responses disclosed a
pattern that was, it seemed to me, nothing more than a reluctance to admit the necessity imposed by moral choice altogether—an impulse to
replace those demands with the deferrals of tolerance and understanding. Where, as for the actions of the SS man, there seemed no way of
judging him without condemnation, exclusion, then the judgment must
itself be flattened, denied: there was, we ought to conclude, neither reason nor the means. Where, with Eichmann, the moral enormity was
more difficult to avoid, let it at least be shared with those who brought
him to trial, perhaps with mankind in general: was Eichmann, after all,
so different? What stirred these reactions could best be understood as an
enlargement of the principle of tolerance: from a precept governing relations *among people* to a precept governing judgment *within the individual*.
Tolerance appears first in Mill's account, for example, as a social ideal:
people (others no less than oneself) have a right to self-determination,
to choose the careers they want, their friends, even, finally, their own
characters—however well or badly any of these later turn out; thus, no
possibilities should be excluded beforehand (except for those imposed
from the outside that harm the capacity for choice). But then, this ideal,
intended for relations *among* people becomes internalized—as if the individual person, in the attempt to be fair and just, had the obligation also
to see *himself* as a society, as if he should renounce his own agency, admitting all possibilities and declining to make judgments or discriminations
on the ground established by the principle of tolerance, namely, that all
potential actions share equally the right to be summoned.

To be sure, exactly the opposite conclusion might be reached from
this same appeal to the principle of tolerance: that just *because* of their
freedom to act as they choose to, people then are accountable for the
choices they make and for the differences between those choices and the
alternatives that had been possible. But in order to draw this conclusion
and so, later, to judge the actions for which the principle of tolerance

initially provides a means—*this* requires the collaboration of quite a different principle, something in addition to, indeed beyond, that of tolerance. There would have to be a basis here to which individual agency might look for particularity and exclusion, in effect superseding the effort to preserve alternatives. The principle of tolerance initially provides a basis for generality and inclusion—but if a choice between alternatives is to be made, a principle must be available which is even more fundamental than that basis. The acknowledgment of such a principle, it seemed clear, was for these students alien, disfiguring.

Admittedly, when, in desperation, I asked the students to imagine themselves as Jews threatened by genocide, their response was quick and assured: *of course they would have acted*—to oppose, even to attack the machinery poised to destroy them. (And why—the question confidently presented itself—had not the Jews been more vigorous in their own defense? But this question represented only naïveté, not principle.) But this, too, they persisted, was not a conclusion based on principle but an instinct for self-defense. One could, they thus held, understand *why* people would resist or condemn—but that was far from claiming or demonstrating a reasoned justification that would indict those against whom the reaction was directed; they too, after all, were victims of circumstance.

This halfhearted, half-minded conclusion, it seemed clear to me, embodied the same dilemma posed more generally by the tacit assumptions that underlay the educational institution as a whole—the university—in which our seminar was acting a small part. The point here is, not that tolerance and pluralism are not authentic values, but that *by themselves* they cannot do the work of moral judgment or action. (All this, of course, leaves to one side the possibilities of hypocrisy and the fact that pleas for tolerance and pluralism often serve as a disguise or means for self-serving particularity.) What tolerance and pluralism teach is mainly how *not* to choose, how *not* to discriminate; and as important as are the moral lessons to be learned here of disinterest and the renouncing of domination, they offer no basis for the positive choices that—often in the same moment—have to be made. This absence is felt especially sharply in the making of moral choices, because without the latter choices there would be no self-determination, no definition of a particular self at all.

Do such grounds for exclusion or particularity exist? Surely, people act and speak *as if* they knew those grounds, as if restricted communities of interests existed within the larger one of humanity, as if individual persons had certain specific obligations and thus also a basis for moral choice. And the "as if" reiterated here is all that is needed to compel acknowledgment of principles in addition to those of openness and tolerance, and perhaps even prior to them. There must, after all, be a *place* from which tolerance can be extended—and that place is not, as a matter of either history or theory, arbitrarily located. It is not easy to become an individual, the master of *that* corporation, but it is not impossible, either, and the choices required in order to do so are neither accidental nor the result of having addressed all possibilities as equal. The individual person is anything but hypothetical.

I knew better than my students did that their reactions went well beyond their own histories, that what I threw up to them as a possible example of moral blindness (still only "possible," so the idiom of tolerance continued to prevail) had broader, social origins; that the seminar in which I was addressing them and for which *I* was responsible was itself contributing to that same failing. To hope to represent within the walls of a classroom the willfulness and persistence of evil; to place the Nazi war of extermination against the Jews by the side of the worlds of *King Lear*, Dostoevski, *Job*, the Marquis de Sade, Plato; to talk about the varieties of wrongdoing as one might talk about the varieties of an art form: are these not also to affirm the ideal of moral neutrality, to ignore the necessary constraints of the individual moral decision? And the sides of this pedagogical dilemma, it seems to me, repeat the other, more general antinomy that has been mentioned here. For not only does a teacher have what is impressed on him as the professional obligation to convey to students his commitment, as a "universal" observer, to disinterested reflection; he also, in practice, is asked to be a source for the students of the evidence of particularity, to provide them with a model of individual choice or assertion which they do not readily find elsewhere. He has in effect to provide them with *experience* in all its one-sidedness, partisanship, individuality. Even when the facts speak for themselves, their audience must be in a position to listen—and a training in generality affords little preparation for a grasp of particulars or the decisions which they require.

These two kinds of requirements—respect for the many, the commitment to the one—are not easily reconciled even if the independent claims of each are fully acknowledged. When either of them is ignored or denied, furthermore, the other becomes distorted, enlarged, dangerous. The institutions of education are currently there, it seems to me, with the many and the universal—reluctant, almost disabled, to confront the one and the particular. Teaching about a moral enormity like the Nazi genocide in which the facts, if ever, *do* speak for themselves, so discloses the imbalance—that we are not now, in the university, probably also in the culture, in a position to speak about or to enact moral judgment,

large or small. We have the one side of it, the will to universalize; but
then the question arises of what there is to universalize about—and it is,
after all, in the answer to that question that moral judgment begins and
ends.

3. Holocaust Studies

The issues raised by proposals to institutionalize the Holocaust in the
American university are in many ways similar to questions that have
arisen in connection with other recent proposals for courses or programs
in "area" or "ethnic" studies. But there are also important and even obvious differences among such proposals, which have influenced the
discussion of what the status of "Holocaust Studies" should be (whether
at the university or in scholarship more generally), and it is worth considering what these differences are. Any such discussion unavoidably
touches on the institutional character of the university itself (and also
then on the features which the university shares with other social institutions); as the university is often viewed as a microcosm of the
society or culture, furthermore, the role it assigns to Holocaust studies
will also indicate the significance of the events on which those studies are
based in history and social memory more generally.

The questions raised about—often against—Holocaust studies have
been predictable: Is the Nazi genocide not too parochial, too narrow a
subject to provide a focus for scholarship and teaching at the university?
Could a single event (or even a series of them) that mainly affects the
history of a small group of people, in one short period of their history,
qualify as a *field* of discourse? Or: does not the Nazi genocide viewed as a
whole involve such diverse areas of society and culture (e.g., economics,
religion, sociology, the arts, political theory) as to defy the usual academic categories (let alone the possibility of being taught as a single
"discipline")? So also the issue is raised whether there *should* be—even if
there could be—professorships or chairs or departments (or programs
or centers) of Holocaust studies: would these not conflict with the disinterest required by the search for knowledge that the university claims
as an ideal? Would they not mainly serve special interests beyond the university altogether—religious or political commitments that the university not too long ago was struggling *against* in order to assert its own
autonomy?

It seems evident that such questions should themselves be ap-
proached skeptically, that they themselves should be questioned. Much
of what they assert or imply is possibly not true at all, let alone self-
evident—and this holds also for the presuppositions on which they de-

pend. For example: one of these presuppositions is committed to the view that because the Nazi genocide against the Jews is a matter of social concern, this should count against its being accorded a place in the university curriculum. For if, as the academic tradition has argued, the university ought to be insulated from the interests around it that are poised to use for their own purposes any sign of tendentiousness, even topics which in other contexts would be intellectually significant may have to be excluded.

But this formalist definition of the role of the university is transparently mistaken in its own claim to speak with the authority of history. Indeed, if any single fact is clear in the past of the university, it is that the conferring of academic and scholarly legitimacy on a topic or discipline has characteristically occurred *first* as a function of social and cultural— or even practical—interest, and only then as an expression of the academic or scholarly issues that surround those interests. That this aspect of its history is often repressed in "theories" of the university has been a persistent feature of its own institutionalization; to bring this into the open in respect to the question of the legitimacy of Holocaust studies, furthermore, is also to recall other relatively undisputed areas of study which have by now left far behind the objections that accompanied their initial appearance at the university. Had someone told a nineteenth-century American university president that his twentieth-century successor would be signing diplomas for degrees in business administration, dance, physical education, painting, or journalism, he would have been not so much critical as incredulous. He—and the president *would* have been a "he"—would not, however, have thought to question the fact that the majority of the degrees that he himself certified were clerical or that he was himself almost certainly a cleric (and not, of course, of just any persuasion). To move back further to the medieval origins of the university in Italy and Spain does not alter this character; there, too, it was the faculties of medicine, law, and theology that provided the impetus for the higher learning; none of them were free of strong social and practical motives.

Admittedly, such claims about the history of the university are distinct from the question of whether the purposes which thus shaped the university were warranted. But *then* what is at issue is much more than the status of Holocaust studies. So far as concerns the latter, it suffices to note only the fact itself that from the time of its institutional origins, the university has been closely tied to the historical interests and practical needs of the context in which it was set. To recognize this does not mean that proposals for courses of study in the university have not been scrutinized (or should not be), but only that the criteria applied in this

process have consistently been less single-minded, less purist, than the
now standard claims of scholarly disinterestedness would suggest. Indeed, that principle of disinterestedness has often served to defer a
question which, cynical as it seems when directed to academic discussion
and in particular to the issue of Holocaust studies, is nonetheless crucial
to understanding how decisions in the academy, like social decisions
more generally, are made. This is the question "Cui bono?" ("Who ben-
efits?")—and the answers to it in this context provide a warrant for the
question itself. There can be little doubt that disputes about the institutionalization of Holocaust studies at the university, like the disputes
concerning women's studies or black studies or the more conventional
"area" studies, have been carried on largely between those who believe
that the presence of those issues should be maintained in the civic as well
as in the scholarly consciousness and those who deny this. The latter
characteristically base their response on the ground that the questions
relevant to those areas would be more fruitfully or properly raised elsewhere—which is at least sometimes a way of saying that they do not
deserve to be raised at all.

Finding a place for a discipline or "area" at the university is thus also,
or even first, a form of social validation or institutionalization; it is unlikely that this side of its function would not be a deliberate part of the
purpose as well. Insofar as this is acknowledged, moreover, the justification for Holocaust studies also extends then to the question of what the
status of such studies would be *outside* the university—what practical
and moral claims they make or where they stand in respect to the large
group of social ideals among which the role of the university is but one.
To reject such questions as irrelevant to the character of the university is
to obscure the history of scholarship itself, to refuse to admit that it suffers history as well as speaks about it. Undoubtedly, individual questions
arise which seem to be disinterested, independent of the historical turns
of culture or consciousness; but these, too, looked at more closely, reveal
their institutional origins and affiliations, their contextual presuppositions. Recent developments in the field of the history of science—
beginning with the acknowledgment that science *has* a history—have
provided a striking example of the role of institutional power and constraints in the legitimation of "academic" questions: it had before this
served contemporary science and technology well to be thought of as
existing *without* a history. The question, then, of what constitutes a field
of study even among the most theoretical or systematically rigorous dis-
ciplines cannot be understood metaphysically: the categories of the
academy are social, contextual, temporal, historical—even if the subjects
which they define are alleged not to be. This is not a tendentious way of

arguing that whatever makes its way into a university curriculum is vali-
dated by that fact; but it does mean that the decisions responsible for
such appearances are practical and social no less than intellectual. Arguments for or against the institutionalization of any particular topic or
field cannot afford to ignore this fact.

Predictably, then, the issue of Holocaust studies resolves itself into a
single and brief question: how important—outside the university or inside it—is the phenomenon of the Nazi genocide? And once the issue
appears in those terms, also those who are doubtful will have to confront
what it is that they are doubting. Whether its formulation is part of a
general analysis—of totalitarianism in the twentieth century or of history as such—or whether it is set within the specific contexts of Jewish or
German history, the fact of the Nazi genocide is not only a possible example or occasion of evidence, but an unavoidable datum in the
testimony of moral history and in this sense in the history of mankind.
The crux here is not the issue of uniqueness, but the features of extremity
and innovation. As, under stress, the criteria of moral significance most
clearly reveal the elements (and fractures) of conceptual complexity, the
justification is evident. History, to be sure, is prolific with examples, and
it is unlikely that any single example will be decisive or irreplaceable. But
one does not need to deny this in order to demonstrate the significance
of an example. It would be enough only to bring into view the many and
central aspects of human experience on which the example impinges—
and this indeed is what the studies in the present volume of the Nazi
genocide, as act and idea, have attempted to do.

Emphasis on the issue of the legitimacy of a discipline or area of study
often serves to conceal another question of legitimacy which is of special
relevance to Holocaust studies. For it is not only the validation of a *subject* that matters in relation to its institutionalization, but also the role of
its "professors" and the assumptions on which their role depends. The
economic status of the teacher or writer is admittedly only one among
these assumptions; it is an assumption, moreover, that is rarely thought
to be worth mentioning at all, although that, too, is part of its importance in judging the prospect of Holocaust studies. It may seem only a
mild irony that a large number of teachers—and so also academic admin-
istrators, book publishers, advertising copywriters—now support
themselves by interpreting (and often, advocating) the thoughts and
words of Socrates, who himself refused payment for his teaching; or
more generally, that thinkers, poets, and artists who often lived ne-
glected and in poverty now provide a steady means of livelihood for
critics or teachers or performers. But if the unspoken issue of academic
and artistic commerce in general deserves to be raised more than it has

been, that question is of still more obvious importance for Holocaust studies. To be sure, the issue defined in this way does not bear only on the institution of the university: it extends even more stringently to the writers of fiction, of popular history, and of film whose "success" depends on the representation of an event that "appeals" because of its moral enormity, because of the combination of criminality and suffering that constituted it. Whatever might be said about the justification for teaching or writing about Plato or Shakespeare as the means of earning a living, could anyone claim that there is not a moral issue *here*—that professors, artists, writers about the Nazi genocide are free simply to assume a just relation between their profits from their work and the subject that provides them?

It seems to me evident that the most forthright response to this question is that no one should gain personal benefit or profit from such work—that there is here, between its occasion and the writer's own interests, a basic incommensurability. If the Nazi genocide as a subject affects the forms of discourse in which it is set, should not that subject also make a difference in the purpose and consequences of his work for the writer or teacher? To be sure, without such efforts the Nazi genocide would soon be erased from memory, and so the work *needs* to be carried on, if only, given its likely deformations, as the lesser of two evils. But this does not mean that it should be carried on with, let alone for the sake of, personal profit. The students of Holocaust studies ought then to consider the future of a "volunteer" discipline, and perhaps an anonymous one as well.

I think here—it is an equivocal justification, a reformulation of the issue itself—of the traditional account given of the Hebrew *melamed,* the teacher who would make his living by teaching children the language and texts of the Jewish tradition. The justification for that teaching had appeared first in the biblical commandment "And you shall teach these words to your children, speaking of them when you sit at home and when you go on your way, when you lie down and when you rise up." Such a commandment ought, it seems, to be freely heeded and observed: could one accept payment for fulfilling a religious obligation? And so a further justification appeared: the teacher's salary would be paid to him, not as compensation for his teaching, but for the time that he would have spent, if he were not teaching, on work that would have been remunerative. The teacher is paid, in other words, for *not* working; his teaching he does freely, on his own, fulfilling an obligation.

The explanation will seem sophistic, a joke. But it does not have to be accepted at face value for us to see that it takes the question to which it responds seriously or to recognize that that question *is* serious. In this role, the question serves as a reminder to the teacher that it is not his own work which engages him, but work that ought to be done; that he is not doing it for himself, but for its own sake. So he is not to be compensated for his work—how *could* he be? So, too, other credit that may come to him from his efforts is also likely to be a misrepresentation, easily misunderstood by others and even by himself. When Rabbi Tarfon, in *Ethics of the Fathers,* warns that "the day is short and the work is great . . . and the master of the house presses," he does not describe what "the" work is which needs to be done or why it is important that the need should be met; these will, he believes, be evident. The definite article he uses here is as knowing and clear as it is in his reference to "the" master. No one should be in doubt.

Index

Des Pres, Terrence, 159; The Survivor, 159 n. 49

Dewey, John, implicit as well as explicit opposition to fascism, 191

Diaries of Nazi genocide, 127–29

Diaspora: active and creative, 213–14; contribution to positive universalist impulse, 223; danger of assimilation, 225; and Israel, 212n, 215n, 219, 223; Reform Judaism, 208–9

Dickens, Charles, *David Copperfield*, 126

Diderot, Denis, 178, 181

Discourse, relation between subject and form, xix

Distancing, moral, 115, 145; from subject, xiii

Divided self: as distinguished from self with different moral objects, 52–56; as explanation of Nazi psychology, 48–56; Hannah Arendt's distinction between banal and radical evil, 49; illusion of in Nazi policy, 54; split personality, 51–52

Dobkowski, Michael: *Genocide and the Modern Age*, 8 n. 5, 23 n. 19; historical and conceptual background of genocide, 5n; political use of term "genocide," 4n

Documents from the Holocaust (Arad et al.), 71n, 88n

"Doubling effect." *See* Divided self

Downie, R. S., "Forgiveness," 56n

Drama, Nazi genocide as literary subject of, 131–33

Dumont, Louis, *Essays on Individualism*, 195, 195n

Duras, Marguerite, *The War*, 135

Eagleton, Terry, *Criticism and Ideology*, 122 n. 6

Eberhardt, Helmut, *Euthanasie und die Vernichtung "lebensunwerten" Lebens*, 38n

Eichenbaum, Boris, *Aufsätze zur Theorie und Geschichte der Literatur*, 120n

Eichmann, Adolf, 23; author of *Endlösung*, 85; claim to be a Zionist, 208; Hannah Arendt's representation of, 148–49; principle vs. economic interests, 17

Einsatzgruppen, 85; and euthanasia program, 27; and Russian campaign, 87

Eisen, Arnold, *Galut*, 225n

Elman, Richard, trilogy of *The Twentieth-eighth Day of Ellul*, *Lilo's Diary*, *The Reckoning*, 135

Else, Gerald, *Aristotle's Poetics*, 117n

Elster, Jon, *The Multiple Self*, 52n

Emancipation of Jews in the Enlightenment, 183

Endgültige Lösung. See Endlösung

Endlösung, 85–92; act opposed to connotation, 88; denotation and connotation, 90; historical use before Nazis, 85–87; persuasiveness of term, 87. *See also* Final Solution *Endziel. See Endlösung*

Enlightenment: growth of social sciences, 181–83; moral judgment, 187; Nazi attack on, 193

Enlightenment and conceptual framework for Nazi genocide, 189–95; causal evocation, 169. *See also* Enlightenment and the Jews; Kant's Enlightenment; Universalizability, principle of; Universal self as moral agent

Enlightenment and the Jews, 183–89; oblique threats, 169n. *See also* Universalizability, principle of; Universal self as moral agent

Epstein, Leslie, 106; impulse to historical truth and *The King of the Jews*, 127, 134; "The Reality of Evil," 127 n. 12; salvaging the world through imagination, 153; "Writing about the Holocaust," 153 n. 42.

Erlich, Victor, *Russian Formalism*, 120n

Esh, Shaul, "Words and Their Meanings," 85n

"Eternal Peace" (Kant), 178

Ethical imagination, 64–65

Ethical practice, 63–65

Ethics, philosophical: divorced from ethical practice, 63; inventive rather than historical examples, 63; will for generalization, 62–64

Euthanasia program, Nazi, 27; pressure against, 44; relation to Final Solution, 27n, 28n

Evacuation, as synonym for execution, 68